# Teaching as Believing

# Teaching as Believing

## Faith in the University

CHRIS ANDERSON

Baylor University Press
Waco, Texas USA

Series in Religion and Higher Education 2

*Book Design* by Westchester Book Group
*Cover Design* by David Alcorn, Alcorn Publication Design

Library of Congress Cataloging-in-Publication Data

Anderson, Chris, 1955-
  Teaching as believing : faith in the university / Chris Anderson.
    p. cm. — (Studies in religion and higher education ; 2)
  Includes bibliographical references and index.
  ISBN 1-932792-03-1 (pbk. : alk. paper)
  1. Christian college teachers—Religious life. 2. Catholic teachers—Religious life. 3. Anderson, Chris, 1955- 4. Oregon State University.
I. Title. II. Series.

  BX2373.T4A54 2004
  248.8'8—dc22

                                        2004007264

FOR LEO

# Contents

# Acknowledgments

To Parker Palmer, for his example and encouragement. To Fr. Andy Dufner, S.J., Colleen Dean, and the Nestucca community, for sanctuary and guidance. To the faculty and students of Mount Angel Seminary and the monks of Mount Angel Abbey, for all they've taught me, and to the diaconal community of the Archdiocese of Portland and St. Mary's parish in Corvallis, for making my ministry possible. To my colleagues in the English department at Oregon State University and especially to Robert Schwartz, the chair, who has supported me all along. To my students in the Literature of Western Civilization class, for continually converting me.

To Anna Harrell, Alicia Kleiman, and Patrick Williams for their helpful responses to an early draft. To Tracy Daugherty, Kathy Moore, Mike Oriard, and Richard Wakefield for their fine suggestions on structure and ideas. To Fr. Dave Leigh, S.J., both for his critique of a draft—particularly on the question of method in theology—and for inviting me to speak to the Conference on Christianity and Literature, at Seattle University, April 2003. To Anna Harrell for her great help with citations and bibliography. Especially to Ruth Russo, whose remarkable comments on the first draft so encouraged and guided me.

And to Carey C. Newman of Baylor University Press, for his enthusiastic acceptance of the manuscript and for his strong, editorial presence on my final revisions—what a blessing it has been, what a gift, to be able to speak in my own voice as both a teacher and a Christian.

# Introduction

On Holy Saturday, Barb and I and the kids went hiking in the old growth forest of the Drift Creek Wilderness, not far from Waldport. It was a wonderful day, a day of healing. The fir and the spruce were as huge as we longed for, bigger around than two of us could reach, and they stretched out as far as the eye could see. There was that sense you get in both forests and cathedrals of height and breadth and depth, of the eye being led into deeper and deeper shadow, of intricacy and complexity, and yet, at the same time, of dignity. The sun broke through the branches just like in a poster, shafts of light extending ever further back.

We saw it and it was good. There was mystery and there was order. And it was dazzling, like the two dazzling men who speak to the women at the tomb in Luke's account of the resurrection (24:1–12). To walk in the light of those ancient trees was to feel all at once as if the stone had been rolled away from our lives.

So I report my experience, as the women reported theirs, fully prepared to be doubted, as they were doubted, as I doubt it myself much of the time.

I fall asleep and dream that I'm opening a door to a room that I didn't know was there and inside it there's a forest, a beautiful forest. When I wake up in the morning something has shifted inside of me. Somehow I feel light as a feather, tender, alert. I sit down at the computer and my writing gives way and the words come pouring out. I stop at the New Morning Bakery for a cinnamon roll and there's a friend I haven't seen for months. We sit and talk and I feel such pleasure in the presence of this person, in the sound of his voice, in the way he tells his story. Later in class everybody's excited about the reading, unexpectedly,

1

as if suddenly we're all a part of a story, with a plot and a movement and the hope of resolution.

Or maybe it's summer and the light is in the trees and I'm throwing the Frisbee with the kids, the dogs running around and barking. I stand back and fling that Frisbee as far as I can, and it glides through the air, hovering at the end, and the kids are rolling in the grass, laughing, and all at once I realize I've been praying. All morning I've been praying and I didn't know it.

I believe that the world is charged with the grandeur of God.

I believe that our hearts are restless until they rest in God.

I believe that Jesus Christ is the way to this God—the way, the truth, and the life.

—————

How then do I teach the Bible at Oregon State University, and Augustine, and Dante, and the other Christian classics? How do any of us who are Christians teach what we teach, in whatever field, at the public university, or at any university, even religious universities—the American university, the postmodern university, the university where it sometimes seems that everyone is welcome except believers?[1]

It's not that there's necessarily a conflict, because as Christians we also love our teaching and our writing. We are devoted to the intellectual life. We care deeply about our students. We respect and admire our colleagues, who are people, too, after all, with their own spiritual struggles and joys. The problem exists more in the culture of the university than in our own heads, though sometimes it's in our heads, too, and our hearts. There are days when the university seems to want to drain all of us of our humanity. To use Parker Palmer's terms in *The Courage to Teach*, his landmark study of the spirituality of education, how do we live in "integrity" as academics if our "identity" is also as believing Christians?

By being ourselves. By professing who we are.

By professing who we are while also respecting the good and necessary boundaries—boundaries that are good and necessary *for us*, as Christians. These are our boundaries, too. The university honors the many ways and truths and lives of human experience. So do we. The university insists that the grandeur of the world is difficult to read and that no single reading suffices. So do we. The university believes that the human heart should be restless, that the mind should always be open and searching. So do we. Christianity doesn't deny the methods of the intellect but moves beyond them, to a greater level of particularity, and what's important for us and our colleagues is that we always keep this in mind, both the commonality and the difference.

Thus: the way to be a good Christian is by being a good professor, and the way to be a good professor is by being a good Christian. But it's more than that, too. There's a greater urgency: we *need* the university, and the university needs us.

————

This is my argument in the book that follows, a book that is part teaching memoir, part argument and analysis; a book that dramatizes my own experience teaching a particular course at a particular place and time; a book that interprets this experience as representative for other Christian faculty.

Palmer says in *The Courage to Teach* that we should all tell each other stories, describing two kinds of moments, moments when we knew we were born to be teachers and moments when we wished we'd never been born. Technique is of "marginal utility," the advice of experts of little help (141). To grow as teachers and live "divided no more," we must first turn inward, exploring our own inner lives, then come back together and share what we've found (166). It's from these stories and from nowhere else, Palmer believes, that we learn the most about the complexity and the challenges of teaching. It's through these stories that we form "communities of congruence" within the larger institution, communities that can reform the university, slowly and incrementally, by giving us the strength to stay healthy within it (172).

I am not a biblical scholar. I am not a theologian, and the theology I know is Catholic, grounded in my training and experience as a Catholic deacon, though I am in the process of learning about a new postmodern evangelical and Protestant theology that has much in common with my own tradition.[2] I write as an amateur in all the disciplines I draw on, as a generalist, an essayist. My observations about faith and the Bible will be obvious to anyone with much experience—what I say about literature is what I say to sophomores. What follows in the next six chapters are simply some of my own stories and the inferences I make from them, inferences about the nature of education and the role of faith in the intellectual life. My hope is that by sharing these experiences I will encourage you to share your own. My hope is that for a moment we will draw together into our own brief community of congruence, or what Palmer's late friend Henri Nouwen would have called a "community of resistance" (*Seeds of Hope* 176).

Here in the introduction I map out my argument in more detail and explain its underlying assumptions, drawing in particular on the theory of Paul Ricouer. I also tell the first of my stories, the larger, framing story of the last ten years of my life, since what I have to say grows out of this experience of retreat and return, conversion and reengagement. This is my most important assumption—the assumption underneath Palmer's call for stories, the assumption that Ricouer helps us better understand: that ideas always grow out of experience, that what we think is grounded in who we are.

The issues take shape for me during a sabbatical year, when I leave the university to teach at a Catholic seminary. They come to a head when I return, the first day of the Literature of Western Civilization, the sophomore survey course that I enact in the chapters that follow. By this point, inspired by my experience at the seminary, I have gone on to be ordained myself, and it's in the tension between these two vocations, as a minister and a teacher, that I come to understand the line that we are always crossing and that we have to cross.

## A Teaching Moment

The first day of fall term. Leaves are turning. Students are filing into the room, a long line of backpacks and caps, and I'm standing at the door, handing out the syllabus for the class, a sophomore survey course called "The Literature of Western Civilization." Most public universities offer a course like this, a survey of the great books from Homer to the Bible to Dante to the moderns, and mine is much the same. I use an anthology. I assign journals and papers. I break the class up into discussion groups. There are as many nonmajors as majors in the course, good, smart engineering and forestry students without much experience reading literature.

People sit down and the room grows quiet. As the stragglers keep coming in I start explaining how the course will work, the reading and the assignments. Maybe leaf blowers are already going out in the quad. Maybe the rain has already started, students sitting in their desks with wet hair and soggy Polartecs. First days are important. Impressions are made, an atmosphere set. Usually I ask the students to do a freewriting exercise recording their expectations, the first of many freewrites in and out of class over the term, bursts of raw, unedited writing good for warming up and capturing what people are really thinking.

And when I'm done with the requirements and the reading and the grading, I always tell these classes that I am a deacon.

I am a full-time English professor, I say, but I am also an ordained minister for the Catholic Church and active in both parish and campus ministry. Deacons are usually married men and usually work full time in their own secular professions, but they are called out of these professions, as I have been, to baptize babies and witness marriages and preside at funerals and communion services and to proclaim the gospel at Mass and to give the homily, a reflection on the Scripture for that day.

I joke that students should come to Mass now and then—at least if they want a good grade—then, seriously, that of course atheists can get

A's, Catholics F's. Most of my students are unchurched, without a lot of background in organized religion, and it's tricky to talk about religion right away, particularly Catholicism, which even now, in my part of the country, draws out an instinctive anti-Catholic bias. I always feel a little nervous, as if I've brought up something risky and personal, which of course I have. Universities, even public universities, in America as in Europe, were established jointly by both church and state, no strict separation assumed. Clergymen were the first teachers of literature as of everything else, but that sense of the relation between faith and reason has long since pulled apart into all our current pluralisms. The extreme religious right has captured the public discussion, the newspapers reduce the issues to easy oppositions, and the average person assumes that faith must be merely a private matter, not a subject for discussion in Moreland Hall, Oregon State University, or any other public place.

Like all faculty of faith I of course understand the real boundaries: no preaching. In a classroom at a state university I must be open to all points of view, to all faiths and varieties of doubt, as I am, and I must teach as "objectively" as possible, which of course I never do. No teacher can. Objectivity isn't possible or desirable, in the teaching of the Bible or in the teaching of any other subject, and that's the reason I talk about my own situatedness as a reader. Partly, I'm trying to be honest. Partly, since our focus will be the Christian classics, I'm hoping to suggest a kind of personal competence, on the same principle that an engineering class should be taught by an engineer—or appropriateness, as in a woman teaching women's literature, an African American teaching African American literature.

But deeper than that what I'm trying to do on that first day is to begin the process of complicating how my students understand the nature of meaning and of truth. That's what I take to be the purpose of the university: to complicate, to show that there's more than meets the eye, that the world is a much bigger and more interesting place than we often assume it is. Not everyone thinks as we think, not everyone takes for granted what we take for granted, and coming to know this is the beginning of humility and so of wisdom. What we know is rooted in who we are. Knowledge is always grounded in faith, in belief, of one kind or another, and by talking about mine I am inviting students to think about theirs.

I talk about my faith in the classroom both the first day and throughout the term—talk about it, not urge it on anyone else, not try to convert—because I want to help students think past the assumptions implied in the following response from Will, a freewrite from several weeks later in the term. I had asked the class, in light of our discussions to that point, to return to the first day and to think about why I had confessed to my

own faith. Should I have talked about being a deacon? Should I refer to
my faith as I often do?

Will responds:

> *What I really want from you is an objective look at the reading. I understand
> that the Bible has played a large role in your life, which I consider personally
> admirable. But I do not think that you should express how much effect the
> book has had on you as much as you do in class. I think we would all be able
> to think clearly about it if we could further detach from the religious impli-
> cations of what we are reading. I think you should supply as many multiple
> interpretations of the Bible as you can, even if they are negative.*

This is an intelligent and courteous paragraph written by an intelligent
and courteous student, a student who did well in the class. Its views are
not uninformed and neither are they unrepresentative. Many good people would agree. Which is the point. What this freewrite expresses so
clearly are the unexpressed assumptions of many in the university,
assumptions that students learn from teachers and classmates, that they
take in both through what their classes are teaching and how they are
taught: that knowledge is true knowledge only when it's "detached," that
effective reading is reading that never shows the "personal effect" of the
text on the reader. What this freewriting expresses are the apparent
assumptions of many students and colleagues about religion an religious
life, that a faithful reading of the Bible isn't "multiple" but singular and
dogmatic, that a faithful reading of the Bible never engages anything
negative or complicated or fully and really human—that religion is both
one dimensional and unrealistic—that the only mode of religious discourse is preaching and that this preaching must be pushy and narrow, a
knock on the door and a tract shoved in the face—that faith is divorced
from reason, that religious life and religious texts can't be seen as in any
way related to the intellectual life of the university.

## The History of This Moment

The first day of the term is not of course the first day of the university
but one of a long line of days, and it's important to have a sense of this
history:[3] how the university began in the Middle Ages in the monasteries, the learning of Greek and Latin literature seen as a means to the end
of reading the Bible and understanding the Mass; how this system of
education expanded beyond the monasteries to parish schools and then
further into the larger community, including more and more of the laity,
until the establishment of the great medieval universities in Bologna
and Paris and Oxford and Cambridge; how for centuries faith and the

university were seen not as opponents but as allies, as necessarily inter-dependent.

From the beginning there was tension, and this is key. A tension is inherent. Rather than "ally" it might be more accurate to see reason as the servant of faith, but a servant that more and more begins to resist the master, getting stronger and stronger in the Renaissance, under the influence of science and technology and the rise of the middle class, until finally, in Modernism, the servant breaks away and becomes the master. The church is then in the subordinate position, still involved if less influential, until finally it is excluded altogether, pushed to the boundaries.

This process of reversal has taken place more gradually than we might expect, even in this country, even given the first amendment. But it has taken place, as my student Will demonstrated. The founders never intended the separation of church and state to become the wall that it has become in the last fifty years of American law and politics. Harvard and Yale were founded on a Protestant ideal of the church serving the state and the state the church. Even into the twentieth century land grant colleges like Oregon State required chapel attendance and offered courses in the Bible, not as literature, but as a moral guide for citizens. Campus ministries have only recently been pushed outside the university and across the street. For two centuries there was an assumed, often unconscious alliance of Protestantism and democratic values in this country—but an alliance that gradually drained religion of any but its most generic moral qualities, until finally even those qualities were drained away. Led by John Dewey and other reformers, American education set out to eliminate the irrational influence of religion.

For a moment, as Christianity began to lose its influence, university professors became conveyors of general spiritual values, liberal education a substitute for catechism and creed, before the German model of professionalism broke up the disciplines into pseudo-scientific specialties more and more removed from real life concerns. Now, in the twenty-first century, the paradigm for the university has become the global economy, students reduced to customers and education to product, regulated not by values but by profit.

A tradition of important books critiques and resists these movements and forces, a tradition that extends from Cardinal John Henry Newman's seminal *The Idea of the University*, written in the nineteenth century but reflecting the high medieval synthesis; to Walter Moberly's *The Crisis of the University*, actually written by a group of English clergy after the Second World War and reflecting a modernist approach to Christianity; to David Tracy's *Plurality and Ambiguity*,[4] a defense of Christianity in the terms of postmodernism, building on the theory of Paul Ricouer. My argument is theirs, and before them, Augustine's, who is at the heart of this tradition as he is at the heart of Christianity. What Newman and Moberly and Tracy do in their own terms is to work out Augustine's first intuitions, in the *Confessions* and later in *On Christian Doctrine* and the *City of God*, about the relation of reason and faith, education and conversion. Augustine is at the heart of this book: his longing for God, his sense of the otherness of God, his struggle to understand the logic of the incarnation. His joy.

Those who argue for a return to some uncomplicated union of intellect and belief are arguing for something that never existed and wouldn't be healthy anyway, true either to the university or to the moral life, least of all in twenty-first-century America. Yes, it's silly that Christianity is the only "ism" excluded from public discussion on campus. Yes, it's silly that even the name "Christian" can make colleagues uncomfortable. The creative tension between faith and reason has been reduced to an easy opposition, the reversal of the binary has gone much too far, and in response there is now a powerful and healthy movement in this country, led by Palmer, to restore the place of spirituality in the lives of faculty and in the intellectual life of the campus—spirituality in appropriately general and inclusive terms.

But like Palmer, I am not arguing that one set of values be made dominant again, in the university or in the country.[5] Campus ministries are right where they should be, on the boundaries, separate and distinct, because however recent a development, however American, such a distancing and separation is in keeping with the aims of Christianity at its origins. It circles back to the deepest nature of faith, which is to be prophetic, which is to exist in a creative and complicated opposition to power, a role that was understood even when the universities were the handmaid of the church, a role that defined what it meant to be a handmaid.

Whatever their time and place, Christians at their best have always professed the radical humility of faith. Augustine was postmodern sixteen centuries ago. "Since it is God we are speaking of," he says, "you do not understand it. If you could understand it, it would not be God" (Wills xii).[6] I rely heavily on Newman's *The Idea of the University* in the chapters that follow, reflecting on its claims in my own context. I rely heavily on Ricouer and on Tracy, in their insistence on the limits of knowledge. But underneath their thinking for me is always Augustine's clear and pervasive sense both of God's inexplicability and of his searching love.

Orthodoxy is the insistence on the limits of our knowledge and our language and our traditions. What is infallible is not human judgment or creativity, but the mystery of God. Thus our need for pluralism. Thus our necessary respect for people of other faiths and variety of doubt.

## The Controlling Metaphor: Crossing the Line

My argument, then, depends on paradox.

Christian faculty too often feel discounted and excluded by the university. That's been my own experience as a professor of English who is also a Catholic deacon: The university either ignores my faith or sees it as a potential problem. But this is wrong. Faith isn't irrelevant to the intellectual life. Faith isn't a threat to pluralism. In fact, Christian faculty are necessary to the public university, central to its mission, because they call the intellect to humility.

Intellectuals too often feel discounted and excluded by the church. That's been my own experience as a Catholic deacon who is also a professor of English: The church either ignores my profession or sees it as a potential problem. But this is wrong. The intellectual life isn't irrelevant to faith. Pluralism isn't a threat. In fact, the university is necessary for the church, central to its mission, because it calls faith to humility.

The tension underneath these two parallel claims is the tension that defines Christianity, the creative and redeeming tension, and to represent that tension in the structure of this book I've used the central image of Christian faith, the cross itself, organizing the six central chapters into a chiastic design.

On another level these chapters progress as readings of certain central texts in turn. My conceit is to dramatize my teaching of the Literature of Western Civilization—Genesis, Mark, and Homer in the fall, Augustine in the winter, Dante and the resurrection in the spring (though I don't necessarily teach these texts in this order, and of course I teach more texts than this—*Oedipus*, for example, and later *Don Quixote*, *The Prelude*, others—not focusing as much on the Bible as I do here). My concerns are first the concerns of pedagogy and of literary study, centered on the teaching of literature and writing.

But I believe that what's true for the teaching of literature and writing is also true for teaching in other disciplines, not just in the humanities but also in the sciences. What applies to the critical reading of Genesis or Homer applies to the reading of a culture, or a forest, and deeper than that, applies to an understanding of what it means to be a believer, what it means to come to a faith. By recreating my own teaching of the Bible as Literature and these other great literary texts I mean to establish ideas that can lead both to a theory of higher education and an understanding of faith.

This is where the chiastic structure comes into play. The image of the cross can help us understand the creative tension between faith and reason not just in the reading of literature but in all reading, all living.

Think of the three parts of any cross: the horizontal beam, the vertical beam, and the place where the two come together.

Chapters 1 and 2, under the heading *The Way of the University*, work along the broad horizontal beam of that cross. Here I reflect on my experience teaching Genesis and Mark as a way of talking about the secular work of the public university in any department, in the sciences or the humanities. This line is "horizontal" in the sense of being earthly and everyday, without benefit of meaning that might come from "above."

Chapters 5 and 6, under the heading *The Way of Faith*, work along the vertical shaft of the cross, the beam of commitment and of love, ours for God and God's for us. Here I reflect on my experience in the classroom and in the church as a believing Christian, experience that is "vertical" in the sense that it has to do with meaning that does come from "above" or "beyond" the everyday work that we do in universities.

In between, in the two chapters I include under the heading *Intersections*, I describe several moments in the fall and winter term of the course, when in discussions of Homer's *Odyssey* and Augustine's *Confessions* my faith seemed to intersect my life in the classroom, to cut right through it—startling moments, challenging moments—moments when the way of the university and the way of faith didn't seem at odds but somehow, scandalously, in harmony.

The image of the cross serves as a powerful way of thinking, suggesting both limit and connection, intersection and divergence, and using a passage from Newman's *The Idea of the University* in the beginning of each of the six chapters, I keep returning to its possibilities. The metaphor isn't static. The six chapters shouldn't be read out of order, as I've described them above, with *Intersections* emphasized last. The book has a plot and a plot that builds, moving from one through six in a sequence based on Ricouer's idea that "mystery gives rise to story gives rise to thought." The work of the university is not to endorse a particular interpretation of a story but to show that any one interpretation is always provisional, one among many. This is the theoretical model that I establish in the next chapter, blending Ricouer's heuristic into my own, and it leads through the complications of the middle chapters and then to the final claims of the fifth and sixth, and beyond, into the conclusion, a final reflection on the faith of my students. The line of faith passes through the line of the university, powerfully, but then it keeps on going, further and further, and sometimes my students, too, follow where it leads.

The endnotes consider a number of more academic and background issues, issues that I've wanted to keep out of the text itself, engaging in particular the history of the university and questions of postmodernism.

Faith can be the test of diversity. As Christians we should join in the multicultural and inclusive and chaotic world that has become the university in the twenty-first century. We can deepen this diversity. But at the same time there is a limit, there is a line between church and state, however fuzzy—the line between "story" and "thought" in Ricouer's sequence—and that line is necessary and good, for both sides. Diversity is also the test of faith. Faith and the university need each other exactly because of the tension that exists between them.

Yes, we should cross the line, I will say in the end, but not in the classroom. We should cross it by leaving the classroom, walking away from the limitations of the intellect and finding completion in what only faith can provide. This is how it is in the *Divine Comedy*, where Virgil as the symbol of reason can take Dante only as far as the Earthly Paradise, the pinnacle of human achievement. Only Beatrice, the symbol of grace, can carry him into Paradise. Even at religious schools, as Pope John Paul II says in *Ex Corde Ecclesiae*—in a comment that applies to religious schools of all kinds, Catholic, Protestant, and evangelical—"emphasis is placed on how human reason in its reflection opens to increasingly broader questions, and how the complete answer to them can only come through faith" (18).[7]

What's at stake in this crossing isn't just the welfare of another special interest group. As Moberly put it a generation ago, Christian faculty, exactly as Christians, have an obligation to "call the university to *be* the university" (26). Our campuses are in crisis, more now than in the last century—the reversal has gone even further, intensified by the market forces of the global economy—and as Christians we have it in our power to form a "creative minority" within the institution, as Moberly says (141), a minority that sounds a lot like Palmer's communities of congruence or Nouwen's communities of resistance, a minority that can help renew and reform higher education. As Christians we have a separate source of strength and authority, one outside the structure of the university, and it's exactly because of this that we can and should speak, exactly because of our distance. We have a contribution to make, a unique contribution, from the other side of the line.

## The Circuitous Journey

Within the logic of this "crossing" design, I work through narrative and reflection on narrative in the chapters that follow, in the tradition of spiritual autobiography, of "confession" in Augustine's own sense, not of confessing one's sins but of "testifying," as Garry Wills explains (xiv–xv), reporting all the ways in which God has been active in my life and heart and mind. Though my purpose is to make and sustain a larger argument, and though I devote the bulk of this book to that purpose, my argument begins and ends in my own experience—not because I think that my experience is unique but because I know that it isn't, because the truths that I am trying to understand are embodied in the concrete moment, available in their fullness only there.

Form is the shape of content. A certain style is appropriate for certain subjects. "Pride asserts, humility testifies" is how Augustine puts it (Wills xii), which is to say that for him the very perfection and mystery of God requires the humility, and edginess, and imperfection of his own rough autobiographical style, just as the Incarnation requires the telling of his own story. If God reveals himself within us, if God makes himself known in what Augustine calls "drops of time" (*Confessions* 258; 11.2), we most honor and describe him when we honor and describe our own experience, in all its particulars. *That's* where God is, in the mirror in the morning, on the street, in the green hills. As James McClendon puts it in *Biography as Theology*: "Narrative or *story* is a means of expression uniquely suited to theology or at least to Christian theology" (158). Or as novelist and memoirist Frederick Buechner says of his own writing, "if I talk about these things less as lecturer than as storyteller, more anticly than academically, more concretely than conceptually, it is not only because I can do no other but because it is also the way I believe I have heard my life talk to me if my life talks to me, the way even God talks to me if God talks to me" (*Alphabet of Grace* 12–13).

This is how it is in my own life. A personal history leads to that moment in the classroom, too, the first day of the Literature of Western Civilization. My argument grows out of a story, a story that began several years before when I took a leave from Oregon State to teach at Mount Angel, a diocesan seminary run by Benedictine monks, fifty miles northeast of town. The abbey and the abbey church rise up on a hill above the valley, among the seminary classrooms and dorms, and my wife and I would commute there every weekday, to the monastery, through the rolling fields and farms, from one world, one time, to another, back and forth. She took classes towards her Masters degree in theology and I taught introductory literature courses to small groups of seminarians in the undergraduate and pre-theology program, men from all over the world studying for the priesthood.

I leapt at the chance to escape the hiring committees and the library full of esoteric and pointless scholarship, the bickering and the quiet enmities of any English department, any institution, public or otherwise, and I was fleeing, too, a deepening clinical depression, a slow, deadly paralysis of mind and heart, though I didn't know this at first. What renewed and refreshed me about the seminary was partly its provincialism, its small scale, its ignorance of the critical debates and increasingly dispiriting theoretical discussions that have long been draining English studies of their purpose and life. I *was* the English department at Mount Angel Seminary, it was just me and *The Norton*

*Anthology*, and sitting in a circle with Brother Sipho and Brother Dominic, with Michael and David and José, the fountain playing in the courtyard, the fields all around us, I felt for a while that I had escaped into Narnia. It was an illusion, of course, and temporary, but it was a pastoral illusion in both senses of that word: an experience of a green and softening world; and an experience of being ministered to, of being soothed and healed.

It was here, at this time, within this culture and the kinds of thinking and awareness that this culture makes possible, that I felt myself reconverting to Christianity and then being called to ministry. Depression was also a part of the experience, catching up with me at just the moment I was sensing the joy that religious life makes possible, and somehow this didn't feel like a contradiction. Somehow it was both the presence and the absence of God, both joy and despair, that led me to abandon the sense of self that had governed me for nearly forty years and to enter instead into this new and radical freedom.

When I came back to the university—after going on to train and then become a deacon—my Christianity seemed at first a private thing, separate from life in the classroom and with colleagues. It was my rock, my shield, my secret source of strength, what kept me centered and whole for the buffetings and diminishments of so many days on campus. The stark language of the Psalms made a deep sense, the language of enemies encamped around us and of enemies laying snares for us and of God as refuge, God as fortress. I respected, too, in an unconsidered way, the separations of church and state, not wanting to violate the accepted boundaries. When I brought the Eucharist to school on Wednesdays for a weekly communion service, carrying the consecrated hosts in a small pyx hidden away in my Lands End attaché, I was carrying something precious and personal and set apart. When we sat together at the Memorial Union at lunch time, praying and sharing communion, we were drawing together among ourselves for solace and perspective, staying quiet.

My reconversion to Christianity and my experience at the seminary had given me new clarity, new pedagogy, and new anger as a teacher— anger at the hyperspecialization of English studies, its grounding in a false notion of professionalism, its devotion to research understood narrowly and arrogantly, its false objectivism, its tendency to ignore the needs of the student, its tendency to divorce the reading of stories from anything that might matter in the world or in the heart. But at first I didn't see how that anger could be made public or acted on. My pedagogy was my own, opening up my own classrooms without influencing anyone else's. This is the way of English departments, as Gerald Graff has observed (6). We specialize and then distribute. We don't reform curricula but let each person do his or her own thing, hiring a feminist, hiring a ecological critic, and letting them teach their private courses side by side with the traditionalists and the Marxists and the others, each of us locked away in our own insulated classrooms and offices, attending our own conferences and reading our own journals.

My Christianity was just another option among all the other options, tolerated because ignored, or seen, if seen at all, as another eccentricity. In Benedictine monasticism, in my knowledge and experience of the tradition of the church, in my experience of the Mass and the liturgy, I was coming to know a radical alternative to the atomization and emptiness of the contemporary university. I was coming to know a radically transforming model of community, but I didn't at first see this as transferable, as a model I could talk about to others, an experience I could reflect on and share. When I first read Palmer urging teachers and students to live "divided no more," to act with "integrity," no longer disguising their real identity and commitments, I said, yes, of course, in a general way. But for a number of reasons "congruence" like this didn't seem to apply to me as a Catholic Christian in a contemporary university. In my case congruence seemed more dangerous and problematic than for a feminist or an environmentalist or a person of color.

And it is problematic. It is dangerous. But what began to surprise me on my return, what has led to the claims I make in this book, were little moments of congruence, of continuity, in the classroom, in conversation with colleagues, in reading. For brief moments the barriers in the institution or in my own mind seemed to fall away as they still seem to fall away and what I was professing quite properly as a professor at a state university seemed disconcertingly, unnervingly, altogether congruent with what I also professed at Mass on Sundays, when I stood up and proclaimed the gospel. At least in my own classrooms, at least in my own experience, some deep intersection seemed to be taking place, some disquieting overlap. Christianity was beginning to support the work of critical reading, and from there it couldn't help but move outwards, towards feminism and environmentalism and multiculturalism, joining in their prophetic analysis and critique.

This journey of mine away and then back towards home is a version of what David Leigh would call the "circuitous journey" (see his book of that title), and it is the journey of Augustine himself, and later of St. Benedict, a journey away from the schools and out into the wilderness, then a journey back to preach and reform. It is the mythic journey, the journey of the hero, which is the frightening thing about it. Odysseus is a hero not because he goes away and has adventures but because he comes back. He doesn't remain in the enchanted worlds but returns to his own to purge and reform it. Jesus of Nazareth doesn't just die, he rises again and gathers the people into the church.

I haven't slaughtered any suitors. My clarities are too modest, blurring too easily into uncertainty and confusion, and the very values I have come to profess, the Christian values of dying to self, of self-emptying, make me uneasy about claiming to know the truth. But I believe that the stages in my cycle are in some sense universal: from retreat to renewal to return to reform—then to renunciation, then to release, before the cycle repeats again. "Below our cultural inheritance," Northrop Frye says, "there must be a common psychological inheritance" (xviii). This is the cycle of the intellect, this is the cycle of a career, this is the cycle of a life. In entering the world of the monastery I was also traveling back in time, to the Middle Ages and so to the world of Newman's *Idea*. In returning to Oregon State I was entering again the world of postmodernism and skepticism and doubt and science and technology, a world that Augustine wouldn't have understood on some levels and that Newman resisted on others but that both would have seen through, to the God we all need.

The circuitous journey, then, could provide another image for the theme of this book, an alternative to the image of the cross—though not an alternative, but another way of saying the same thing, a way of describing where the image of the cross really comes from. It comes from our lives. The circuitous journey of my own life involves many crossings of the border, from the university to the church and back again, and in the act of crossing I am in some small way experiencing both crucifixion and resurrection, over and over again. So are we all.

## A Theory of Story and the Idea of the University

Ideas, I am saying, emerge from experience. Ideas are the result of reflection on the stories of our lives. Mystery gives rise to story gives rise to thought. This is the center of the theory of Paul Ricouer, in his seminal work, *The Symbolism of Evil*, and in the rest of this book I use it to make clear what I think I've learned from Augustine and Newman.[7]

First comes great sadness, Ricouer says. First comes great and shattering joy. First comes the night sky and all the stars, their vastness. Then comes the natural human act, the first instinctive response to the mystery of a world and a life and a presence that seems so much greater than we are: we tell stories. We don't philosophize, we don't theorize, we don't assert. We begin, "Once upon time." We begin, "A funny thing happened," because funny things do happen. Life happens, concretely, moment by moment, and all our theories and interpretations of it, though necessary and important, are always secondary and inadequate and if useful at all merely return us to what is impossible to translate out of the moment itself, what we can only experience, in our bodies. "Thought" is the last step, it is always last, and it is always provisional and self-consuming.

Ironically, this was the central insight of my time at the seminary. The "thought" that emerged was precisely that "thought" is always last and least. The stale smell of cigarettes in the halls. The sound of rap music on some distant stereo. Doughnut crumbs in the coffee room. After the euphoria of my first few weeks at Mount Angel my delight in the warmth of the people and the scale of the place, I moved into the stage when details came into focus. Mount Angel became a real place, the monks and seminarians real people, with their own particular names and faces. Students yawned there, too, and slouched at their desks. There was the same tension and tightening a month into the term, the same resistances and the same need to convince. What struck me at a faculty meeting was how familiar things seemed, despite the flowing habits and opening prayer. People were nicer than I'm used to, trying harder to listen and cooperate. But there was still the wrangling about procedure and the bumbling around about dates and times, the talking at cross purposes, the reinventing of wheels. What seems solid from a distance never is up close.

The church is often presumed to be some vast, monolithic, impersonal institution, a system of dogma enforcement so old and powerful that it can't be felt as human. The image seems to be of long, hushed corridors and echoing chambers—the church as nothing but the tradition in the abstract, nothing but ideas: the Immaculate Conception, celibacy, patriarchy.

But what I experienced every day at the abbey wasn't the priesthood or the crisis of the priesthood or the male-only celibate-only priesthood. It was José and Mark and Maselino: their individual stories, the sound of their laughter in the halls. As we worked together on Wordsworth or the *Iliad*, I wasn't thinking about these people as future priests, but as students trying with varying degrees of sensitivity and intelligence to understand the language of literature, no different in many ways from any other group of students I've taught, no less capable of insight or misreading. There were some differences, good ones for me as a teacher: a greater respect for authority, a greater willingness to work hard, a greater openness to imagination and feeling. Yet in its daily give and take the teaching seemed just as haphazard and messy as it always does. I felt right at home.

Each day at noon prayer, my wife and I watched monks trail in from wherever they'd been, bowing to the altar and taking their places in the choir. Each day we joined them in the chanting of the Psalms. What we were experiencing wasn't the "Benedictine tradition" exactly. We were standing at that place, at that time, with the noon light streaming through the windows, that monk on the back left coming in on the wrong measure. And we knew that monk now, his name, his quick frown. When we looked at the choir we didn't see "monastic life." We saw Dominic, Konrad, Joachim. What we joined every noon was grounded in centuries-old tradition and a spirituality worked out in every detail—dignified, structured, beautiful. And yet there also seemed something wonderfully amateurish and ad hoc about the whole thing—something specific and local, as if a bunch of guys had just gotten together and agreed to go through those odd motions for a while. Voices cracked, shoulders shrugged, someone hurried in late. It seemed made up, spontaneous.

I sat in on a class in "Fundamental Theology" that year. What we learned, among other things, is the grand structure of the church as it is laid out in *De Verbum*, the Vatican II document on revelation, a powerful summary of the church's belief in apostolic succession and the teaching authority of the magisterium. Somehow, I know, this structure is underneath what drew me to the abbey and keeps drawing me back: the silence and the peacefulness, the holiness at the center, the reverence. Yet at the same time I wonder if the church ever really exists on the level of council documents, whether there really is a church in this sense or whether there is just a whole series of moments and glimpses and individual acts carried on day to day, informed by tradition, informed by theology. I wonder how the church would change if we started seeing it this way. It would certainly be a lot harder to dismiss or evade responsibility for. It would be too vulnerable. It would be too complicated.

I bet the disciples had sore feet and growling stomachs sometimes, and it is clear from the Gospels that they were often making things up as they went, making mistakes and doing the best they could. The Gospels are stories, after all, good stories, full of the complexities of character and the concreteness of scene. There are all these distracting place names: Capernaum, Caesarea Philippi, Bethsaida, Tyre. What Christians most centrally believe is that God intervened in history, came, that is, to a certain place and a certain time. We miss the point altogether if we don't imagine the dusty roads and the smelly donkeys and the hawking of the sellers in the marketplace. I think we're too quick to generalize, to read past the contingent to the transcendent, when the contingent matters just as much if not finally more. What's astonishing about the stories the church is meant to preserve and interpret is their claim that God came into a haphazard and bumbling and continually reinvented world exactly like our own—in fact, that God has come into this world, right now, the world of the rolling fields and the doughnut crumbs and the slow, sweet chanting of the prayers at noon.

This is why Augustine had to write an autobiography, the first in western tradition, because he believed this, he knew this, in his bones. "Whatever is revealed in Jesus," George Dennis O'Brien says in *The Idea of a Catholic University*, "theology and doctrinal statements are finally and only validated by the presence of that actuality. We don't start with theological doctrine and then instance the reality; we start with the given reality and then try to understand what there is about it that theologians may be pointing to" (48). This is what I came to know at the seminary and what, ironically, I have brought back into my teaching at the public university—not my faith itself but my intuition about where it comes from and how it evolves. "The secondary role of doctrine is vital to understanding biblical religion," O'Brien continues. "What leads the religious believer is not a statement of belief, a dogma, but some lived actuality" (49).

Thus the stories and reflections that follow. Thus a discussion of the form of the book becomes a discussion of its content. Because "mystery gives rise to story gives rise to thought" describes what I experience and so act out in my writing, at the same time it provides the theoretical basis for the argument I make.

I report my experience in the monastic world of Mount Angel as a time of conversion and grace, but someone else may see hierarchy and patriarchy and clericalism only. I report the moment in the old growth in the Drift Creek Wilderness, the light and the healing, but someone else may see board feet and acreage. Because our "thoughts" are inevitably partial and temporary, because the fullness of meaning is located in story itself, there is always a line between story and thought, and this line, I argue, is the line between the university and faith (chapters 1 and 2). We sometimes cross it whether we mean to or not (chapters 3 and 4), and eventually we must cross it (chapters 5 and 6).

We must—but outside the university, in faith.

# PART ONE

# The Way of the University

CHAPTER I

# Teaching Genesis as Story

In the beginning of *The Idea of the University*, Cardinal Newman considers the possibility that even when the university is sponsored by the church, a "line" exists between the way of the university and the way of faith. For a moment he identifies a clear boundary:

> It will be said, that there are different kinds or spheres of Knowledge, human, divine, sensible, intellectual, and the like; and that a University certainly takes in all varieties of Knowledge in its own line, but still that it has a line of its own. It contemplates, it occupies a certain order, a certain platform of Knowledge. (29; 1.2.3)

*It will be said.* Newman raises this point only to deny it in the next sentence, insisting that to separate faith and knowledge is finally too easy. In the end, at the Catholic university that he is charged with creating, in nineteenth-century Ireland, a university grounded in faith, the distinction won't hold.

But in the beginning of my own discussion, at a state university in twenty-first century America, the distinction between faith and reason does hold. Though the university "certainly takes in all varieties of Knowledge," though the distinctions will start to dissolve before long, in an obvious way, in this time and place, Oregon State University can be said to occupy a "platform" or "sphere" of analysis distinct from that of St. Mary's Parish. It can be said to have "a line of its own," and intuitively we know what it is: the line of inquiry rather than of advocacy, of analysis rather than of dogma.

21

This is where to begin, with the broad, horizontal beam of the cross, the beam that describes the work of critical thinking that is the work of a public university or any university. In this chapter, I explain how the teaching of the book of Genesis as literature can simply be seen as another way of doing that work, how the Bible can serve as a particularly rich text for the kind of analysis that defines higher education. In Ricouer's terms, the aim of the university is to keep demonstrating the many possible "thoughts" that can be inferred from the "story" of our lives, our culture, our literature, our science.

The paradox is that my identity as a preacher becomes a very useful way for me to demonstrate exactly this point.

This chapter and the next argue that we need to leave out our stories (in a sense), setting them aside and focusing instead on the texts themselves. But I want to begin by returning to my time at the seminary, reflecting on the differences between my experience there and at the university because these differences prepared me to return. They gave me tools for doing exactly what the university is supposed to do, what I feel called to do, as both deacon and professor.

## Fall

Often in the fall when I was teaching and studying at the seminary I'd walk out on the bluff beyond the monastery buildings. There is a rutted road and then a path through the blackberry hummocks and dry grasses to an oak grove where I would read and watch the birds. Sometimes a downy woodpecker was going about its work in the branches. Chickadees bickered and fluted lower down. From beneath the trees I looked over the brow of the hill to the wide fields of the valley floor, sprinklers arcing in the distance.

One afternoon I brought a book by the Anglican theologian and patristic scholar Andrew Louth, *Discerning the Mystery*, and reading it there in the oak grove I had one of those profound moments that we all have now and then when our intellect and our life and our faith come together. It happened when I read this passage:

> The central truth, or mystery, of the Christian faith is primarily not a matter of words, and therefore ultimately of ideas and concepts, but a matter of fact, of reality. To be a Christian is not simply to believe something, to learn something, but to be something, to experience something. The role of the Church, then, is not simply as the contingent vehicle—in history—of the Christian message, but as the community through belonging to which we come into touch with the Christian mystery. (74)

I remember how the oak trees broke up the light. I remember the smell of the dry grass. I remember the intellectual joy I felt when I realized that this is the faith of my tradition and that it makes sense, it answers to my experience. It's about my experience, and all experience—it says experience is more important than dogma, more important than systems. The whole point of religion and theology, Louth says, is to affirm their own inadequacy, to give way to experience, and yes, I thought, yes and yes, and though I was alone in that moment, apart from the community on the other side of the hill, the community I had prayed with that noon, that I would pray with again each noon of that fall term, I felt in relationship to them, too, because this is what we all believed, this is what we were there to affirm and explore and live.

I will come back to this passage again in chapter 4—it's central to the argument of the book—but the point for now (ironically) is that the moment of my reading it was both an experience, a "story" in Ricouer's terms, and at the same time a story that I was interpreting, that I was coming to understand intellectually and in a sense doctrinally—and it was the doctrine, the "thought," as much as the experience, that was giving the joy. For so long I had resisted the obscurity and what seemed to me the arrogance of contemporary postmodern theory, but here it was again, humble and prayerful and in the service of all that I most loved. It liberated me. It helped me name the moment and name it specifically, as Christian. I wasn't just experiencing. I was affirming. And I wasn't affirming all the possible meanings of the experience, of the birds and the oak grove and the page in front of me, the sprinklers in the distance. I was affirming one and one only: Christ, the way.

This is what the seminary was doing, too, of course, from the outset, as its initial premise, much like the university that Newman was forming in Ireland in the nineteenth century: promoting a particular interpretation of experience, insisting on one particular thought, even if that thought was about all the multiplicity that can be found in Christ, who is inexhaustible. Faith and reason are united in a seminary, the one leading to the other, back and forth—we must believe in order to understand, we must reason and so arrive at faith, and the two paths intertwine, circle back, turn into each other. There is a kind of reasoning that is theological reasoning, that is reasoning on what is first accepted as revealed truth, and this is the kind of reasoning that we were all united in doing at the seminary, the kind of reasoning that John Paul II celebrates in *Fides et Ratio* and *Ex Corde Ecclesiae* and that my experience in the oak grove affirmed. This is the understanding of the relation between reason and faith that defines the mission and curriculum of religious colleges and universities.[8]

And it's not just at the seminary that these experiences take place, and not just that fall that they have taken place for me. They are happening all the time. For me as a believing Christian, as someone who has traveled through Ricouer's sequence and come out the other side and made the choice I have made, chosen the interpretation I have chosen, Christ is lovely in ten thousand places, Christ is present everywhere.

One weekend in the fall we got a call from our oldest son. His truck had blown an engine and he was stranded on I–5, halfway between Corvallis and Mount Angel. I drove over to help him, and soon I was sitting there, too, in the grass by exit 244, beneath some apple trees from an old orchard, waiting for the tow truck. The autumn sun was shining on us. Cars were barreling down the freeway and we watched the faces of the people, how worried and unhappy they looked, like me a few hours before, when I was so pressed for time. And suddenly I was glad I was there, on the side of the road. There was this peace seeping into me, this slow, gradual feeling of the presence of God.

It seemed to me a moment of grace—but not just a moment, because at the same time I was interpreting it. I was inferring a thought from it. Given my tradition, given my knowledge of the Bible, given my commitments, I thought of the great "*Kenosis*" hymn in Philippians, some of the most magnificent poetry in all the Bible or anywhere else. *Kenosis*—self-emptying. The rhythm of those lines is so beautiful: "Though he was in the form of God he did not regard equality with God something to be exploited, but emptied himself, taking the form of a slave" (2:6–7).[9] That's the center of our faith: that we, too, must die to live, that only by letting go are we truly free. "Do not worry about anything," Paul says later, at the end of this letter, "but in everything by prayer and supplication, with thanksgiving, let your requests be made known to God" (4:6). Paul's no silly idealist. He's in prison as he writes this, in danger of losing his life, and yet there's this magnificent calm in his words, this quiet joy. And I have felt this myself, through grace.

It's a joy that comes in part from recognizing the subtle signs of God's presence day to day, in "whatever is true, whatever is honorable, whatever is just, whatever is pure, whatever is pleasing, whatever is commendable" (4:8). Such a lovely series of words! We tend to think of the spiritual as separate from the ordinary. But Christ is present in whatever is excellent—a book, a face. Listen to Mozart. Look at the leaves falling. Whenever we take someone's hand or make something right, the spirit is rising up. Whenever we turn away from the shoddiness of the junk culture and reach for what is gracious and true, we glimpse the coming of the kingdom.

There are reasons to be happy, in other words, even now, but the peace that Paul describes is still deeper than that. The peace he describes "surpasses all understanding" (4:7), because it comes from God, who is greater than all evidence. Even when the subtle signs have disappeared, even when we are overwhelmed by the human capacity for violence and stupidity, somehow, in faith, a deeper calm can come. There is a love and a wisdom beyond what we can understand—and yet a wisdom we can feel. It seeps into us. It settles into our bones.

This is the thought that I have come to—even though I am always losing it, too, failing to believe it.

Once I was asked to do a graveside service for an elderly lady. It was a fall afternoon, very hot. Before the service began I went over to visit the grave of a young boy who had died several years before. I remembered where it was, beneath a large tree. I knew it even from a distance, because someone had recently placed a little soccer ball, a real little soccer ball, in the grass by the grave stone. Amos was thirteen when he died of leukemia, the son of a dear friend, and I will never forget the sight of his body in the casket, dressed in his school sweater, the sight of the open ground, the mound of dirt.

But in that moment, looking down at the marker, I was moved by this obscure sense of something precious and tender and very real. There was an enormous sadness, too. I can't even begin to imagine the grief of parents—I would never want to cheapen it with false piety or sentimentality. But somehow—I have to report this as true—this really happened—somehow I sensed something else gathering there, in me, in the air. It was peace. Of all things to feel at the grave of a child, it was peace—like a presence, like something palpable.

And I thought then of the closing blessing from the Catholic graveside service, the blessing I was about to give to the mourners waiting up the hill, a beautiful, beautiful blessing, based on the passage from Philippians:

> May the peace of God
> which is beyond all understanding,
> keep your hearts and minds
> in the knowledge and love
> of God and of his son, our Lord Jesus Christ.

---

To be at the seminary one fall and at the university the next was to experience a difference, a line. What I felt was culture shock at first, to reenter the world I came from and was called to be in again. My first week back I sat in a meeting and watched one professor cut another to ribbons. On the way to my office I was walking behind two women students. One girl was saying that she'd been having a lot of sex lately, even though she hadn't been using the pill. She shrugged her shoulders and then said, laughing, pointing to her womb, die-die-die, and I think she was talking about the sperm in her body.

I don't mean to idealize the seminary, which, as I've said, is a real place with its own failings, the people as sinful as anywhere else. The recent scandals in the church, and the often defensive clericalism of the church's response, have made this painfully clear. I don't mean to caricature OSU, where, as I will discuss later, Christ is also lovely in ten thousand places. I feel called to the university. I feel that this is where I should be, not in a monastery, not on a hill, but here, down below. What I mean to note is simply the difference in the two cultures, in what Augustine in *The City of God* would call the two cities. People organize themselves into societies around what they love, Augustine says. In the City of God as it's mirrored on earth, we sinful people are organized around love of God. In the City of Man, we sinful people are organized around a love of ourselves, a love that can't help but become selfish and grabby at times, and this is what I experienced on my return. This is what I knew in my bones and what shocked and saddened me, this difference.

But what I experienced on my return was also a conceptual difference, a difference in the nature of the intellectual work that the university does as opposed to the intellectual work of a seminary or monastery, a proper difference, a good difference, a powerful difference. At OSU reason is not supposed to lead to faith and it's not supposed to proceed from faith. It's supposed to be distinct from it. Of course. I know and I accept this: I am not to bless my students, I am not to proclaim my own conclusions, I am simply to demonstrate the process by which we all come to the many different and conflicting conclusions that we all come to. All the love and the joy and the beauty—and the sadness and the struggle and the humor—the oak grove and the apple trees, the soccer ball and the grave—all that I most centrally am and believe in and aspire to be—all this I have to take off, I have to remove, I have to set aside.

But *that's* the value of my faith. That's precisely its value: that I can take it off.

———

One day in class in the Literature of Western Civilization I come in with an exercise in one hand and my alb and my stole in the other, on a hanger. I hang the alb and the stole on the top of the open door, without comment, and hand out the exercise, a list of questions asking students to think about how they've been taught to read the Bible even if they think they know nothing about it—what they've heard about it, what they've experienced of Jews and Christians, the kinds of books they read, if they do read, the movies they see and the work they do, the majors they've chosen. Their hometown. Their parents. Their gender.

As the class is working in groups filling out this questionnaire, I am putting on my alb and my stole. *Alb*: Latin for white, to symbolize my spiritual purity (at least sacramentally—I'm wearing jeans underneath.) My stole: diagonal from left shoulder to right hip (as opposed to the horseshoe-shaped stole of the priest), to symbolize my office as a deacon, as an ordinary minister of the Eucharist and a servant of the people. I slip my arms into the sleeves of the alb, tie up the waist, and snap the buttons on the neck until I am covered from my chin to the tops of my scuffed Clarks in polyester white. Students are watching, looking up as I do this, and I'm embarrassed and nervous as I go, not sure I should have tried such a stunt in the first place. Oddly, it feels like I'm taking my clothes off, not putting them on.

There I am, standing in a white lace robe in front of 75 college students, big as a tent. But I keep going, and as I place the stole over my shoulder—green now, for ordinary time, like the altar cloths in the church three blocks away—I start talking about the group exercise very matter-of-factly, explaining the idea of it and the purpose of it, how what I'm trying to demonstrate is simply that we all bring things to the text, that we are all conditioned. I don't mention the alb. Some of you come from religious backgrounds, I say, Jewish or Christian, Protestant or Catholic, evangelical, fundamentalist. Some of you have stopped going to church. Some have started. Some of you wouldn't be caught dead in churches or don't know a thing about it one way or the other, but that's a way of reading, too. None of us come to this or any text naked. Human beings live, I quote from Frye:

> Not directly or nakedly in nature like the animals, but within a mythological universe, a body of assumptions and beliefs developed from [our] existential concerns. Most of this is held unconsciously. [. . .] Practically all that we can see of this body of concern is socially conditioned and culturally inherited. (xviii)

When I ask students to share what they developed in groups, I identify each answer as evidence of this unconscious "body of assumptions and beliefs," this "mythological universe" that we inherit and that conditions us whether we know it or not. "I didn't do much reading as a kid," someone says. "I mostly just watched TV and played video games." So, I say, you come to the Bible conditioned by SuperSmash Brothers and by a way of interpreting information, visually, quick image by quick image. "I'm an engineering major." "I'm a biochemistry major." So, I say, since you probably spend most of your time reading textbooks in your field, you may come to the stories of the Bible the way you come to a linear equation, as if it's a problem to be solved rather than as story to be experienced. You may make assumptions about the nature of what counts as evidence, what counts as true, and though those assumptions are not necessarily invalid, it's important to become aware that there other possible assumptions, other ways to proceed.

"I was raised in a church but I hate it all now," someone says, and then another jumps in, defensively, "I'm a Christian, and that's the most important thing in the world to me." The word "Christian," I know, means that the student belongs to a nondenominational group on campus, probably Intervarsity Christian fellowship, but I suggest that both students have a kind of faith. Both have a set of attitudes they bring to the text. Both have assumptions, to read literally, to reject all literalism. Both are wearing albs of their own, really, the kind of cultural clothing in which Frye says we all live and can't help but live.

Which is of course why I'm standing wearing a lacy white robe, and now I start explaining this, what my alb is, why and when I wear it— preaching or doing baptisms or weddings and funerals—and I joke as I do this, to relieve what seems to be the unease in the room. We all wear albs because we all make assumptions. Ever since the expulsion from the garden, the fall that Genesis describes, none of us have walked through the world without something to cover us. My garment is only whiter, only longer. Mine just has lace.

But the unease in the room is also the point. When several students volunteer, nicely, respectfully, that my putting on the alb made them uncomfortable, I respond that of course it did, of course it seemed silly and wrong, because it is. A professor shouldn't act as a minister in a classroom on a public campus, a professor shouldn't begin class by making the sign of the cross, a professor shouldn't preach. That's to mix up roles that shouldn't be mixed up, and students shouldn't mix them up either. There's a difference between reading the Bible as literature and a Bible study somewhere outside campus. I lead Bible study, too, I respect it, but the value of reading the Bible as literature comes when students set aside their assumptions and come at the text fresh, as if they've never seen it before, as if they know nothing about it.

There are gaps in the Bible, lots of them. The Bible shows rather than tells, in minimal language, and so stories that we think have one interpretation have many, there's always more than one, and these interpretations come from all the assumptions we make, conscious or unconscious, all the assumptions we've been taught.

Not that our assumptions are necessarily wrong. Not at all. "The Bible as Literature" often causes students to rethink some of what they've taken for granted. I hope it does. But to say that something is biased or that it's an interpretation is not to say that it's mistaken. Bias is what I live by. I live by the Catholic bias, the Catholic interpretation, one reading out of all possible readings, and all of you (I say) have made similar choices, whether you know it or not, even if you might change your mind again, and again. The point is simply to be aware of that. The point is simply to be aware that our interpretations are interpretations, not facts. (And I am taking off my alb as I say this, putting it on the hanger and hanging it back up on the door.) The point is for all of us to take off our albs and hang them up, then to stand back and look them over. Not to burn them. Not to throw them away. Just to become aware of them, as garments, as one set of clothes hanging up here among so many others, clothes of so many shapes and designs, coats of so many colors.

Though in another way we can never do that. Because our faith isn't finally a garment. It's our skin. It's not our glasses, it's our eyes. My alb isn't white after all. It's brown and green—brown like the hill beyond the monastery, brown like the oak grove. Green like the apple trees, like the grass on Amos's grave.

## The Genesis Quiz

To bring home the idea of the "nakedness" of the Biblical text, I give a friendly quiz the next day in class. The Genesis Quiz. Now is the time to move from the preliminaries to the text itself. Now is the time to stop reading ourselves and start reading the stories, in their wonderful starkness and strangeness—though in the end, of course, to read the stories *is* to read ourselves.

It doesn't seem to matter whether the class has read the first few chapters of Genesis in advance. Their responses are the same, and that already suggests the point: that our reading of this text, above all other texts, is conditioned from the start. It's situated. We come to it with interpretive frames, Burke calls "terministic screens," a screen of words and assumptions that lets in certain meanings and blocks out others (44).

For example, when, according to Genesis, was woman created, before, after, or at the same time as man? Nine out of ten students immediately answer: after, from the rib of man. Even for people who have never opened a Bible in their lives, the story of the creation of woman seems to belong to a store of common knowledge, its details as familiar as a nursery rhyme or commercial jingle. The lonely man is made to fall asleep and out of his side the Lord our God fashions Eve his helpmate and companion. Of course.

But in fact this is only part of the story—or it's only one of what seem to be two different accounts of the same event. It's the apparent second version, in the second chapter, in which God takes the rib and brings to man a helper. Animals were his first attempt to provide companions for Adam but that isn't quite enough and Adam is still longing for intimacy. Thus Eve. But in the first chapter, in the twenty-seventh verse, men and women, plural, unnamed, are created simultaneously and after animals as the final and crowning achievement in a vast, stately, majestic sequence of creative acts beginning with the creation of light itself: "God created humankind in his image, in the image of God he created them; male and female he created them." No Eve here and no Adam either. No garden and no snake. God in this version is not the intimate God who walks in the garden in the cool of the day but the God of cosmic power and unimaginable reach, and when he makes human beings he makes them in his own likeness and image, the male and the female equally and apparently in just the same moment. The *imago Dei* is the Latin phrase, the image of God, and it's the cornerstone of the Jewish and Christian understanding of human dignity and worth, of our original blessing, as Matthew Fox famously puts it, in his book of that title.

It's not that the Bible is full of discrepancies, badly made or unreliable. It's that the people who wrote it weren't from around here. The consensus among Biblical scholars is that the first five books of the Bible are composed of layers of originally oral material from a variety of sources gradually stitched or quilted or "redacted" together over centuries. These are ancient stories, handed down from a culture so different from our own that even the composition of texts didn't happen as it happens for us. We take out paper and write. We turn on the computer and we're surrounded by books and written information produced just as quickly, the distribution of knowledge a given, a fact. But in the ancient world stories were first oral, told and retold and memorized over generations before being preserved, painstakingly, in parchment scrolls so difficult and time-consuming to produce they were regarded in their rarity as sacred themselves. In a world like this authorship is not claimed, texts not signed. This is cultural knowledge, the wisdom of the whole people, and those who record it, for all their artistry and skill, see themselves not as "writers" as we understand that word but as nameless servants doing the work of God, preserving only what is important enough to have been handed down again and again.

A more particular sense of the authorship of the creation stories can only be inferred: that the first creation account, from 1.1 to 2.3, is probably the work of a group of "Priestly" writers operating under the pressures of cultural crisis and disintegration somewhere around the sixth century, possibly after the destruction of the temple in 587 and the Babylonian exile; that the second creation account, starting from 2.3, is probably the work of a group of writers we might call the "Yahwist" writers, after their name for God, writing actually much earlier, somewhere around the tenth century, at the time of the prosperity and cultural confidence of the Davidic monarchy. These two strands of material, along with two others, the Elohist and the Deuteronomist, are woven together throughout the first five books of the Bible, the Pentateuch, redacted perhaps by the Priestly writers themselves, who seem to have wanted not only to tell their own story but to preserve those that had gone before and who seem not at all disturbed by what strike us as discrepancies of fact or detail. This is sophisticated theology, not primitive science, and those who have brought it to its final form seem quite unlike us in their preference for multiple interpretations. When there are two or three apparently conflicting accounts, the ancient mind doesn't censor one but includes them all, side by side, expertly collaging and sequencing the different types of material, interested, apparently, not in exact historical rendering but in subtle literary patterns, in larger structures of tone and image and theme.

The God these stories hint at is too great to be seen from any one angle. The God these stories hint at is paradoxical, both vast and intimate, both cosmic and local. To include multiple versions of creation and of all the other events in the faith life of this people is by juxtaposition itself to honor that greatness and paradox, to suggest through redaction both creative joy and interpretive humility.

In an essay on Homer in *Great Books*, David Denby describes the paradox at the heart of a course like "The Literature of Western Civilization" or "The Bible as Literature," that there are at the source of Western culture, in Homer for example, values and ways of being very different from our own. "Academic opponents of the Western classics constantly urge readers to consider 'the other,'" he notes, "but here, at the beginning of the written culture of the West, is something like the 'other,' the Greeks themselves," in their violence, in their ritual (39). Our ancestors are alien, and this is true of the Bible as well: multiple where we are singular, rough-edged when we are streamlined, concerned with tension and paradox and image where we are most desiring of information or truth.

But I am getting ahead of myself, beyond the details of the text and already beginning to interpret them, to infer from their arrangement an ideology or a value that might fit my own or challenge those of my students. The real point is more basic still, more fundamental: that the details of these stories require interpretation—that these are stories, not sermons or treatises, that they show rather than tell, and so require us to draw from them each time we read certain meanings that exist always among a range of other possible meanings, a set of possibilities, all of them contained within the image itself.

The great Hebrew scholar Robert Alter has said that the Bible exhibits all the sophistication and literary technique of any contemporary piece of fiction but that those effects all take place "microscopically" (*Art of Biblical Narrative* 46). The Bible is radically condensed. It's spare. Stories we imagine on an epic scale pass us by in a line or two. But still more fundamental is the fact that this spare language is spare story, spare narrative, and like all narrative, even long winded and prolix narrative like Homer's, it requires a certain kind of reading, a certain kind of filling in of gaps. "The story of Adam and Eve is very, very short," Gary Anderson says in *The Genesis of Perfection*, his study of early Jewish and Christian interpretations of the book of Genesis. "Yet the very brevity of the tale, along with the knotty questions it leaves unanswered, cries out for some sort of interpretive expansion," which is exactly why the early Jews and Christians wrote so many commentaries on these stories, to fill in the blanks, to say what isn't said (20).

We've already spent several pages unpacking or interpreting Genesis 1:27, a single verse of translated Hebrew prose. We've pulled out of it, from between its lines, a volume of interpretive language many times the number of words in the lines themselves. Genesis doesn't say any of what we've been saying or inferring. It doesn't say "here are two different accounts and here are their historical contexts and we the redactors are putting them together in this way for these reasons." The stories are just given to us, in their spareness and concreteness, not two different versions at all, for all we know, just words on a page, saying what they say and not saying far more.

Two more questions on the Genesis Quiz. *According to Genesis*, why does God create the world? *According to Genesis*, when God is walking in the garden in the cool of the day, he calls out to Adam, "Where are you?" Why doesn't God know where Adam is? The answer to both questions is: *the text doesn't say.*

It doesn't say. Students come up with all kinds of answers to these two questions, all kinds of interesting interpretations of the condensed and narrative details. God is lonely, some say in response to the first. God was overflowing with love and so creative he could only create another being to live with in relationship and community. God was bored. The second question inspires even more ingenuity and reflects even more assumptions: God is testing Adam and Eve, God isn't all powerful, God is being playful, God is angry. But as valid or invalid as these interpretations are, what they are is just that, interpretations, inferences drawn from the narrative facts. The text of Genesis contains certain details, is composed of certain images and pieces of narrative information, regardless of whether you believe that it's redacted from multiple sources over time, even if you believe it to be composed by Moses himself, dictated to him by an angel of the Lord: here are the details, concretely, and there's not a word about God's creativity or manipulativeness or his motives, only words about what he does, what happens. God creates the world. God forms human beings from soil, breathing into the mud he has shaped. God walks in the garden in the cool of the day.

According to Genesis, Eve's eating of the fruit is the first example of "original sin." True or False? False, at least if we're being pedantic in the way this little exercise encourages us to be, at least if we look just at the words themselves, at what they actually say. The phrase "original sin" is nowhere used in the Genesis stories, nowhere, and in fact when you consult the standard concordance for the New Revised Standard Version of the Bible you discover that the phrase is nowhere used in the Old Testament, nowhere, and in fact is nowhere used even in the New Testament, even there. In Romans chapter five, Paul does read back into the Genesis story and does interpret Jesus as the New Adam, redeeming as a man what the first man made to happen, but this is a complicated passage, syntactically shifting and densely metaphorical, and it's only later, in the second century, that the early Church Fathers begin using the phrase "original sin" in a way that Augustine, in the fifth century, seems to take for granted. It's a powerful phrase and crucial to Christian theology. It's a phrase that as a Christian myself I believe to be a convincing way of understanding what I have experienced in my own life and what I see in the world. But it's not in the Bible. It's not what the Bible *says*, only what it *implies*—implies among other possible implications.

Human beings are fundamentally sinful: true or false? Does Genesis actually say human beings are sinful? No. Whole systems of theology have been erected on a faith in humanity's essential vileness, its loathsomeness, whole ways of life, and certainly the narrative details of the Genesis stories can sustain that interpretation. Human beings do exercise their freedom in the midst of all perfection to do precisely that which they are forbidden to do, and things continue to get more and more profoundly screwed up as the stories proceed, through Abraham and Sarah and all their deeply dysfunctional offspring right up to the present moment, stupidity after stupidity.

But there's also the *imago Dei*. There's also Genesis 1:27 and the astonishing idea that God has created human beings in his image and likeness, fundamentally and originally good in the way he is good: creative, ordered, playful, self-restrained and limiting, delighting. There's a whole tradition of interpretation, beginning in the second century, that stresses not the fall but this first spontaneous act of identity and love, this freedom, this relationship.

Or let's return to the notion of gender. God's own gender in the opening chapters is open to interpretation. The pronoun used is masculine, but if God is said to have created humans "in his own image," "male and female he created them," it's possible to infer that God is both male and female. Nowhere to this point is God called "father." As for the subjugation of the woman, the patriarchal assumption that Genesis sustains a belief in the superiority of the man, the *imago Dei* is again the sticking point. The patriarchal interpretation seems to ignore the first chapter and privilege the second, focusing only on what comes from Adam's rib, although even here it's possible to draw different conclusions. If woman is drawn from the rib of the man she is drawn from the center of the man, from his essence, which is why Adam's first words proclaim that at last here is "flesh of my flesh" and "bone of my bone," an apparent celebration of identity and commonality—a celebration, too, that is made in poetry. The first words of Adam, the first human words in Scripture, are poetry, are arranged in the form of line breaks, a formality that doesn't suggest degrading lack of respect. Oppression of the sort justified by extreme patriarchal interpretations is in fact the result of the fall. The woman is told that the man "shall rule over you" only after the great lapse in the garden, as punishment for what happened there: oppression as the first sign of sin, as the condition of it, not an expression of what was meant to be and what we should strive to regain.

An ecological interpretation of the Genesis stories is also possible. In the beginning the Lord our God creates everything as related to everything else, observing its proper place, beautiful and bursting with life each in its kind, nothing eating anything else. Into this ecological balance the Lord comes walking, entirely self-limiting, restraining his great power in order to enter into relationship with human beings. To be created in the image and likeness of such a God, both vast and intimate, both powerful and subtle, is to be creative ourselves and to be restrained ourselves, likewise powerful and yet self-limiting. The prohibition in the garden, against the eating of the tree, is a prohibition against overconsumption, we might say, an invitation to be like God in not doing all that we are capable of doing—the garden like a wilderness area perhaps, walled off to be preserved in its wildness. From this perspective our violation, our sin, is not that we have acted like God but that we *haven't*. It's the serpent, after all, who tells Eve that God is afraid of our being like him, and the serpent, we know, is not to be trusted. We already are like God, in the beginning, and when we choose in our God-like freedom to eat of the tree we are at precisely that moment choosing not to be God-like anymore, a choice that by its nature leads us out of the garden we have destroyed and out into a world we must continue to fight and to manage and to tame. Like sexual inequality, in this interpretation the domination of the land is a result of the fall—"cursed is the ground because of you" (3:17)—not the way things should be. It's ecological balance we must strive to return to, "dominion" not in the sense of an exploitive and domineering dictator but in the sense of a wise leader carefully husbanding the resources of a delicately balanced "domain."

---

Am I suggesting that this environmentalist interpretation, or the feminist interpretation, or the idea of "original blessing" rather than "original curse," is the only interpretation of these stories, the right one, the one we must obey? By no means—only a possible one, only one among a number of interpretations that the details support, and an interpretation that of course reflects my own cultural situatedness, my own values, here in the twenty-first century, knowing what I know, seeing what I see, being who I am. Of course there are other possible and powerful readings, as witnessed by the very answers my students instinctively give. A harsher, sterner, more patriarchal interpretation has been so dominant for so long in Western culture that even my students who haven't read the Bible at all, from fundamentalists to feminists, assume that it's the interpretation required, the one to be accepted or resisted. Who tempts Eve, I ask, and over half the class says "Satan," or "the devil." All the text says is "the serpent," the snake in the grass, but the sense of the snake as devilish or Satanic is so strongly in the air that it's the devil over half the class always sees there—even though the word "devil" is never mentioned in the Hebrew scriptures, anywhere, and the word "Satan" is mentioned only twice in passing and only once in any detail, in the book of Job, where he is a very different character than we assume Satan is, simply a clever angel, a figure in a folktale, not the fallen angel and rebel of Revelation or Milton.

So many of my students have been taught that Christians think of God as a harsh and reproving judge that they can't engage the evidence to the contrary: the God who creates a structured and beautiful world bursting with life; who gently fashions the man from the clay and gently breathes him into life; the God so moved by the loneliness of the man as to create for him a mate, later so moved by their nakedness as to make for the two of them garments of skin; an intimate, loving, creative God; the God I see when I read the opening chapters of Genesis, the God who moves above the waters and who moves me, too, being who I am, living when and how I do.

Do I mean that anything goes, that every interpretation is equally valid? By no means. A valid interpretation has to take into account the actual details of the text. It has to take into account the fact that in the first chapter animals are clearly created before man and in the second chapter clearly after. It can't claim that the phrase "original sin" actually appears in the stories. It doesn't. To say that the Bible is patriarchal or that it is feminist is simply wrong. The only valid claim in light of the text as it really is is that these are possible interpretations among others, inferences based on detail that can lead to a variety of inferences, some of them conflicting.

Palmer uses a simple image to describe the act of knowing, a large circle surrounded by smaller circles, like a planet surrounded by satellites or a table ringed by chairs. The truth is the "great thing" in the middle of every class, from geology to literature to economics, the complicated subject matter and all its traditional methods and forms of interpretation—it's the world the way it really is, in its messiness and irreducibility (*Courage* 102). And we are the satellites, we are the chairs, individuals who see what we can see from our own particular perspectives, individuals in relation to the great thing but always in relation, in process, catching glimpses and figuring out pieces but never owning, never capturing the great thing itself because it can't be captured. It's too big for that.

The great thing in the text of Genesis is the text itself and all that's behind it, what we can infer about its history and social contexts and so use to help us limit its meanings, what we know about the nature of language and human nature as well as the language itself, as well as our own human nature, as well as each other, all the rest of us around the table or in the class, sharing what we see, what we glimpse, and learning from each other.

A four panel comic. In the first an old woman in a polka dot dress bends over with a dish of dog food. In the balloon above the dog: "She feeds me every day and cares for my every need." Next panel: "She must be God." In the third panel the woman is bending over again, this time with a dish of cat food. In the balloon above the cat: "She feeds me every day and cares for my every need." Final panel: "I must be God." In both situations the facts are the same. The woman isn't beating her pets, she isn't ignoring them, she is bending over them, feeding them, though her motives are never stated. The cartoon captures her actions, not her interior state, and so either interpretation, the canine or the feline, is possible. What determines the different readings is their context, of course. The readings come from somewhere, from the nature and identity of the viewer, just as the interpretations of my students come from their own natures and identities, identities shaped by centuries of interpretive moves and conclusions, whether students are aware of these traditions or not.

Genesis is like the cartoon in that it gives us pictures, not analysis; two points of view, not just one. It shows rather than tells, and finally this is the most important point of all. The most important expectations that students bring to Genesis are expectations about the nature of texts and of reading, expectations that come from ignorance and lack of experience. Another cartoon, a single image: a man standing at a bookstore counter, the clerk behind him, apparently looking something up on the computer. "The Bible . . . . that would be under self-help." Well no, not at all, because the Bible is 80 percent narrative, 80 percent consisting not of sermons and theology and lists of do's and don'ts but of language like the stories of Genesis, the language of story. It's a surprise finally. The Bible doesn't answer life's questions, it questions life's answers. In its concreteness it raises more issues than it settles. It is self-help only in the sense that each reader must help herself, must take the initiative, filling in the gaps with imagination and reason—but what each self does, how each self goes about the filling of those gaps, is determined by traditions of reading that filter into our consciousness and even deeper long before we open the book itself.

## Showing and Telling

Part of what the Genesis Quiz demonstrates, then, is the rudimentary fact that the Bible is concrete rather than abstract. It uses images. It tells stories. That seems like a simple point. But once it's granted, once we've seen it, the whole discussion of the Bible is completely changed. With that in place it's clear why the Bible as Literature belongs at the state university and why it's appropriate for me as a Catholic deacon to admit that I'm a Catholic deacon and to make that admission, that fact of my own person, part of the experience of the class.

Let me clarify what I mean with a crude distinction between "imagistic" and "propositional" language. When I say that "my love is like a red, red rose" I do not mean that I am in love with a rose. I mean something, literally, that I have not said. I have used a concrete image from the poet Robert Burns, the image of "rose," which suggests a whole range of possible, unstated ideas: that, let's say, "my love is beautiful and temporary and always evolving, a beautiful and precious thing that can also be dangerous or prickly." There's the distinction. "Red, red rose" is concrete, physical, and sensory. My interpretation of it—"beautiful and temporary and always evolving"—is an example of propositional language, abstract, direct, and explicit. The poet gives us an image and we have to supply the ideas. Propositional language supplies the ideas for us, ready made—it does just the interpretive work that the image otherwise forces us into ourselves. To use Frye's distinction in *Anatomy of Criticism*, "rose" is an example of *mythos*, or narrative discourse; "beautiful and temporary and always evolving" an example of *dianoia*, or reflective discourse (77–79).

"Story" or "narrative" might be understood, again crudely, as imagistic language in motion or in sequence. A story is the concrete description of people, places, and events in time, and so, too, is distinct from the propositional. A man finds a dead deer on the side of a road one night and decides to roll it over into the canyon. "To swerve might make more dead." In this opening stanza from his poem "Traveling Through the Dark" William Stafford gives us details, not theories, dark roads and canyons and the wilderness all around, although from those details we can quickly infer larger possible meanings: that we are all traveling through the dark, perhaps, all on a dangerous road, and that sometimes we must swerve for fear of going over the edge (*Selected Poems* 177). But what defines this little piece of narrative is its refusal to make such possibilities explicit, its fidelity to the experience itself, as opposed, say, to this example of propositional language from one of Stafford's own essays:

> Art has its sacramental aspect. The source of art's power is one with
> religion's: the discovery of the essential self and the cultivation of it
> through the act of its positive impulses. (*Writing the Australian Crawl*
> 51)

The first concrete, the second abstract. The first giving us images and inviting us to reflect on whatever theories they imply, the second giving us the theories themselves, the ideas.

To say that Genesis is imagistic or that it's story is not to say that it's merely "literature" in the sense of form apart from content, mere style; or merely "literature" in the sense of untrue, in the sense of something made up, mere fiction. It's to observe what the language actually does, how it actually works, what's on the page and what isn't. It's to observe that the Genesis stories don't provide us with elaborate theology or abstract terms but the earth, the seeds, the surging waters, the flowering tree, the Lord of all gently blowing breath through the very nostrils of the man he has made.

In this rudimentary sense it doesn't even matter whether the story is "true," whether the world really was created in six days, for example, historically, scientifically. Let's say that we add a third piece of language to the Stafford poem and the Stafford essay:

> Once upon a time there were three bears, a papa bear, a mama bear,
> and a baby bear. They lived in a snug little house in the forest. One
> day a little girl came to the house, a little girl with golden hair.

Among these three examples of language, which two belong together? Which one doesn't belong? It's the propositional piece that stands apart, the theorizing about the sacramental dimension of art that's distinct, as language, from the other two. The poem would have us believe that

Stafford actually did find a deer dead on the edge of the Wilson River Road and was confronted with the choice that the poem later describes. The poem asks us to believe that it's "true," while the fairy tale, of course, in its conventional language and rhythms, announces from the beginning that it's not, that it's fantasy, a children's story. But in its basic structure the description in the poem is far more like the fairy tale than like the theory proposed by the essay exactly because it's description. It's story. True or not the fairy tale does just what the poem does. It describes things in the world, actions in the world, movements, objects. Whatever those movements and objects might mean, whatever the story implies in a Freudian or Jungian or whatever other sense, whether it's just a bedtime story without a larger meaning, is left to us to decide. The author has observed, as Stafford does, as the authors of Genesis do, an "authorial silence," to use a term from Wayne Booth's *The Rhetoric of Fiction* (271–309). Literally: they have not said what the details mean. "By this image of water what I intend is. . . ."

Even the writers of poems and stories don't necessarily know what they intend by a particular image or can't necessarily articulate what they do know except in the words of the poem or the story itself. They don't sit down and say, I have these ideas and so I'm going to use this image to clothe them, to carry them. It's the image that comes first, instinctively, spontaneously. It's the image that comes in response to the experience of joy or sorrow or the world the way it is day to day in its textures and ordinariness, and the writer writes it down and shapes it through intuition and spontaneous creativity, not at first or mostly through conscious control. The image comes from somewhere deep down and carries with it some sense of that inner vastness and depth, untranslatable, not reducible to abstract propositions or a single interpretation.

This is the huge and important implication of the English-teacherly showing versus telling distinction: not just that we as readers have to act, have to do a brief second of intellectual work; but more, that whatever interpretation we come up with is always partial and provisional, one possible meaning among a range of possible meanings not even the writer herself can pin down once and for all or would even want to. This is how literature works. This is how images and stories get produced and why.

This is the simple issue at the heart of the process of storytelling and image-making that Ricouer sees as central to human nature, the first, instinctive response that all of us have to the way things really are. All around us is mystery, all around us is the inexplicable, the messy, the beautiful, the tragic, that which must break all our hearts, as I explained in the last chapter: the stars and the trees and the visible world that Genesis claims was created by God in all order and intimacy; or within us, our memory and our desire, our longing, our tenderness, our need. Whenever that mystery breaks in upon us or we are suddenly made aware of it; whenever we experience such joy or sorrow or laughter or chagrin that we have to do something about it; the something we do, Ricouer believes, is tell stories, is make images. We respond to the vastness in the world and in ourselves not first with philosophy, not first with literary theory, not first with theological propositions and moral debate, but with words and sentences made up of the earth and the sky and the water and the living things. Theory is important and we need it, but it comes later. There's a deep sequence here, from mystery to story to thought, and the movement is crucial. Story comes first and "gives rise" to thought, Ricouer says.[11]

Think of childhood. The child's first form of language isn't philosophy but the simple, babbling stories of fairies and heroes. Think of dreams, where what comes first always comes in images, dark roads and huge oceans, an old woman in the middle of a forest—a woman who turns into a snake, perhaps—images that come to us unbidden and that we sometimes puzzle over for days, moved somehow but not quite sure what they mean. Later in Genesis Abraham falls asleep, Jacob falls asleep, and what they dream isn't a set of ideas but a flaming coal, a brilliant ladder. In the Gospel of Matthew Joseph twice falls asleep and what the angel brings him isn't the Nicene Creed, it isn't Trinitarian theology but instructions: marry this woman you doubt, take your wife and your son and flee. As the philosopher John Smith puts it, when the angels appear over the stable in Bethlehem they don't say, "Behold I have brought you a topic of discussion" (qtd. in O'Brien 118). Think of any experience now, as an adult, falling in love, grieving. Our first response to the beloved is love letters, not critical interpretation. What we tell our friends isn't a psychoanalytical theory but the color of her hair, how she walked on the shore. What is told at every funeral are first the stories of the one who has died, the funny stories and the sad ones, the stories of how this person moved and lived in the world we touch and taste and feel, and somehow this nearly suffices. The theological consolations come later.

This is the movement of a culture, too, of a whole society. First there are stories, then there are philosophies. First there is Homer, then there is Plato, and later and always as the culture seeks to renew or sustain itself, it must return to the poets and the storytellers, to those who are living and perhaps even more important to the first storytellers, those who first put into words the first, great, instinctive images of the people.

Odysseus, naked, stripped of his hero's cloak, his men dead and gone, his little raft destroyed in the waves, is "adrift on the heaving swells," "quite lost," "the whole sea shrouded—sheets of spray," lost and broken, entirely defeated in all the "waste of water." "The sea had beaten down his striving heart," Homer tells us, and it's at just this moment, just this moment of complete surrender and despair, that suddenly, miraculously, he is cast onto shore. Naked and alone, he buries himself in the leaves beneath two olive trees, where later, in the morning, he throws himself on the mercy of a beautiful young princess, come to wash clothes in the stream nearby (*Odyssey* 5.390–547).

What does this beautiful scene mean? What does Homer have in mind here? What is his theme? A Christian critic can answer that there's implicit here the great notion of dying to live; the psychological critic that there's implicit here the great notion of transcending the ego; the anthropological critic that there's implicit here the great theme of all the heroic myths, that only in surrender can we find our strength. All these themes are there, and it's important to read between the lines of the story and to find them there, to infer them, to tease them out, but what Ricouer insists is what every writer and every dreamer and every person finally knows: that first comes the scene itself, comes the images, and finally not even the dreamer or the poet can say what they add up to because finally they don't add up but open out, expand. In the experience of telling or hearing a story we are plunged into the sea with Odysseus, stripped, at first, of analysis and critical apparatus.

This is the importance of the ancient myths for culture, that they are ancient, that they are first. Their priority is like the priority of dreams or of childhood memories in psychoanalysis. They are first, closest to the original impulse, to the mystery itself, and so in a sense truer or more transparent.

"Symbols precede hermeneutics" is how Ricouer puts it. A symbol "presents its meaning in the opaque transparency of an enigma and not by translation" (16). The meanings of a symbol are somehow "bound" to the symbol itself (17), so that even though we are always teased into trying to pull those meanings out—we are always invited into trying to untangle and fix them—we never can. Images and stories are, in the words of John Shea, a interpreter of Ricouer, "flush tight" with the experience of the mystery itself, as close as we can get to it in words and so infused somehow with the nature of the mystery itself, so somehow mysterious themselves, eluding formulation (60). "Myth," to return to Ricouer, "has a way of revealing things that is not reducible to any translation from a language in cipher to clear language" (163). By myth Ricouer means the first primitive stories of our beginnings. He would call the Genesis stories "myth," as would most believing Biblical scholars, an inspired myth conveying spiritual truths rather than a scientific treatise intended to describe the physics and biology of creation. But the idea of meaning being "bound" to the symbol or the image itself, of the

image being closer to the mystery and the explanation and the philosophy always coming later, always secondary, always provisional—that idea
applies to all stories, from primitive myths to contemporary novels and
autobiography and even to student freewriting.

This is why a story or myth can never stand alone, why it always
demands interpretation. This is why we do what we do in an English
class, carefully teasing out the meanings implied in the grammar of a
story. Stories, in other words, suggest their own interpretations, inviting
and limiting what might be said about them.

To make this point in class I sometimes ask my students to freewrite
about their earliest memory. Think as far back as you can go. Wait for
the first image that comes to mind and start writing, nonstop, not worrying about grammar and punctuation, just letting the words come and
come. Try to put yourself there. Describe everything you touch and taste
and feel. So the words come tumbling out and with them the first images,
the images of light and dark, of water and earth, of a father, of a mother,
of transgression, all our first stories somehow alike, somehow sharing
certain essential elements.

I remember, as I write myself, my father taking me in his arms and
out into the cold dark air of the mountain we lived on, halfway up in our
crackerbox house with the fence and the swings, trees and darkness to the
open top. He was a policeman then, and I think I remember him shifting
my weight against his shiny badge and pointing to the C on the top of
the mountain, the great Colville C all lit up with the lights, and to the tall
white cross floating above it, phosphorescent, as if hanging there in the
dark. It's a vivid memory. I feel myself being pulled into it as I continue
to freewrite, some deep emotion being tapped. Towards the end I suddenly remember, too, the feeling of being held in his arms, and the smell
of his aftershave, and the cold air, and then, maybe, although I'm not
entirely sure I'm not making this up, I'm not sure this really happened in
fact, but maybe, maybe, the feel of my slippered feet brushing against the
top of his gun belt. The softness of my feet. That gun belt, that broad,
black gun belt. The butt of his pistol.

The process of freewriting mirrors the sequence Ricouer describes.
First the freewriting, the spontaneous pouring out of the words, the good
mixed in with the bad; then the editing, the going back and taking out
what makes sense, discerning an implicit structure, trying to bring out
what might be hidden or partial. Symbol gives rise to thought.

Jacob wrestles with an unnamed figure by the river Jabbok, struggles
with him all through the night, never yielding, never gaining the upper
hand, and it's only when it's all over, when the "man" has refused to tell
Jacob his name or who he is, when Jacob is wounded and limping, that

he, Jacob, names the place where all this has happened: Peniel, because here he wrestled with God. The figure was a man at first, just a shadowy form. It's after the fact that Jacob understands him to be God (Gen 32:22–32). Dante is being led through the horrors of *The Inferno*, confusion and tumult and suffering wherever he looks. Here a whirlwind swirls and sucks, people are being swept around in its funnel, and Dante describes all this first, he sets it out before us, concretely, as if a travel writer. It's only then, after the description, that he turns to his guide, to Virgil, who is standing there always beside him, and asks him what the image means, what the details signify. And Virgil always answers, clearly and succinctly, explaining that the image in its nature implies this idea in its nature, the whirlwind the chaos of love, of uncontrolled passion. First the image, then the idea. "After the gift, the positing," Ricouer says (349).

In the wrestling and the whirlwind of the little freewriting, I begin to discern the implications: it's a cross, I think, on the top of that mountain. It's a Christian image my father is pointing to, and so perhaps my earliest memory says something about Christianity and its place in my life. If I wrote a poem about this memory I could perhaps shape it so that the cross was at the center, the structuring principle, although how then can I account for the most vivid image of all, the image of my father's gun belt, of his gun, the image that came near the end of the freewriting, when I least expected it? It's a negative image. It runs counter to the mistier, more impressionistic mood the memory has invoked, of the dark mountain and the cross. It might imply a complicated relationship with my father, something I'm not sure I want to imply or fully understand. But there it is.

Although it's a soldier, a centurion, a Roman policeman, say, with a sword on his belt, who stands at the foot of the cross in the synoptic gospels and looking up says, "surely this was the son of God" (Mark 15:39).

It's important not to oversimplify the sequence Ricouer describes. Though the symbol is spontaneous and its meanings bound to the image, finally not fully recoverable, a symbol is "already speech." A symbol is not entirely free of "idea," but in some fundamental way created by it from the start. "A meditation on symbols starts from speech that has already taken place, and in which everything has already been said in some fashion; it wishes to be thought with its presuppositions" (348). I can't sit down and do a freewriting without being influenced by Christianity and my experience of the cross. My faith is influencing the spontaneous choice of words at the first moment of composition and so constructing it just as it does more explicitly after the fact, in my reflections on what the freeewriting might mean, my thoughts in my act of editing it. Meaning is always mediated, as is experience itself, by culture. The world my father brought me into, the world he was pointing out to me, was already constructed. It was a cross he was showing me, not a Muslim Crescent. It was the letter "C," not a Greek symbol or mathematical sign. The "thoughts" the symbol give rise to always come back and inform our consciousness for the next time we spontaneously invent, the sequence finally bending into a circle, a cycle of meaning.

"We must believe in order to understand," Augustine says, translating Isaiah 7.9 (*Teaching Christianity* 137). Without the names for things we can't see those things in the first place. Without first assumptions we have nowhere to look. Even a mathematical problem depends on posited first principles that can't be proven. The great Catholic novelist Flannery O'Connor puts it matter of factly in a wonderfully clear and concise essay on her experience as a Catholic novelist. Of course Catholic faith influences how she writes, from the very beginning. Her "theology," she admits, has a "direct bearing" on what she says and doesn't say, influencing her choices of character, setting, mood, even when she's least aware of that influence. She can no more avoid a Catholic coloring or framing of her fiction than she can avoid being a southern writer, and it's still deeper than that. A writer has an obligation not only to find "a symbol for feeling," she says, but to find "a symbol and a way of lodging it which tells the intelligent reader whether this feeling is adequate or inadequate, whether it is moral or immoral, whether it is good or evil" (156). It's this sense of the moral meaning of a work, its point, its implications, that is most influenced by the writer's faith.

But O'Connor goes on to make it very clear that this moral theme, this judgment, is not a sort of abstract idea that can be taken out of the context of the work itself or reduced to a simple set of propositions. The novelist writes stories, not treatises, and in that sense fiction "escapes any orthodoxies we might set up for it" (192). A writer begins in experience, in the world as we know it through the senses. "You don't write fiction with assumptions. The things we see, hear, smell, and touch affect us long before we believe anything at all" (197), at least consciously, at least in words we can reduce to creeds, and the novelist always begins at this first, primal point, always goes back as much as she can to that origin, that moment, that genesis. Fiction, in short, is concrete, it shows rather than tells, and so "renews our knowledge that we live in the mystery from which we draw our abstractions," O'Connor says, anticipating Ricouer's sequence (152). Mystery gives rise to story gives rise to thought. She herself is everywhere influenced by her faith in Christ, in the dogmatic truths of Catholic faith, she says, and that faith in a sense inspires all that she writes as it inspires all that she is. But the "real meaning of a story does not begin except at a depth where these things have been exhausted.

[. . .] there always has to be left over that sense of mystery which cannot be accounted for by any human formula" (153).

Now, it's startling enough to discover that big parts of the Bible, many of the most important and controversial parts, like Genesis, don't give us answers but stories, give us gaps. It's startling enough to discover that the act of reading Genesis doesn't involve the passive reception of do's and don'ts but the active filling in of those gaps. What O'Connor is insisting as a working novelist, what Ricouer is insisting as a literary theorist and anthropologist, is that our filling in of those gaps is always necessarily limited. There are many other ways of doing it, many other meanings, and all those meanings are so intricately bound up in the details themselves that all we can do finally is return to the story itself. All we can do is recognize our limitations and celebrate the image.

It's humility they are urging, interpretive humility, by necessity, and this humility, I want to argue in the next chapter, should be the defining attitude of university education. It's what a university education should be designed to do: to humble us.

CHAPTER 2

# Teaching the Ecology of Mark

This chapter continues the discussion of the line that Newman momentarily considers between the way of the university and the way of faith. As I argued in the first chapter, reading Genesis as story not only honors that line but makes it even clearer. Ricouer's theory helps unthicken the images in these ancient texts, and there's a way in which this "unthickening" can be seen as exactly the work of the university. Or to return to my metaphor of the "alb," the work of the university is to make us aware of the vestments that all of us wear, to show that none of us are ever naked. Literature is a particularly good way of doing that work simply because it shows rather than tells.

What's good about the Bible is that it does this showing rather than telling when we least expect it. We expect sermonizing. We expect all the propositional theology we've heard about or been exposed to directly, and although that theology is "in" there in a sense, in another sense it's not. The text *is* naked in some sense, and this is as true for the gospel of Mark as it is for Genesis. Though Mark is written in Greek, centuries later, it shares with Genesis, as Reynolds Price has noted, the same devotion to the devices of "story." "What matters to Mark," Price says, "is what mattered to the great J writer in the Hebrew Bible." Their central concern is with "the literal line which human action makes on the surface of time and place, and with the degree to which we can infer from those writers' words alone" greater and more suggestive meaning (60).

This chapter, then, continues the discussion of the last through an analysis of Mark, then steps back to talk about the process of writing more generally, then concludes—drawing on the thinking in both this and the last chapter—by developing a theory of education both Biblical and ecological. What we do here with Mark is what we do in all classes at the university, or should, and to reflect on this is to inquire into the idea of the university.

## Mark as Story

Genesis, then, shows rather than tells. That's all. It works through image rather than explicit commentary, at least most of the time, and it does this in very few, though very artful, very crafted, words. This is the sense in which the gospels, too, can be understood as literature. This is the sense, O'Connor's sense, in which they are "fiction," exactly fiction: not because they don't try to tell the truth but because they do, the messy, recalcitrant, irreducible truth of the concrete life we actually live.

Students are surprised when the Gospel of Mark begins without the Christmas stories but instead with John the Baptist thundering in the wilderness and the baptism of Jesus, and they continue to be surprised. Mark's language is spare to the point of choppy, his quick cuts between pieces of narrative nearly collage-like. "The style is terse," David Rhoads and Donald Michie say in *Mark as Story*. "The narrator 'shows' the action directly" (44–45). This happens and then this happens, immediately and without preamble—the phrase "at once" and the word "immediately" appear nearly fifty times in the story—and much is unexplained, simply presented, starkly and vividly, without Mark intervening as narrator and explicitly interpreting the details. In novelist Price's contemporary translation, without chapter and verse notations, the text not in columns but moving across the page like any other book, the baptism is described with a moving awkwardness and economy:

> It happened in those days Jesus came from Nazareth in Galilee and was baptized in the Jordan by John. At once going up out of the water he saw the sky torn open and the Spirit like a dove descending to him. There was a voice out of the sky, "You are my Son the loved one. In you I have delighted." (87)

Mark's Roman contemporaries, trained like Augustine in the *Confessions* four centuries later in the long oratorical flourishes of Greco-Roman rhetoric, found language like this ungrammatical and undramatic and unconvincing, a reason for ridicule, and Price captures this roughness in what he claims is a literal, word-for-word translation, not pasteurizing the prose into the more familiar cadences. But still more striking is how little is said, roughly or not, how little is explained, how much is left for the reader to infer—and how much the reader does infer, conditioned as we are by centuries of interpretation and devotional practice.

A student raises his hand: why does Jesus need to be baptized? He's the Son of God, he's God himself, without sin, the savior of the world. Why does he have to be baptized?

My answer: who says that Jesus is divine? Not Mark, at least not explicitly, at least not in the sense that the Son of God equals "one in being with the father," in the words of the Nicene Creed. If we take just the words before us, if we try to set aside everything we think we know about Jesus already and read Mark from the beginning, inferring only what he allows us to infer, we have to say that so far at least there's nothing in the text to establish exactly who Jesus is. Mark says in the very first line of the gospel that this is "good news," not just the news, so it's clear that he's not being "objective," not simply trying to convey a flat, uninterpreted history. As we keep reading it's clear from the energy and drive of the prose, its headlong enthusiasm, that Mark is tremendously compelled by this figure of Jesus, mesmerized, head over heels, convinced in some way of his greatness and uniqueness and authority. But all that he actually says here about Jesus is what Jesus does, that he comes from Nazareth and is baptized in the Jordan. Just that, just those words. There's a buildup to that action, in a passage from Isaiah and in John's promise that one "who is stronger than I" will come after him, one who will baptize in the "Holy Spirit," but if we have just the words on the page to go on, just those words, it's not clear what "the Holy Spirit" means and or what "stronger than I" means and not necessarily obvious that "stronger" means "one in being with the father"—to quote the Nicene Creed—that it means "divine."

The very first line of the gospel also calls Jesus the "Messiah," a word that all of us, Christian or not, assume that we know and understand, but again, if we return to the deliberate pedantry of the Genesis Quiz, restricting ourselves to a narrow and close reading of the words themselves, what's clear is that Mark doesn't define for us what that word means. As Price explains in a fine introductory essay to his translation of the gospel, it seems that Mark assumes a great deal about what his readers know, as if he's writing in the midst of a community where certain understandings can be taken for granted (50). He's not, in a sense, writing for us, as outsiders, but for insiders, but even so, the starkness remains, the narrative fact of what isn't said, isn't defined. A little historical background will quickly explain that "messiah" denoted for most Jews of the time of Jesus a new David, a new earthly king, come to restore the political power of Israel. "Son of God" doesn't necessarily imply divinity but is most likely a messianic term as well, implying divine favor towards a special human being. But again, this is a footnote, and it's a footnote required by the terseness of the page.[12]

In a sense we have to forget about history even as we forget about traditional theological interpretations. History can be an evasion, as Tracy argues (*Plurality and Ambiguity* 39, 69). Understanding cultural context is crucial, of course. We have to know in at least a general way what historical forces have influenced the text. But historical research can also be a way of evading the strangeness and complexity of the text itself. Students tend to think that if they only learn what was going on behind the scenes, all the interpretive problems will be solved. Oh: all these stories are really an effort to understand the exile and the problems of Israel's own identity as a nation. I get it. And then they move on, the issues settled, entirely in the past. Oh, the gaps can be explained away by the history of redaction—the history of composition as a kind of code that neutralizes all the interpretive problems, reducing them to a single meaning or pattern. But no. The gaps remain, there really are contradictions and absences and enigmas, the tensions exist, and they exist here and now, in the present of the reading. The real payoff lies in deliberately "forgetting" the historical background, Tracy says, as in deliberately "forgetting" our own biases and preconceptions, and confronting the work itself, head on, with all its strangeness and challenges.[13]

The sky is "torn apart," Mark does tell us, and the Spirit descends like a dove upon the man coming up out of the water. There is a voice sounding from the sky, "You are my Son, the beloved; with you I am well pleased" (1:10–11). There is a theophany, a moment of light and rending, of revelation, this man Jesus named somehow, marked as beloved, as the source of delight. For all its choppiness and awkwardness there is in this brief passage a movement and a dramatic power, a deliberate positioning of language, as there is throughout the gospel. More and more, on closer study, the gospel seems to be intricately, carefully collaged and sequenced at every point, brilliantly paced, emphasis repeatedly put on key and dramatic moments through juxtaposition and repetition. "The writer has told the story in such a way as to have certain effects on the reader," Rhoads and Michie say, using "sophisticated literary techniques" to develop character and build narrative suspense (3). Here that literary genius points us towards the uniqueness of Jesus, his special identity and power, but it also leaves the exact nature of this uniqueness, the exact nature of this power, deliberately and subtly up for interpretation. Mark even seems to be careful not to say exactly whose voice is sounding from the sky. It's just "a voice," its location not specified, simply there.

The student who asked the question about the baptism is obviously conditioned by the theological tradition surrounding the gospels, the centuries of inferences and interpretations, even though he isn't Christian. We are all of us influenced as we look at these words on the first page of the gospel by the words of the Nicene Creed, written three centuries later, in 325, or if not by those words by the tradition they represent and engendered. We all look at Mark through the understanding hammered out then, in the creed, that Jesus is "one in being with the father," *homoousios*, in the Greek, and that's a valid understanding, a valid inference, teased out of Mark's deep and powerful attachment to the charismatic figure he describes, as well as teased out of the other three gospels. But Mark doesn't use the phrase "one in being with the father," at any point in the gospel, and neither do the other three gospel writers, neither does Paul, just as the Genesis authors never use the phrase "original sin." In fact, part of the debate at the council of Nicea was over the question of whether a nonbiblical term like *homoousios*, a term taken from Greek philosophy, was appropriate to use in a creedal statement drawn from the Bible. Many resisted, just as many people for centuries read the gospel of Mark and the other gospels and from those words drew the conclusion that Jesus was a great man, that Jesus was uniquely related to the Father of all, the Creator of Genesis, but not himself divine, not himself God sent to earth. This is why the Council of Nicea was necessary in the first place, because the gospels themselves are stories, they are narratives, they are committed first and most of all to the details of what was thought to have happened, and do not in their commitment to this showing, this dramatizing, spell out in complete and satisfactory detail a full Trinitarian theology.[14] The text is not self-evident. "The sacred text was never intended to teach doctrine," Newman says, "but only to prove it" (*Apologia* 29–30); that is, only to be used in the act of interpretation. If it were sufficient unto itself, if it contained all the explicit dogma and doctrine we need, three centuries of Arians would not have read it the way they obviously did and it would not have been necessary to convene the Council of Nicea in the first place.

Far from being a crude and sloppy writer, as he was believed to be for centuries, Mark is careful and deliberate, and what he is careful to do is to present the figure of Jesus as doing and saying mysterious and controversial things that the people don't understand and even resist. He shows us a Jesus who doesn't explain himself and he doesn't as a writer fill in those gaps. He leaves them there. The Jesus of Mark's gospel is a man who performs miracles that scare people, tells stories that confuse people, expels demons and heals lepers and never comes out and says why, forcing the people to interpret his actions for themselves. Mark imitates him. In its spareness, Mark's prose forces us into the position of the people inside the story, left to puzzle over what we've just seen, left to figure out what hasn't been said.

A violent wind storm comes and the waves pour into the boat but Jesus is sleeping. The disciples wake him and say, "Teacher, do you not care that we are perishing?" (4:38). And he warns the wind and silences the sea and the wind falls. There is a great calm, but not in the disciples, not in those who witness the miracles. Readers inexperienced with the gospel or with faith come to it with the assumption that miracles somehow settle the questions. We see a miracle, we're convinced. We witness something spectacular like this, Jesus calming the storm, Jesus walking on water, Jesus healing the blind and the lame, and that's it. We've got it. He's the one and we understand all. But no, not here, not in this scene and not in any of the scenes that Mark so carefully orchestrates, one after the other, piling up examples to make the point: "They were filled with great awe and said to one another, 'Who then is this, that even the wind and sea obey him?'" (4:41) This is what happens again and again. The teaching and actions of Jesus lead to questions, not answers; they upset people, not remove their burdens. And until the great speech about dying to live before the central moment of the transfiguration, Jesus never explains to the disciples or to anyone else why he is doing what he's doing and exactly who he is. Those who seem to get it he tries to silence: don't tell anyone. Keep this to yourself.

One of the synagogue leaders named Jairus comes running up to Jesus and begs him to heal his dying daughter, but on the way to Jairus's house Jesus is stopped by a hemorrhaging woman who reaches out to touch his garment. Jesus turns around as he feels the power flowing out of his body, faces the woman, blesses her, and sends her on her way, only to discover that in the delay the daughter of Jairus has died. And in this great example of Mark's technique of sandwiching one episode inside another, the technique of *inclusio*, of inserting one narrative event inside another in order to call attention to their relations, Jesus comes to the little girl and tells her, "Little girl, get up," and she gets up, she is alive, she lives (5:41).

But far from settling the question for those who witness the miracle, the actions and words of Jesus invoke amazement and questions and even offense. "Where did this man get all this? What is the wisdom that has been given to him?" And "they took offense at him" (6:2–3), and Jesus lets them be offended. He does nothing to interpret his actions, to surround them with theological commentary or softening explanations and reassurances. Neither does Mark. The scene is dramatized in convincing and powerful spareness. The words leave no doubt about the charismatic power of this man and certainly infer Mark's own attractions, but his strategy as a writer is never to intervene, never to do what Jesus himself rarely does, which is to explain, which is to move from story to proposition, from red red rose to the language of criticism.

He works the way writers work, by showing rather than telling. His sense of what the events mean is implicit in their juxtapositions, in his frequent use of *inclusio*, or rhetorical sandwiching. By placing the story of the hemorrhaging woman inside the story of the daughter of Jairus Mark must be inviting us to think through comparisons. The dying girl is twelve years old, the woman has been bleeding twelve years; he addresses both the girl and the woman as "daughter." But the girl is the daughter of a synagogue leader, a daughter of power and influence, while the woman is just a woman, and a poor woman, and a woman who is bleeding, anathema and impure to Jews. Yet Jesus allows her to touch him, he turns and addresses her by name, she, too, is healed, and this carries through a pattern throughout the gospel not just of *inclusio* but of Jesus welcoming the poor and the marginal and the outcast to his table and to his presence, into the kingdom—the very reason he is killed.

Mark's artfulness and craft extend over the whole gospel, which is structured, as are the other two synoptic gospels, Matthew and Luke, around three parallel events: the baptism, the transfiguration, and the crucifixion. The transfiguration is in the exact middle of the story (9:2–8). Everything leads up to it and follows it. It's the moment where Jesus is revealed fully and completely for who he is. Right before it, in his great pretransfiguration discourse, he finally explains fully and completely who he is, though only to the disciples and though they don't understand. I am the messiah, but not in the way you understand that word, he says. After that point, after Jesus walks up the mountain and is bathed in the blinding light, seen in the company of Elijah and Moses, he walks back down and into Jerusalem, the action accelerating now, the controversy increasing as he argues with the religious leaders on the steps of the temple itself, until finally he is arrested and tried and nailed to a cross, the last of the three structuring events. It's a clear, symmetrical, climactic structure, and each of the three scenes that defines it has just the same elements in just the same sequence. There is "tearing," there is a "voice," and there is a naming of who Jesus is. The parallel of the baptism and the crucifixion is especially clear: the curtain tears at the end as the sky is torn at the beginning; the voice of the centurion is heard as the voice of God is heard; and the voice says this is "God's Son" as the voice from the sky had named Jesus the beloved son (15:37–39). It's as if the whole gospel is bracketed by one big *inclusio*, one large artistic device, and within it, at exactly the center, the transfiguration repeats the same pattern with only slight variation: the light instead of the tearing, then a shadow passing over, then the voice from the cloud with the identification, the naming, "this is my Son, the beloved" (9:7). Similar and subtler patterns weave all the stories together—images of "tearing" repeated every few pages, for example, as a hole is torn in a roof or people tear their garments or demons are torn out of bodies; scenes of table fellowship, repeated images of Jesus eating, and eating with those not welcome anywhere else; scenes of buildings entered or left or taken down, Jesus coming and going, turning the world inside out and taking all things into himself. To say that Mark's gospel shows rather than tells, that it doesn't posit a propositional theology, is not to say that it's not intended, not shaped, not informed by a sensibility both believing and highly artful. It is, just as the book of Genesis is.

Alter's notes to his careful new translation of Genesis abound with explanations of the authors' sly punning and patterns of imagery: concealment and disguise, clothing and nakedness, the favored second-born, the ritual blessing and the ritual meal, the barren and the prolific, the call and the dream and the subsequent doubt, all of it carefully orchestrated and collaged until the climax in the book of Exodus, in the story of Moses, which repeats all the patterns. Students begin their reading of Genesis asking irritating and distracting questions about what seem to be narrative inconsistencies. Where did Cain's wife come from? Where did the people who threaten Cain come from? As if the writers of the stories are concerned with that level of detail, as if they are writing an objective family history or historical tract. My task with Genesis as with Mark is to move students toward an appreciation of the literary structure of the work, the larger consistencies of theme and image as signaled in patterns over the course of the book. Surely if we can see these many uses of the imagery of clothing and concealment, for example, extending across multiple stories and even material coming from multiple sources—if we see all this disparate material stitched together like this, with such obvious care, it might be that this is the writer's concern, the level on which the writer is operating, the level of the image, the level of the literary. The writer must not care, as we do, about these smaller inconsistencies—at least this is a possible inference—and perhaps in these little details we are being encouraged to understand the work as literary, not historical; we are being given clues about how to read it and what it is.

Leaving intention aside, there's a greater intellectual payoff in looking at literary patterns than in looking for historical inconsistencies. We gain more from the work if we assume it is a literary whole, a shaped and intended work, than if we keep trying to poke holes in it. We start being able to infer its meanings. We move from the question, did this happen, to the question, what does this mean?

But what's even more important than understanding that the gospel of Mark is crafted is understanding *how* it is crafted. It is crafted through detail. It is crafted through showing rather than telling in very much the way of the parable, Jesus' central way of teaching. Parable, of course, is story, as John Dominic Crossan explains in his important study of the form, *The Dark Interval*. A parable is a simple story, drawn from everyday life and so familiar to the hearers and in a sense easy to understand. Yet it's not easy to understand finally because Jesus as storyteller rarely explains the moral directly. The listeners must fill that gap themselves. It's not easy to understand finally because the meaning of the story varies, is layered and multiple, depending on the situation of the hearer, varying as the context varies. This is the moral of the famous parable of the sower, which is, among things, a parable about parables, a parable about story and so about the gospel and what it demands from the reader (4.1–9). The sower goes out to sow and some seed falls by the road where birds come and eat it up. Other seed falls on a rocky place, other seed into thorns, other into fertile ground, and it's the ground that makes the growing possible. It's the listener, as Jesus explains when he explains the parable to the disciples, one of the few times he does this. But the explanation is only to explain why explanations are not forthcoming. The seed is the word, he says. It's the word, and because it's a seed it's small, it's tiny, and it's hidden in the ground where it grows slowly and over time, not all at once, yielding fruit only in due season and only if the listener has received it openly and with grace, and even then it dies back again, there's a cycle of growth and dying back, as there are ups and down, as there are "undulations" in our faith life, as C. S. Lewis puts it in *The Screwtape Letters* (37). Reading the Bible, the parable might imply, isn't a matter of receiving simple lessons for living once and for all, immediately, full grown, so that no thinking ever has to be done again. No, reading is slow, it's a process, it happens over time and only with cultivation, and it all depends on how the reader works and what the reader does. The fruit isn't handed to us.

Even in the great pre-transfiguration discourse, when Jesus finally comes out and says who he is and why he comes, the language is difficult and elusive, however propositional. I am the Messiah, he tells the disciples, but not in the way you think. I am the Messiah who must die, who must be crucified, and if you want to follow me you must be crucified, too, you must die to yourself because only in dying can you live. This is what Jesus tells his disciples in a language at once propositional and tersely, densely packed, and as in their reactions to the healings and the miracles and the parables, the disciples just don't get it. The light of the transfiguration has barely faded when Peter, overwhelmed, wants to build a booth and reduce it to what he can manage and contain. The disciples are barely off the mountain when they're back to arguing about who comes first and who is the best.

What dying to live means can only be demonstrated, not explained. It can only be acted out, and that's what Jesus does in the end, on the cross, spreading out his arms and in silence suffering a painful and degrading death that his Jewish contemporaries could not have understood as the death of a messiah. Jesus falls silent and is raised up on a cross, a final image for the people to contemplate, a final gap to be filled, and Mark doesn't answer the question for us. He shows us the centurion, the Roman soldier, at the foot of the cross, the one who says, looking up, awed, surely this was the Son of God. But the centurion is only one viewer of this image, of this symbol, and Mark is careful to arrange a number of others around the cross as well, those who laugh and jeer, those who mistake Jesus for someone else. All possible views are available to us as readers because Mark in his spareness, in his powerful spareness, sticks to the scene itself, respecting the silence of Jesus in his own authorial silence, forcing us in the end to answer the question Jesus put to his disciples before the transfiguration: Who do you say I am?

Even the resurrection doesn't answer that question for the reader. So true is Mark to his strategies of silence and showing that he ends the gospel with the empty tomb and the women running away, afraid. Later commentators added a quick summary of the post-resurrection stories elaborated in Luke and Matthew, but Mark apparently ended with a young man dressed in white sitting in the open tomb who reports to the women, secondhand, that the one they seek is raised: "He is not here," the man says, and that blankness, that gap, that opening in the tomb, is like the gaps and the openings in the narrative itself. It terrifies the women: "So they went out and fled from the tomb, for terror had seized them; and they said nothing to anyone, for they were afraid" (16:6–8).

Afraid. Afraid is one of the last words of the gospel of Mark, an ending so ambiguous and open-ended that apparently it's not only self we must die to but certainty, interpretive certainty.

After considering a number of possible reasons for Mark's silence about the resurrection—what he and his community might have taken for granted, what they assumed—Price insists that finally the motives must be literary. They must have to do with a fidelity to story:

> Mark's final reason for the omission of a resurrection scene is surely part and parcel of his bedrock narrative strategy, his narrative faith throughout his book. Masterful as his writing hand has proved to be from the start of his tale, here at the end he faces the inexorable fact that words on a page, however attentive and carefully arranged, cannot of themselves produce belief and trust of the sort that a phenomenon like palpable resurrection from the dead demands of an audience. (80)

"The supreme narrators," Price says, trust finally in the power of the story itself, in the force of description and scene, and he includes Mark here with the Yahwist writer of Hebrew scripture, as we have seen, as well as with Homer and Shakespeare. What Mark shares with these writers is what Price calls the "ancient trust of all those who bet their entire hand on story, whether oral or written: the thin compelling thread of an action that is worth our attention." What Mark knows is that "the first thing a listener or reader craves from the teller is clean-lined portrayal of mighty [. . .] acts" (60). And this, I think, is itself a theology, or itself carries a theological content, because it implies a faith in a mystery that cannot be named in any other way, a mystery that story and only story can get close to, a mystery that can't be resolved into simple lessons for living.

Price is a southern novelist as O'Connor is a southern novelist, and a believer, too, though Baptist, not Catholic, and what he says about Mark as storyteller sounds much like O'Connor discussing the faith of the novelist. He brings us back to O'Connor's analysis of what a story does, which applies at every point to the gospel of Mark. O'Connor says that the writer must be faithful most of all to the concreteness of the world the way it really is, and this is Mark, describing what Jesus does, what he says, how he moves in the world, and staying out of the frame, avoiding propagandizing. O'Connor says that in his fidelity to the facts the Christian writer must never oversimplify or pretty up, describing only the good in a person, describing only the saint and the saccharine outcomes of saintly behavior. This is Mark, insistent on the stupidity of the disciples as well as of the people as a mass, the stupidity of those who lived and worked with Jesus everyday, people Jesus tried to teach directly and intimately and who still so radically missed the point as to have abandoned him entirely by the end. Even Peter, in fact Peter most of all, the manic depressive rock of the church, the one who in a moment of inspiration recognizes who Jesus is—you are the Messiah—and the next is so wrong about what that means, who so misunderstands the weakness and the foolishness and the sacrifice that this will involve, the humiliation not the glory, that Jesus calls him Satan himself. Peter, the favored one, the special one, who not only foolishly tries to erect the three booths but who later denies Jesus three times.

"We Catholics," O'Connor says, "are very much given to the Instant Answer. Fiction doesn't have any" (184). As Mark, too, doesn't have any, as Mark, too, avoids the easy cliché, the dismissive tag line, the false promise. To follow Christ is to be lost, not found, to enter more deeply into the messiness and the misery and even now and then the glory of the world created by God reputedly in six days. What comes from following Christ is mystery, not solutions, certainly not political power, and Mark so believes this to be true that he won't even end his story in a way that makes his readers feel certain or content.

Students who read the Bible in a course called the Literature of Western Civilization need to know the finer points of genre as well. They need to know that the Bible is a library, an anthology, containing all kinds of discourse and writing just as any library contains all kinds of books, not just history but biography and fiction and fantasy and instruction manuals and reference works. They need to know the scholarly consensus that parts of the Bible were intended to be read from the beginning as folktales and comic short stories and fables every bit as conventional and in a sense unreal as the story of the three bears, and that to read the Bible without knowing this, without a preliminary sense of the kinds of language and the nature of conventions, is to read it naïvely and incorrectly. Star Trek is not the same as the evening news. Aliens monitoring our transmissions from a planet far away would have to understand the nature of genre not to mistake the various truths these kinds of discourse intend to tell, the conventions they assume we all understand, and the Bible is no different.

In other words, students need to understand that not all the Bible was intended to be read as history in the first place and that those parts that were intended to be read as history were not intended to be read as objective but as faith-filled histories, intended and shaped from the start, didactic histories, gospels, good news with all faith in the goodness of the news. Students need to understand that the gospels are not eyewitness accounts but redactions of oral stories written down at least a generation later and under the influence of believing and worshiping communities, everywhere shaped by the assumptions and the experience of those communities.

But first, before all these refinements, maybe what students most need to understand is that the Gospel of Mark, like the book of Genesis, is a story. Maybe the first and most important thing of all is not that Mark was a believer but that he was a writer; that when he sat down to write he went about his work the way all writers go about their work, wild and shuddering and full of grace as well as fear, caught up in the struggle and joy of the act of composing.

## The Empty Net

When my youngest son was small I went to one of his soccer games and came home so moved that I had to compose a poem. What moved me was hard to explain. I couldn't put it into words, really, and that's why I wrote the poem, because I didn't understand what I was feeling. What I could do was record the event itself, as clearly and directly as I knew how to:

*The Empty Net*

What I saw on the flushed
and sweaty face of my son
as he waited for the throw-in

was a giving up of himself
to the play of the ball and
the boundaries of the field

and the exact position of
his friends so complete and
generous and brave that it

was sadness bursting out of
me like cheering, it was grief.
For sacrifice like this no

honor is commensurate, no
moment sufficient. The shadows
would have deepened even if

he'd won the game, the mothers
and the fathers folding up the
lawn chairs and hurrying home.

Sleep would have come in any
event and with it the darkness
and the dreams, the ball shooting

back into the ropes again and
again, falling and falling into
the empty net. Oh my beautiful

son, I never would have given
you up so freely, I never would
have given you up at all.

It was the image of my son's face that moved me to write, the image of
the empty net, the image of the field. It was a feeling that moved me, of
grief and of loss, although from the beginning, too, I was shaping that
feeling. I had almost from the moment of first feeling that grief intuited
as well a structure or design for the poem. Simultaneous with the emotion were a few of the words, a couple of the sentences, and as I sat down
and began composing them I wrote as a Christian man, a Catholic man,
with some awareness of how my experience of losing my son was perhaps
analogous to the theology of the Father and the Son. That little bit of
Trinitarian theology was so embedded in me that it helped shape what I
was thinking and feeling from the beginning, even on the sidelines, even

as I stood and watched my son losing the game. All this, and then the line breaks, the arranging after a while of the poem into three line stanzas, which I couldn't help but think of as in a small way Trinitarian.

So it was image first and thought second except for how my previous thoughts and the existing culture and theology shaped the image in the first place, until finally the poem was ready to send out, I thought, and I sent it to the Catholic magazine *America*, a choice of course reflecting my awareness of the Christian themes in the poem. But still it was the image, it was the experience, it was that sense of the empty net and the ball falling and falling into it that moved me to write the poem and to send it out and that was all I could have told you about if you'd asked me. All I could really say about the poem was the poem itself finally, the concrete images I had written in the order in which those images had come, which is why I was both surprised and delighted when the poem was accepted and the editor wrote in the acceptance letter saying how I had invoked the theme of the sacrifice of Isaac, that great story later on in Genesis, a story also not explained, also left starkly and mysteriously on the page by whomever the author was all those centuries ago, God in his mystery requiring for no reason that is clear to Abraham or to us that his beloved son be brought upon the altar and offered up, this precious son, sacrificed, and then the last minute reprieve, the knife hovering above the terrified boy (Gen 22). The author in the starkness and power of his language leaves all this for us to figure out, though perhaps the point is that it can't be figured out, that the moment eludes explanation and so is only available to story. Now an editor of a Catholic magazine quite naturally and sensibly suggests how my poem invokes this very mystery when in fact I hadn't thought of it at all, hadn't considered it in any way I could have articulated, wasn't thinking of Abraham but only of myself and my beautiful, beautiful son, given up.

Months later the poem appeared, on Good Friday, distributed to Catholics across the country who if they bothered to read it would quite naturally read it from the perspective of their Catholic faith as I now read it from mine, as in a sense I wrote it from the beginning with my faith as the motive and the frame.

———

C. S. Lewis's *Chronicles of Narnia* are so obviously Christian in their implications that people think Lewis began with Christian ideas and then came up with images to embody them. But this is "pure moonshine," Lewis says in an essay about fairy stories. "I couldn't write that way at all," and no writer can. He didn't "draw up a list of basic Christian truths" and then "hammer out the allegories." No. "Everything began with images: a faun carrying an umbrella, a queen on a sledge, a magnificent lion." At first "there wasn't even anything Christian about them," in fact.

"That element pushed itself in of its own accord," was part of the "bub-bling" that was the act of composition for Lewis as it is for every writer of fiction and poetry (*On Stories* 46). Stories always begin with images. There is always an intuitive and mysterious process of bubbling up and surprise. The ideas emerge later, but not in a way that's separable from the images themselves.

"One thing I am sure of," Lewis says in a preface to the Narnia sto-ries written for children, all the stories "began with pictures in my head" and he doesn't exactly know where those pictures came from. "I don't know where the Lion came from or why He came," for example. He just came, and with him, all the stories, almost all at once. "In a sense, I know very little about how this story was born. [. . .] I don't believe anyone knows exactly how he 'makes things up.' Making up is a very mysterious thing" (*On Stories* 53–54).

In an interview about "Traveling Through the Dark," his most famous poem, Stafford claims not to know its theme. "You know, that is not a poem that is written to support a position that I have chosen, it's just a poem that grows out of the plight I am in as a human being," as all poems grow out of that plight. When Stafford writes as when all of us write, "I don't have any program, any idea of any purpose to tell the American people about themselves, or anything like that, or how they ought be." Instead, his writing, like Lewis's is "like a groping forward into an experience of my own" which readers then interpret in whatever ways they interpret it (*Writing the Australian Crawl* 93, 108).

It's dangerous to attribute motives to an author alive right now, let alone an author dead two thousand years. Price is especially good in the introduction to his translation in identifying his speculations about what Mark was thinking as merely speculations and in sticking most of the time to the words themselves, to what's on the page. But what if Mark was a writer just as I am a writer, just as my students are writers, just as Lewis and Stafford and any writer is a writer? Yes, he had the beliefs of his community, his experience of the liturgy, all those framing symbols and ideas, as I do. But what if he sat down and wrote out of his joy and his pain and drawing on all his talent and skill absolutely convinced of the power and the glory of this man named Jesus, absolutely believing in him, but believing in him in a way he could not articulate except in the words of the story he actually tells?

Mark certainly believed in Jesus Christ as the Messiah, as the chosen one, but he would not have understood the language of the Nicene Creed. He would not have been able to understand a language that it took the Christian community centuries to negotiate and get right after long and prayerful and even tortured reflection on just the story he was the first to have written down. He couldn't have had that fully developed

Trinitarian theology in mind when he wrote the gospel. What he had in mind is what he had in his heart—he wrote, I think, out of his love and his longing, and what he wrote was all about the touch and taste and feel of that love and that longing, and the achievement and great, inspired truth of this writing was to capture, as O'Connor puts it, "the mystery from which we draw our abstractions" (152), the mystery which always exceeds whatever we can say about it.

————

I was walking again on the bluff beyond the seminary, another hot autumn day, when I heard what I later read was the first of several shot gun blasts. I didn't think much of it. The sound came from far enough away to be muffled, indistinct. The later blast (a minute later?) reminded me of a large book hitting the floor in some adjacent room. And then the first of the sirens started whining. In the next minute I may have heard the next two shotgun blasts—I'm not sure—since another siren, and then another, and then a dozen fire trucks and police cars started up and began intersecting somewhere close by. I felt as if I were in a tower looking down on the people and movements below me—the seminary hill is about three hundred feet high—except that I was listening instead of looking because a wall of alder and fir blocked my view of the trucks screaming below.

A fire? I came into the oak grove and sat down and ate my lunch, then threw my apple core into the brush and read another chapter of Andrew Louth.

The horror was in the paper the next day: an estranged husband, distraught and angry, had gunned down his wife on the lawn of their house in the little town of Scotts Mills, about five miles up the road, then murdered in turn each of his three children. The last one, a baby, he shot in his mother-in-law's arms before a neighbor dragged him to the sidewalk. The grandmother was only slightly wounded, but the rest—the mother and those three little girls—were dead. Each blast I heard walking to the oaks and looking out at the fields was the sound of a death sudden and senseless and horrible. And the gaps between shots—those gaps as I opened my lunch and took out my sandwich—were the children running across the lawn, scrambling away into the flowers? Was the grandmother begging? There were these two moments one day in the fall: a man walking out into the fields and thinking about theology; another man, not much younger, just up the road, hunting down his family with a shotgun. What do we do with this? What can we possibly do?

In a way the answers are too easy. It's not hard to read a coincidence like this as still another example of the impotence of faith. The constant death of children everywhere denies the Christian claim of the love that so redeems the world. It's only a little more difficult to argue in the opposite direction, explaining away the unexplainable with pieties about heaven and forgiveness: Christ has a special place for the little children; they are now playing in all their innocence on the grassy slopes of paradise. Louth would connect the two moments in a profound way. Christ conquered death by first enduring it, he would say. Christianity doesn't deny suffering but embraces it. The risen Lord is the one who was crucified.

But I can tell you how it seemed to me then. The moments felt separate. They wouldn't fit together in my mind. I kept studying theology, my vague and restless faith just as vague and restless as before, no less secure than before the blasts and the sirens, no more resolved. And yet the sense of the horror of the murders remained in force, too, however muffled. The loss was abstract for me only because I received it at my little distance, up in the tower of my private thoughts and needs. I couldn't make it mean anything.

On the day of the crucifixion, what was going on in the rooms and streets and fields nearby. Who was kneading dough or sweeping the floor? Who was lost in thought? Who was watching the birds?

## The Idea of the University Revisited: The Ecology of Reading

In exploring the Biblical text as we have been doing, reading between its lines and becoming aware of our own presuppositions and shaping beliefs, becoming in a sense "disillusioned" by the text and about the text, we are doing the work of all literary study but also the work of the public university. The nature of the Bible as story makes it a particularly ideal text for teaching the kinds of critical reading skills that all the courses at a university are trying to teach, especially a public university. To paraphrase Palmer in *To Know as We Are Known*, if things were as they seem, education would not be necessary (19). But things are not as they seem. Beneath the surface are structures and histories and forces more complicated than students understand at first. That's what we've been experiencing, through the Bible, and this is true in every discipline, from English to economics to engineering. What we assume is self-evident never is. What we think is universal is one voice among many, and knowing this is the first step toward acquiring the skills and methods of precision, of accuracy, of valid, because limited, observation.

The horizontal beam of the cross is the secular work of the university as it goes on day to day. It's our ordinary, everyday work, the work of discovering evidence and testing conclusions, and on this level the Bible as Literature quite properly belongs at the university. The Bible becomes simply another text—a particularly interesting and rewarding text, a particularly complicated text—but in the end simply one among the many texts being used for the critical reading that universities do. That I am a deacon who happens to teach the Bible, a Christian who teaches the great works of Christian literature, makes my situation a little more compli- cated than that of say a math or a computer science professor, a teacher whose subject matter is not obviously related to issues of faith. When I teach the Bible or Augustine or Dante I feel that certain disclosures are in order. But on this first level, on this horizontal beam, those disclosures only reinforce the methods and ideas that I've always taught and that we all teach.

A forest ecologist, for example, is always searching for clues to the vast systems and structures beyond the cycles of nature—the assumption is always of hidden meanings and the possibility of minute "disclosures," as Aldo Leopold puts it in *A Sand County Almanac* (83), especially in a landscape that seems as otherwise plain and unadorned as the Bible first appeared to Augustine. "In country, as in people," Leopold says, "a plain exterior often conceals hidden riches, to perceive which requires much living in and with" (180). That's the ecological imagination: the capacity to believe in what isn't obvious. That's the skill of ecological analysis, as it is the skill of Biblical interpretation: the skill of reading between the lines, the living in and with.

Like a reader trying to infer the meaning of a passage in Genesis or Mark, Leopold follows the tracks of a January skunk, "curious to deduce his state of mind" (3). He calls the act of cutting wood "an allegory for the historian in the diverse functions of saw, wedge, and axe" (17) and imagines his dog "translating" for him "the olfactory poem that who- knows-what silent creatures have written in the night" (46). The history of conservation is really "written with an ax" and every farm is a "text- book on animal ecology" (73, 86). The spaces between the whorls of branches are "an autobiography" to be read, the howls of wolves a mys- tery to be "deciphered," patterns of erosion like a text "written in gullies on a thousand fields" (88, 137, 198).

The goal in such reading, as in the reading of the Bible, as in the reading of statistics in sociology or empirical evidence in physics, is to "promote perception," as Leopold puts it (290). The job of ecological education is not one "of building roads into lovely country, but of build- ing receptivity into the still unlovely human mind" (295), and the most important result of that building is not just precision of method but openness and humility:

> Ability to see the cultural value of wilderness boils down, in the last analysis, to a question of intellectual humility. The shallow-minded modern who has lost his rootage in the land assumes that he has already discovered what is important; it is such who prate of empires,

political or economic, that will last a thousand years. It is only the
scholar who appreciates that all history consists of successive excursions from a single starting-point, to which man returns again and
again to organize yet another search for a durable scale of values. (279)

Here in the text of nature are just the challenges of the Biblical text.
Before it we must recognize the limitations of our own point of view.
Before it we must recognize matters of importance subtler and deeper
than we realized before. In the Western tradition the Bible and the natural world have always been seen as the two great texts, the two great
books, repositories for all we ever need to know of greatness and precision, and this is why. In fact, Alter uses exactly the phrase "intellectual
humility" to describe the effects of Biblical study. What the Bible should
inspire from its readers, Alter says, is both the closest attention to its formal details and an attitude of "intellectual humility" before the subtleties
of these details (*The World of Biblical Literature* 23).

In an argument over an issue in Scripture the third century theologian Tertullian once asked, indignantly, "By what right are you cutting
trees in my forest?" (qtd. in Grant and Tracy 75). This is what the rest of
the ancient world imagined the Scriptures to be, too, not a box, not a
building, not even a garden, but a forest, a complex and beautiful and living ecology—a "forest of symbols," as the twentieth-century French theologian Marrou describes it (qtd. in Louth 112); or, to borrow again from
Cardinal Newman, "an unexplored and unsubdued land, with heights
and valleys, forests and streams, on the right and left of our path and
close about us, full of concealed wonders and choice treasures" (*An Essay
on the Development of Christian Doctrine* 71).

A modest proposal. Students take only one required course their first
year: Introduction to Reading. The only two texts: the Bible and any
nearby forest.[15]

The reason to study the Bible at a state university is the reason to
study a forest, is the reason to study anything else, because the nature of
its language encourages an attention to detail and a healthy sense of
human limitation. The Bible strives for just the perceptiveness and modesty that the university requires. In a comment on astronomy in *The Idea
of the University*, Newman says of the physical sciences that they should
overwhelm the student: "The view of the heavens which the telescope
opens upon us, if allowed to fill and possess the mind, may almost whirl
it round and make it dizzy." And this is a good thing, Newman says. It's
the goal not just of the physical sciences but of the whole university, this
dizziness, this "intellectual enlargement." What every department in the
university hopes to accomplish as it brings before us its "exuberant riches
and resources" is to "take our breath away," to show us that the universe

is a very big place and that we are somehow caught up in that vastness (90; 1.5.9).

The source of our humility isn't just what we discover in nature or in the text but what we discover in ourselves. The cause of our dizziness is the recognition that much of what we took for granted isn't actually in the outer world but in us, projected outward, imposed as a way of defining and ordering. What we realize and what the Bible is particularly good at showing is that we come to the world with assumptions, with biases and values, and that these values are everywhere framing what it is we see and know. The forest we are in is a forest of voices.

The Bible is good at this for two reasons, the first simply because it's literature. In the implicitness and density of any literary text the reader is forced into close attention. All language exists on a scale of explicitness or transparency, with phone books and encyclopedias on the most transparent end, poetry and story on the least explicit or most nearly opaque end. All language, even language that is explicit and purely propositional, requires interpretation. There are hidden contexts to understand, codes to decipher. What's useful about literary language is that this hiddenness and subtlety is taken up and exaggerated, made denser and in a sense more obvious, called attention to. Everything that is true about all language is even more true in literature, so that the critical reading skills we learn from reading it can help us get in shape for the reading of anything else, in any discipline.

But the second reason that the Bible is especially good at doing the work of the university is that it's both ancient and controversial, a literature layered over by thousands of years of interpretive traditions and much current anxiety and attachment. The reading of any literary text involves us necessarily in recognizing the biases or prejudices we bring to the filling of gaps, but because the Bible is so surrounded with biases and prejudices, because it excites such intense resistance or attraction, all that is true of reading any literature is here made more obvious and denser and more dizzying. People don't meet every Sunday to proclaim *Finnegan's Wake*. People don't fight wars over Wordsworth's sonnets. The "religious classic," Tracy says, carries with it "an excess of meaning," both in the nature of its literary structure and symbols and in the tradition of meaning and interpretation that surrounds that structure (*The Analogical Imagination* 102). The religious classic in this sense becomes the ideal test for postmodernism, its density and elusiveness forcing us to confront the roughness and complexity of all meaning.

This is not unlike Newman's argument in *The Idea of the University* for the teaching of theology. It should be taught because it's true. The university should teach all knowledge, should be universal in that sense, and "religious doctrine is knowledge," he says bluntly (40; 1.2.9). What we have seen about the reading of the Bible suggests another, contemporary way of understanding that statement. We might say not that religion is true but that all truth is religious. What we now agree about knowledge and truth, in every discipline, is that's it never "objective," never just out there, once and for all, free of our interpretations. All knowledge, in other words, has the character of religious experience in that all knowledge is somehow predicated upon a belief. "All deeply held commitments should be treated as religious," Stephen Carter says (218). "There is no philosophy without presupposition," Ricouer says (350). We must believe in order to understand.

Or as Leopold puts it, "it is only the scholar who appreciates that all history consists of successive excursions from a single starting-point, to which man returns again and again to organize yet another search for a durable scale of values" (279). The sciences know what the humanities profess, that truth is never possessed but always sought for, again and again, that truth is search, not object, method, not proposition, a matter of successive excursions toward a single starting point we can never reach. We are always in the act of searching for a durable scale of values, but all that is durable finally is the search itself.

————

It's in this context that I tell my Bible as Literature classes that I'm a deacon. What I'm trying to do is demonstrate through my own situatedness that all knowledge and all reading is situated. I'm not arguing that my students should believe but that I do. I'm not trying to convert, only admitting to my own conversion. I'm holding myself up as a specimen, suggesting myself as an example of the hermeneutic circle that I want them to know they live within themselves.

Once, in a very striking phrase, the philosopher Hans-Georg Gadamer said that the purpose of learning is to produce the "experienced person," the person who is "radically undogmatic," open to the presuppositions of others because he is aware of his own (355). This is why I say I'm a deacon. This is why I share my dogmas: in the service of the radically undogmatic. I'm trying from the start to help my students realize that objectivist knowledge is no longer credible and never has been.

Ann Marie, for example, by the end of the term has come to accept the complexity of the Biblical text, commenting in a final take-home exam question on the effort of certain parents in a Florida school district to require that the Bible be taught as history, as historical fact. The school board has responded that the Bible shouldn't be taught at all because it would violate the separation of church and state. I will talk about the separation of church and state in Chapter 5. What interests me here is Ann Marie's comment that the debate "hinges on two factors, (1) one's culture relative to the contents of the text, and (2) one's sense of placement in relationship to the text." In this sense, both sides of the debate, "share the same cultural influences, and also, oddly enough, the same flaw in their approach to the text." Both sides fail to understand that the Biblical authors wrote from a "different cultural perspective than our own." Both sides fail to "acknowledge the Bible's variety of genres and variety of interpretations available through these genres":

> *The Bible authors used stories as a communicative and exploratory channel to try to convey to the people the wonder and puzzlement of the experience of a relationship with God. The stories are suggestive. The modern literalist reader, on the other hand, tends to conclude that the stories are one-dimensional. To have a place in our modern world, the stories must be solely objective, leaving no room for a myriad of interpretations.*

But this is an "arrogant attitude," Ann Marie concludes, because it never stops to consider that other people might think in other ways. "We want direct causality, which flies in the face of the Biblical style of writing as a way to communicate experiences of mystery."

In fact, "perhaps it is mystery that leads to a lot of discomfort. If something is acknowledged as inexplicable—as mystery—we will, of course, encounter difficulty trying to teach it as if it were history." Perhaps it is fear of interpretation, of the need for interpretation, a need that is always there, whether we like it or not—perhaps it is this fear that drives the debate, on both sides. "In apprehension that one preferred interpretation may arise, opponents seek to abolish the possibility of any and all interpretations."

This is the reason to teach the Bible as literature at a state university, to elicit from students writing of this sophistication and self-awareness, of this intellectual humility. The reason to teach the Bible as literature is to help move students from easy black-and-white thinking to this more complex and insightful acknowledgement that interpretation is always necessary and always comes from somewhere.

What the Bible as literature demonstrates so clearly and so well, what Ann Marie has grasped so insightfully, is that any understanding of a text depends on what Gadamer calls "the interplay of the movement of tradition and the movement of the interpreter" (293).[16] Understanding is a "dialectic" in which the text, the interpreter, and all the traditions and understandings of the community of readers play a part, continually interacting and involving each other. "The historian," Gadamer says, "is separate from his object of study by the infinite mediation of tradition" (217). It's not just that the Bible is a literary text that makes interpretation so difficult, but that it's an ancient text, handed on over so many centuries that it's impossible now for us to imagine the original contexts and inspirations, the people who composed and redacted it in some way radically other, alien. And what separates us from this origin, this Genesis, this otherness, isn't just time but all the acts of reading and interpretation that have filled in the gaps and been handed on as well. "Tradition" becomes the key word. There's no way to avoid engaging these layers of interpretation, no way to purge ourselves of how we've been taught to read, however unconscious those assumptions and techniques may be.

Imagine knowing nothing at all of the Bible and finding a copy of it on the sidewalk. You pick it up. How do you know that it's the inspired word of God? How do you know that people have believed it to be the inspired word of God? The word "Holy" may be written on the flyleaf, there may be claims to its holiness buried deep inside, but other texts claim to be inspired and sacred. How, without tradition, without someone having passed on at least the notion that this is the Bible, that this is scripture of some sort, could you begin to read it the way students always begin to read it, accepting or rejecting or remaining open to the presumption of its holiness?

A Japanese-American student writes about her father's first reaction to picking up the gospels. The family isn't Christian and knows little of the tradition. One day the father starts to page through the New Testament, stopping to read into particular stories. Finally he closes the book and puts it away. "Scary," he says. Students often resist such an awareness. They nearly always resist, brought up as they are in an American culture flooded with ideas and images of independence and freedom. The irony of our tradition is that it blinds us to the presence of tradition. The presumption of objectivity, of autonomy, is automatic.

A full-page advertisement in *Sports Illustrated*. On the left are some blurry hills, treeless. On the right is a large, blocky Isuzu Trooper, moving so fast it seems to be hovering above the edge of the page. The fact of the road is disguised. The ad hides how it got there, claims to be without infrastructure. All we see is the metal square of the machine, a faceless driver, and the caption, running across the middle of both pages, "Outrun Civilization." Outrun civilization—though huge numbers of people at the ad agency had to operate in concert to produce this piece of work, though huge numbers of people had to operate within frameworks of meaning and culture to build the car. Though the ad was reproduced en masse by the staff and craftsman of *Sports Illustrated*, all trained for years in ways of proceeding, then read by millions of people across the country who have access to the magazine only because it's systematically distributed. The caption is written in the English language, for crying out loud, something else we didn't invent. Its two words have ancient origins, a range of meanings passed along and modified for centuries. For us to read them in the first place requires a long history of schooling and a system of institutions. But it's a brilliant campaign. Americans don't like to be manipulated, imprinted as we are by the myth of the free frontier, the image of John Wayne blocking out the skyline, on his way out of Durango. That's why we're always electing presidents who promise to get the government off our backs and why universities feel more and more forced to model themselves after free market corporations, though the result of removing such regulations is only to make us still more vulnerable to the sneakier invasions of the multinationals. We've thrown off the visible controls for the invisible ones, and that's far worse. But it's also the point. Isuzu doesn't want us to discover how deeply we've been had. We might rebel. Nothing makes better consumers than the illusion of freedom.

For finally what Isuzu is trying to sell is the myth of surface itself. Its artifice is meant to blind us to artifice, all that color and boldness and simplicity moving us back down the hierarchies of meaning. It's trying to make us fundamentalists. Otherwise we might not buy the car. Otherwise we might remember the darkening of the atmosphere, the asphalting of the soil, our escape from the search for a scale of durable values.

We are all flooded by images like that of the SUV and the blurry hills, in all the hours we spend watching television and listening to the radio and working on the internet, bombarded by advertisements—over 30 an hour on the average network television program. Then add the labels on our toothpaste and breakfast cereal, the billboards and bumper-stickers on our way to work, the neon brand names at the Taco Bell or Burger King in the commons for lunch. Think of the logos and the labels on the shoes and the clothes in any given classroom, the Nike and the Guess and the Gap all around us. This is the water we swim in, the air we breathe, and the task of the university is to make students aware of this. The task is to make all of us aware of our own values, as values, as acts of faith taken from the start and perhaps worth taking in the end, but only freely, only consciously. The task of the university is to give all of us the critical reading skills that we need to analyze the Isuzu ad, to read between its lines.

Another vehicle and another road, this time a chariot, this time the dusty track from Jerusalem to Gaza. An Ethiopian eunuch is rattling along reading from the prophet Isaiah.

It's not clear what reading means here. Reading, as we've seen, was a liturgical act in the ancient world, the declaiming of the scrolls to the assembled faithful. Books were too rare and expensive for the average person to own, although the eunuch is a minister of the queen of Ethiopia, in charge of all her treasure. Maybe, too, he's reading in the sense of orally repeating what he's memorized, which is how most ancient people read, owning a book internally in the absence of the physical object. Luke tells us in this story from the book of Acts that the apostle Philip hears the eunuch reading (Acts 8:26-40).

In any event, the eunuch is reading, and the apostle Philip hears him, and inspired by the spirit, Philip asks the question that I think all teachers ask their students. "Do you understand what you are reading?" The eunuch replies: "How can I, unless someone guides me?"

This is the key. All teachers at the university are teachers of reading, whatever else they are, and what all teachers know is that reading requires community. It's not a solitary act because the texts we have to interpret are never self-evident. The eunuch can't understand the Scriptures on his own, without context, without an interpretive frame. There's always more than meets the eye, there's always complexity, and when Philip begins to interpret he immediately reads between the lines, looking past the literal meaning of the words of the Hebrew scriptures to how they symbolize the coming of this man Jesus Christ. As we will discuss more fully in Chapter 4, in the Jewish tradition that formed the apostles and the gospel writers and Jesus himself the assumption is that Scripture has multiple meanings, what the founding Christian exegetes thought of as the literal, the allegorical, the moral, and the anagogical. The implications of this tradition are huge: that finally traditional, historical Christianity professes the very values that I am describing, the very critical thinking skills that all of us would agree are central to the university. But here the claim is narrower, simply that this is what Philip is doing. He's thinking critically. He's looking beyond the surface to complexities and nuances that the eunuch can't see because they don't first meet the eye. We need a method and a set of assumptions to see them.

The eunuch's response is enthusiasm. "And as they went along the road they came to some water, and the eunuch said, 'See, here is water! What is to prevent my being baptized?'" The eunuch's response is the experience of freedom, and then, in that freedom, a public commitment to community, a plunging back into the tradition of stories and ways of reading that Philip has brought with him. First reading, then reading between the lines, then freedom, then commitment. The university is the road.

To be stopped as you bounce along can be scary. It can be startling. Many of my students describe the process of first reading Genesis and Mark in these ways as like having a rug pulled out from under them or suddenly becoming stranded. It's painful at first, as Gadamer acknowledges. The process involves becoming undeceived. It involves suffering:

> What [a person] has to learn through suffering is not this or that particular thing, but insight into the limitations of humanity, into the absoluteness of the barrier that separates us from the divine. It is

> ultimately a religious insight. Experience is experience of human fini-
> tude. The truly experienced person is one who has taken this to heart,
> who knows that he is master neither of time nor of the future. (357)

The first breakthroughs in reading can seem very like the expulsion from
the garden, the banishment out into a world where we have to do the
work ourselves, where the forest is dark and deep, where who knows but
we might get lost. But disillusion of this sort is only the first step after the
insights brought through critical reading. It can be followed by freedom
and by joy. It has consequences which can work to deepen our humanity
and our solidarity with others.

For one thing the awareness of our own limitations, the acceptance
of intellectual humility, leads naturally to greater respect and acceptance
of others. We don't have all the answers. The person we judged as wrong
is perhaps no more or less situated than we are. For Gadamer the process
of humanistic knowing is a process of "conversation," of bringing out our
own assumptions and then setting them in relation to the assumptions of
others. It's a process that involves an "openness" and a "listening" to others, not only the others in the same classroom but the others who lived
before us, in the past. We are all gathered around the table, to return to
the image of Palmer, all gathered around the great thing in the center,
seeing what we can see from our vantage point, and listening to the
voices of others only enriches and deepens and fleshes out, only
increases, our sense of this great whole.

Maybe we're even a little stunned for a moment, dizzied. Maybe
we've been stopped in our tracks, silenced, and maybe that's the beginning of ethical action after all. It's at just this moment that we stop doing
damage, at least for a while. We're momentarily too overwhelmed to pick
up a rifle or an axe, and when we do pick them up again, at least we've
had a moment to consider why and if we really have to. We stop and look
around and there are other people. There are other people, doing the
best they can, and knowing this somehow increases our gentleness.

My students have the notion that there's something wrong with
them when they can't struggle through to an understanding of the Bible
or of Homer, these great and difficult works, on their own, at home,
alone in their rooms. They have the sense that they've somehow failed or
betrayed a weakness when they understand the point only after the class
itself and the discussion that's taken place there, only after what I've said
and what the class has said. But no. The other side of the claim of situatedness is that reading requires community. The best thing about a literature class is that it brings fifty people together into a room for thirty
class periods, people who read the same texts together and through reading together help each other see things they couldn't see before. Reading
is a process, requiring others. This is what Ricouer affirms. This is what

Gadamer affirms. What follows from their epistemology isn't the exclusion of the self but its inclusion, its celebration.

Because for Gadamer as for Ricouer as for Palmer and all the great humanistic thinkers, to identify a point of view as only that, a point of view, a "terministic screen," is not to sneer or to wag a finger, not to take away the world of warmth and meaning. Terministic screens are not only unavoidable but good, as I will argue in more detail in chapters 5 and 6. Bias is good, tradition is good. They're human, they're who we are, they're all there is and all we can know. The claim isn't that knowledge is unattainable or that it's only and merely subjective but that it is itself a conversation involving two partners at least, the knower and the known, and that both are valuable, both are to be respected. The subject is dignified, not dismissed. "The circle is not a vicious circle," Ricouer says, "still less a mortal one; it is a living and stimulating circle" (351). The intermediary of tradition is not "a yawning abyss," Gadamer says; it's "filled with the continuity of custom and tradition, in the light of which all that is handed down presents itself to us" (297). Tradition carries valid meaning and that's all that carries meaning. It's the place of the human, where all of us are gathered, sharing what we know and most cherish.

The problem comes only when we're blind to the tradition, when we assume that the circle doesn't exist. The problem comes when we mistake the interpretation for the truth, the map for the terrain, to quote the Polish linguist Alford Korzybski (58). Once we become aware of our map as an approximation, a model among others—once we realize that we are like everyone else, living and moving within the circle—the circle becomes meaningful, the map a living guide. The conversation can begin.

Ricouer repeatedly says that thought must be understood as provisional, the symbol as closest to the mystery. But thinking is still necessary. The thought that the symbol teases us into is necessary and good as long as it's recognized for what it is, interpretation rather than fact. "Everything has already been said enigmatically [in the symbol] and yet it is always necessary to begin it again in the dimension of thinking" (349). Thinking is also what humans do, instinctively, necessarily, every bit as much as storytelling and image making. Without those interpretations of what must remain mystery—I will argue later—we would have no frameworks within which to operate, no names with which to order our world, no commitments from which to move on to the work we have to do.

The kind of teaching that follows from this insight is a teaching that respects the first and second and third thoughts of the students struggling to understand texts. It asks students to record their own experiences as they are invoked and changed by what they read, using their experience as a way of informing and deepening the text. The professor doesn't simply stand in the front of the class professing, merely a talking book, but guides students in the process of discovering and sharing the congruencies, the relationships, between who they are alone and together and who they are in relation to these ancient works.

Techniques like freewriting follow from the recognition of our humanness, from our dizziness before the stars and the texts and each other. Students write and write without first censoring, ignoring the demands of audience, letting whatever comes out come out, dying to self, or at least to self consciousness, but in the process freeing that self. The dying is to false expectations of expertise and certainty. The faith is in the dignity and sufficiency of the underlying voice that emerges in the act of writing, the self in the process of being formed and changed. The student is seen as worthwhile, even the wrong first responses worthwhile: that the Bible is patriarchal, that the Bible is preachy, that woman was of course created after man and in subordination to him. Those first responses are solicited not because they're bad but because they're necessary, the point of departure for the always human and collaborative act of discovering meaning in the company of others.

"What we need," Ricouer says, "is an interpretation that respects the original enigma of the symbol, that lets itself be taught by them, but that, beginning there, promotes the meaning, forms the meaning, in the full responsibility of autonomous thought" (349–50). What we need is to celebrate and honor the human work of interpreting our primary symbols without losing sight of the mystery that only these symbols come even close to capturing. This is the work of critical reading, the promotion of meaning in the full responsibility of autonomous thought. As Ricouer puts it at the end of his long analysis, in a statement that can stand as the mission statement for both the university and the church, for both reason and faith: "A philosophy that starts from the fullness of language is a philosophy with presuppositions. To be honest, it must make its presuppositions explicit, state them as beliefs, wager on the beliefs, and try to make the wager pay off in understanding" (357). In the end, after all the analysis, we each have a choice. That our position isn't necessary means that it's free. We can transcend analysis in the act of faith—achieving what Ricouer calls a "second naïveté"—or we can refuse to transcend it—remaining on the level of disillusion—but in either case we are making a choice, we are naming, and what's key is to know that. The key is to be "honest," making our presuppositions explicit as presuppositions, not as truths. This is the line we have to cross, one way or the other.[17]

But the purpose of understanding this process is not to eliminate acts of faith but rather to show them for what they are. It's to prepare us for making them. It's to show us that we're always making them, that we have to make them.

And what remains are the stories themselves, what remains are the images: the garden and the mountain, the Lord in the cool of the evening, the voice from the cloud. The process of analysis is valid if only because it forces us to return to the symbol and to recognize its primacy, its closeness to what can never be named. It's only through the small suffering and discomfort of critical reading that we learn our original sin, the sin of trying to settle our meanings once and for all, to eat of the apple, to consume all the possibilities, trying to take them into our bodies completely, like the "shallow-minded modern" Leopold decries, the one who "assumes that he has already discovered what is important" or that such discovery is within his power. It isn't. What is set apart from us is what we can never finally capture or clear-cut, what is sacred, what is holy. To consume such a wonder is prohibited because it's impossible, as impossible as building three booths to capture the blinding light. Such light can only be witnessed. It can only be seen.

PART TWO

# Intersections

## CHAPTER 3

# The *Odyssey* as Eucharist

I began my discussion of "The Way of the University," in chapter 1, with a quotation from Newman's *The Idea of the University*, but, as I admitted then, I took it out of context. As soon as Newman considers the idea that "a university has a line of its own," that it has its own "sphere" of knowledge, he denies it:

> It will be said [. . .] that a University has a line of its own. It contemplates, it occupies, a certain order, a certain platform of Knowledge. I understand the remark; but I own to you, I do not understand how it can be made to apply to the matter at hand. I cannot construct my definition of the subject-matter of University Knowledge, and so draw my boundary lines around it, as to include therein the other sciences commonly studied at the university and to exclude the science of religion. (29; 1.2.3)

My task, too, is to draw a "boundary" line between "science" and the "science of religion," and like Newman I find this difficult to do in practice. Ricouer's theory gives me a way to imagine the line as existing somewhere between the concreteness of story itself and the thoughts we draw from it, but right away this linear sequence bends into a cycle, the energy starts flowing back and forth, and faith pours into the classroom after all.

What I described in the last two chapters is the pattern and routine of my teaching, when I'm teaching the Bible or the other classic Christian texts in the Western tradition: my own faith identified as example of point of view. But my first year on campus as both a professor and a deacon, two moments in the classroom complicate and violate this pattern. I'm standing by the board, coffee cup in hand, lecturing in the way that professors lecture and leading discussions as we all try to do, when all at once my faith comes welling up, right there, in front of the students, not an example but a fact. This happens the first time during a discussion of Homer's *Odyssey*, and it has to do with the very nature of literature. If mystery gives rise to story, story is inevitably related to mystery. There's a conduit, and through it a connection is always getting made. If mystery gives rise to story, then literature is intrinsically related to religious experience, it can't help but be, and even if that experience is as yet amorphous and generic and unnamed, it's there, powerful and unsettling and entirely joyous.

Even at a state university. Sometimes the horizontal beam of the university is intersected by the intensity and power of the shaft of faith, a beam of hope and joy that starts deeper than the classroom and extends far beyond it, but that for a moment cuts right through it, at its heart. The vertical beam keeps going, becoming more particular and exclusive, as I will argue in the end. But for now there is a glow around the juncture where the beams come together, a wideness, and it's not two dimensional, as my image may imply. It's broad and deep.

"Admit a God," Newman says to complete this passage above, "and you introduce among the subjects of your knowledge, a fact encompassing, closing in upon, absorbing, every other fact conceivable" (29; 1.2.3). We can't keep God out of the classroom. We can't keep God out of anywhere.

## My Odyssey

October in the Literature of Western Civilization. We are deep into a discussion of the fifth book of the *Odyssey*—the sun streaming through the windows, the students alert, intent—when all at once the divisions and the tensions seem to fall away. My detachment dissolves. We are plunged into the story, plunged into the sea with Odysseus, as he struggles to stay alive in the wide, green, open water, in the great storm-tossed waves, as he is flung ashore, naked and spent, discovered in the morning by the beautiful young princess, a beautiful young woman in a flowing gown welcoming him, honoring him, redeeming him. And the joy that seems to flow out then, the joy and the release in that instant, as we discuss this story, as interest and feeling start to swell in class, as the words keep forming within me, the sense of a gathering together and an opening up is so sharp and intense that at exactly that moment I am inside my own faith, I am living and feeling my love of Christ, he is present and overflowing right there, right there in a classroom on the campus of

Oregon State University where mystery is not to be experienced, Christ not to be acknowledged.

———

But first another fall morning, a year earlier, a morning when I was a student myself, not a teacher. It's a turning point, too, another breaking through, and it helps explain how I end up in the water that day in the Literature of Western Civilization, bobbing in the sea of stories. In the first chapter I told this story in a general way—as my version of the mythic story of Odysseus, in fact. Here I want to return to one particular aspect of that story, one moment in it.

I am sitting in a class in fundamental theology at Mount Angel, beginning the masters in theology required for ordination. I taught full-time at the seminary the year before, on leave, but when I felt the call to ministry I arranged to return for a second year, as a student, even though I'm teaching full-time again at Oregon State. I'm commuting doubly now, not just from the secular to the spiritual but from being a teacher to being a student, back and forth, Monday through Friday. The year that I am promoted to full professor Sr. Timothy is handing my papers back with comments like "where is your paper clip Mr. Anderson?"

The important part of the moment is this: I start to write a poem.

For "poem" insert any creative act, quilting or fishing or baking a cake, any creative act pursued naturally and instinctively without thought of reward or acclaim, pursued for the sake of the act itself, with joy, unseen and on our own, regardless of talent, regardless of whether what we try to make with the best of our skill turns out to be of any quality at all. "The glory of God is the living [person]," St. Irenaeus says (490), and it's in our creativity that we are fully alive.

The monk who is teaching this class on the fundamentals of faith is talking about the early Church Fathers or patristic exegesis or the ecclesiology of the first-century church, and it's a fine, dynamic lecture, it shows as many of my courses do the intellectual beauty and coherence of Christianity, its sweep and its scope, but there in the clear fall light and the fields all around I'm not taking notes. I'm writing a little poem, about the fog I'd seen that morning, the skeins of fog hanging above the autumn fields.

We jump in the van each morning and glide through the country, travel cups steaming. Hills rim the valley. A white house, an acre of lettuce, a willow brake. Emmaus Farms, Corn 10 for a dollar. In the seminary mailroom the cubbyholes are arranged by first name. A dusty globe sits in a corner of my classroom, Russia still the Soviet Union. David, a slight, stooping man from Saskatoon; Alex, a crewcut Korean in army boots; Brother Dominic, a monk from Losotho, muddy black with coffee ground beard, fast asleep every afternoon in my one o'clock class, head back. The linoleum in the abbey church is scuffed, the kneelers worn away, the walls painted aquamarine and muddy rose. As we join monks for noon prayer—"the heavens proclaim the glory of God / And the firmament shows forth the work of his hands"—the smell of fish sticks comes up from the cafeteria.

A grassy road forks behind the warehouse down the hill from the monastery, one path following a wooden fence. The other leads out into an opening of blackberry and arrowood, then to the oak grove where I go to read Louth and LeClercq and all the others.

God creates the vast systems of the heavens and the earth and then turns around, in the next chapter, and walks in the garden in the cool of the day, and this is what Mount Angel is for a while, a garden, and within that garden, in Fundamental Theology, as I sit in my little student desk, my response is to write a poem. It's just three lines, just a sentence, but it opens the flood gates for pages and pages of poetry over the next few years, sonnets and prayers and free-verse poems, unread, written in such spontaneous love of the world, such a sense of freedom, I can't seem to stop myself. They keep coming and coming, important for me exactly because they're small, because I write them so naïvely and foolishly after all these years of straining to be polished and controlled, straining to get published and seen. The condition of the joy in the writing of them is indifference to what other people think, a sense of what on one level is the futility of writing poems about fog and fields and the autumn light.

Freedom. I am inside the Canticle of Zechariah, the song of Morning Prayer in the Liturgy of the Hours. "Blessed be the Lord, the God of Israel, he has come to his people and set them free." He has saved me from my enemies and I am free now to "worship without fear." "The dawn from on high" has seemed to "break upon me," and my response is to sit in a class in fundamental theology and day after day write poems (Luke 2:68-79).

## Learning How to Lose

This is a moment with at least two levels of meaning. The first has to do with the fact and the results of dying to live, of accepting, or being forced to accept, the great pre-Transfiguration discourse of Jesus about what it means to follow him, the one the disciples don't get even when they see him hanging on a cross, opening out his arms to embrace all their small-ness and sadness.

When I first become depressed I don't understand it as a call. I don't understand anything. I've become dumb. I've become stone, staring out the picture window at a world drained of color and meaning and force. Teaching is manageable fifty minutes at a time, before I have to flee to my office, shaken and in hiding, nothing left for talking or listening or being in the presence of others.

One gray day at Oregon State, on the fourth floor of the library, I am staring at two shelves of commentary on Gerard Manley Hopkins. I'd wanted to do some quick background checking for a course, but all I could find were studies of symbolism and prosody and theological influence, book after book: *Victorian Philology and the Poetic Language of Gerard Manley Hopkins*, *The Dialectic of Sense and Perception in the Poetry of Gerard Manley Hopkins*, *The Shaping Vision of Gerard Manley Hopkins*, *A Reader's Guide to the Poetry of Gerard Manley Hopkins*. Hopkins wrote a handful of lyrical poems, occasional records of the joy and despair of his life as a priest—of his own struggle with depression, in fact—many of them poured out in a single, ecstatic summer, and here were dozens of books taking the poems apart and solemnly arguing their significance, each published by some important university press, each solid and weighty and framed with footnotes and endless bibliography, one even arguing in the high, poststructuralist style that the poems are really parodies of religious experience, the opposite of what they seem to be, a send-up, a joke. Enough. I grab the shortest, plainest biography and run away.

On an English Department hiring committee we read over 600 applications for an American Literature position, pile after pile of brilliant dossiers, dissertation after dissertation: "Disturbances: Figures of Hybridity and the Politics of Representations," "Masochistic Pleasures and the Sentimental Voice: Gender Politics in American Literature of Domesticity, 1830–1860," "Chronoschisms: Temporality and Contingency in Postmodern Narrative," "The Anxiety of Production: Writing the Modernist Male Body." It isn't just the abstractness and jargon of the dissertations that depresses me or their cookie-cutter sameness but their sheer volume, the sheer volume of bright, earnest young people out there adding to the thousands of books and articles written about writing every year. My colleagues sit around the conference table during our late afternoon meetings, doing their best to be fair, and I join in, weighing one numbing vita against the next, but I can't help feeling that we've got it all backwards, preferring dissection to creation as we do. I can't help thinking that the citizens of our state have a point after all voting for all the tax reduction measures, slashing our budgets, and threatening to throw us all out of work. How many literary critics can a society sustain?

My version of depression may seem a little literary, a little academic, but all those who've been depressed will recognize the basic symptoms underneath—the self-loathing, the despair about the world—as I come to recognize them in therapy, reassured by how common they are, physiological as much as mental. But I come to understand, too, that my ways of thinking are also to blame, my striving for success and approval that can never take away the emptiness for long, never save me from death. Finally I have to face that death. Finally I have to embrace it. "If any want to become my followers, let them deny themselves and take up their cross and follow me. For those who want to save their life will lose it, and those who lose their life for my sake, and for the sake of the gospel, will save it" (Mark 8.34-35). What comes clear to me in therapy is that whatever else it is, this central teaching of Jesus is a lesson in psychological growth and wholeness. Until we give up the illusions of self we've been taught in childhood and carry into our early lives as adults, until we "decenter the ego" or "abandon our ego" for the healthy recognitions of maturity, accepting our limitations and mortality, we can never be happy, never be whole. Those constructions aren't realistic, they don't describe the way life really works.

It's when we do give them up that the freedom comes rushing in. We don't have to be the hero, we don't have to make everything in our own image. It's not up to us, blessedly, wonderfully. The burden is off our shoulders and we are in the clear, smaller at first but lighter, too, buoyed up. The scales fall away and we can see the beauty of what remains, of what was always there in the world we'd been rushing through, always there in us. The poetry flowing out in the theology class, the little poems about the fog and the corn, are one sign of the life on the other side of that death, one gain of that dying. Exactly when I let go of my ambitions and give up entirely, the writing comes rushing back, diminished and more sustaining. Writing can't save us. Writing can't take the place of prayer. But when prayer comes first, really comes first, joy and sadness and tenderness well out in waves, and those waves are the condition of any writing that matters. Writing becomes possible in the wake of prayer, a side effect, possible because no longer necessary or important, pure play, pure praise.

Poetry is possible—useless, childlike, enthusiastic poetry—because I have been called to the diaconate. The call to diaconal ministry not only humbles the writing but gives it a structure and an orientation. *Diakonia* is the Greek for servant. To be a deacon is to be in service to others, in relation to something other and greater than ourselves—Mary in relation to the angel of the Lord, saying yes to the great and impossible request; John the Baptist announcing the one even whose sandals he is not worthy to strap. *Diakonia* defines the breakthrough of therapy, that we are not the first but the last, in service to the world, to time, to the succession of things, listening to what really is.

Writing should be diaconal, too. It should be second, stooping before the one who comes down to the water—the one who then stoops himself, to wash the feet of his clueless disciples, the deacon of all deacons. And so the words come. There is a tearing in the sky and the spirit comes down like a dove, a voice, a new naming. Even the uselessness is revelatory, the silliness, the failure, because it's then that in a very small way we share again in the suffering of Christ, in his own great and saving failure. Even in the act of writing itself, in the moment of composition, O'Connor says, "the writer learns, perhaps more quickly than the reader, to be humble in the face of what is" (146).

One Sunday, late winter. In the morning at Mass, a visiting deacon drones on about a conservative morality not true to the openness and generosity of the gospel. But the homily is not the Mass. It ceases and the Mass continues. For me as a Catholic, the Eucharist is what matters, the body and blood of Christ, the suffering of Christ offered up for us to eat and take into our own bodies, and it's offered regardless of how good the homily is. The homily can only point to it, even at its best.

That afternoon a visiting writer speaks on campus, a writer of creative nonfiction, writing as many nature writers and vaguely spiritual writers do about vaguely spiritual things but in a way that is offensive finally not because of its vagueness but because of its arrogance, its condescension. All this person does is poach on the tradition, taking what she likes and sneering at the rest, borrowing the intellectually and aesthetically pleasing and making fun of the people in the pews who prefer what she thinks of as the superstitious and the kitschy.

I find myself on the side of the superstitious and the kitschy, resisting the writer in her talent and her slickness because in the end it's only her talent and her slickness that have brought us to listen to her. It's only her talent that anchors this gathering, and that's not enough. Suddenly I realize that I prefer the droning deacon. For all his stiffness and straining piety, it wasn't him that we had come to hear, his talent that brought us into church, and he knew that. He was doing his best to place himself at the service of the other, the service of the Eucharist, and suddenly I realize that this is what I prefer, this is what I'll choose on any given Sunday, any given day: the piety not the poetry.

———

Look, I say to my students at Oregon State. Look at this poem by Mary Oliver. "Personal writing" isn't really personal but describes instead a moment of being caught up in something larger and more generous, a moment of losing oneself. The speaker in "Five AM in the Pinewoods" describes two deer stepping shyly into a clearing "like two mute and beautiful women," nibbling "some damp tassels of weeds," then going off again into the trees, so close to her at one point that "One of them—I swear it!— / Would have come to my arms." There's an "I" here, and that "I" is describing her own experience. But the nature of that experience is to be drawn into a beauty and a tenderness that the poet didn't create and doesn't fully understand. What inspires her is the absorption into something so much vaster and gentler than personality that the effect at the end of the poem is silence and in silence joy: "So this is how you swim inward, / So this is how you flow outward, / So this is how you pray" (32–33).

Look, I say: good personal essays are also impersonal in this way. Lewis Thomas sees beavers and otters at the Tucson zoo and is "swept off his feet," he is "transfixed" (6), and the rest of the essay remains flabbergasted, it remains dazed, not trying to reduce the experience to a thesis. Annie Dillard confronts a weasel, "a muscled ribbon, brown as fruitwood" (31), and like Thomas her response is not to indulge her preexisting self. It's to be devastated, so immersed in the mind of this other that the forest seems to fall around her. Augustine called such moments "drops," Wordsworth "spots" of time, and their defining characteristic is how they seem to transcend both time and self-consciousness.

All good writing is about "joy" rather than "pleasure," in C. S. Lewis's sense of that opposition. Joy is never "in our power," Lewis says, though pleasure often is (*Surprised by Joy* 18). There is in joy a "disinterested self-abandonment to an object which securely claims this by simply being the object it was" (77). What should lead us to the keyboard is abandon, is falling in love, because it's disinterest that always shapes the best writing anyway, disinterest that always governs craft. John Keats has called this capacity to be moved "negative capability," which he defined in two ways—first as the ability to enter into the mind of another, second as the ability to endure unresolved contradictions. As he says in 1817 in a letter to his friend Benjamin Bailey, "nothing startles me beyond the moment. The setting sun will always set me to rights—or if a Sparrow come before my Window I take part in its existence and pick about the gravel" (261, 259). That sounds like generosity, like humility, and it's the other side of the capacity to live without resolution. When we are startled only by the moment there's no need for "the irritable reaching after fact and reason" (261) that Thomas, too, tries to avoid, there in Tucson, startled as he is by the beavers and otters, that Dillard tries to avoid as she stares at the weasel, that Oliver tries to avoid until the deer run back into the pine wood.

Good personal essays have the very structure of joy: first the description of a drop of time, then a thinking aloud in the now of the essay, tentative and not imposing, trying out one thesis and now another, searching for answers, though in the end the answer is that life is a mystery, one thesis never captures it all. Symbol gives rise to thought but the thought is always provisional, a reaching back to the fullness of the original mystery that knows it can never succeed. Oliver's poem has this structure of joy. First she describes in careful wonder and precision the coming of the deer through the pinewoods—she gives us the symbol—then she shows us herself teased into thought, trying out possibilities in what Ricouer calls "the full responsibility of autonomous thought" (350), uttering what she believes the experience to mean without presuming that her meaning is the experience. This is her claim, that there's mystery, something beyond sanity.

"You think you swallow things," Friedrich von Hügel says, "when they ought to swallow you" (3).

Be swallowed, I start telling my students. Don't find your own voice. Lose it. To write well first stop caring about writing and about what other people think of it, give it up; and when you do start again write small and write clear, learning to lose your fine fancy phrases and special effects. Cut your best sentences. Cut and cut. And write about being swallowed. Write about the self enlarged, the self absorbed, the self made dizzy, as Newman puts it, dizzy before the stars.

Write like the gospels, in fact, with the spareness and roughness that so offended Augustine before his conversion (*Confessions* 57; 3.5). Write with that absolute attention not to your own language but to its object, to what it loves. Luke doesn't cry out to God, "Oh allot to us, at this point in time and on a per diem basis, a sufficient and balanced dietary food intake." He doesn't ask God to "rationalize a disclaimer against our negative feedback as we rationalize a disclaimer against the negative feedback of others." It's: Give us this day our daily bread. It's: Forgive us our trespasses, as we forgive those who trespass against us. And of course the message underneath this stylistic advice is also the gospel message. This is my faith leaking out into the classroom, crossing the line, though only implicitly.

Something very like this Christian dynamic leads students to better writing, as Peter Elbow argues. It's the principle of freewriting, this letting go and trusting. "Almost everybody interposes a massive and complicated series of editings," Elbow says, "between the time words start to be born into consciousness and when they finally come off the end of the pencil or typewriter onto the page." We think too much. We fail to trust "the sound, the text, the rhythm, the voice" that we all have inside of us, the source of our power and fluency as writers if we will only let it out (5–7). We all have our voice, we all have a power somewhere inside of us, a unique frequency—the *imago Dei*—and the key is to write so much and fast and unflinchingly that we can get that voice onto the page. It will be mixed up with bad and mushy sentences, all the good stuff is entangled with the bad stuff, but that's just the point. We can't get one without the other so let it all go.

A student writes in the beginning of the term in the Literature of Western Civilization, "one can readily concede the psychological importance of imaginatively engaging in the interpretation of mythological structures." What? I ask in the margins. Weeks later, in a freewriting journal, the sentences are coming out like this wonderful retelling of the exodus story, told from the point of view of Miriam:

> *We left Egypt ready for anything. We couldn't believe that we were finally free. God DID remember us. He heard our cries and promised us a peaceful life away from the slavery we were subjected to by the Egyptians. For once people trusted Moses and the God he spoke of, our God, to lead us to safety. Moses warned us to be ready for battle, and we were. But we figured that if we could survive the Egyptians we could conquer anyone, especially with God leading the way as a great pillar of cloud by day and fire by night. I'd never been so excited or scared in my life! You know what it's like doing something without your mother for the first time—you are excited but a little worried and scared because it is all so new and different to you? That is what it felt like, but I trusted Moses and my brother Aaron, even when they told us to turn back and camp alongside the sea.*

This is why the dying-to-live hidden in Elbow's pedagogy is acceptable in the classroom, to a point, because it works, because the writing gets better even as it gets looser and more colloquial.

But it's really a way of being in the world, not of writing, that students experience in the process of freewriting and revising, and it's a way of being in the world that has much in common with Christianity, however generalized and implicit. Through what they discover about style and form and the power of words on a page students come to glimpse the Christian paradox of what Stafford calls "Learning How to Lose." For years we learn to win, he says in this lovely poem, competing with others and judging others, figuring out "who counts." A friend we make is "conquered, like an enemy." But someday we'll stop. We'll "rest" and "have faith." Someday we'll learn to say to the world: "Leave me alone, Hours. [. . .] Let now now win" (*Oregon Message* 30). This is a message that students are willing to listen to and even accept in a classroom at a public university, at least some of them, even though in a way it's a clearly spiritual message, even though it's just as radical a critique of the university as the dying-to-live speech in the gospel. It's the same speech. Universities don't train students how to lose but how to win, how to get and keep jobs, how to get ahead, and in the pursuit of these goals it's not the now that wins but the future, always the future. It's not friends that are made, it's not community, and many of my students are hungry for community, longing for what they know the university lacks but what they don't trust traditional institutional religion to provide for them anymore. They long to express a "self" they feel is denied them in many of their other courses. They long to imitate the gospels, to write simply and honestly and roughly in a way that they usually can't across campus, in a way that would be graded down, dismissed as unsophisticated. They long to slow down enough to hear and see and feel the now, to experience in the moment what in their forced competitiveness and grade-conscious-ness they are too strained and blocked to hear and see and feel.

There's a radicalism in the pedagogy of freewriting and journals, a radicalism that was there before my call to ministry, that was in a way part of that call, only now it's been deepened and sharpened, taken up into a Christian faith that when it's strong and flowing makes me increasingly unable to accept the limitations of a university classroom.

The paradoxes of dying to self apply not just to writing but to teach-ing, and not just to the teaching of writing but to the teaching of litera-ture. When I flee the jargon and the infighting of English studies to teach at the seminary, I rediscover the wonderful naïveté and sentimen-tality of a literature class devoted to the idea that literature might really be about something.[17] All those books in the monastic library, spiraling up to the skylights, are spiraling from and to the one source, the source of love, the source that is love. All reading is divine reading, every office divine. The love of learning is always in the service of the love of God. Though my students at Mount Angel come from all over the world— Samoa, Viet Nam, China, Africa, the most diverse group I have ever taught—they enter the enclosure of the seminary and the monastery because to varying degrees they share a faith that radically centers the energy of the self. "Prefer nothing whatever to Christ," is how St. Benedict puts it, simply, without compromise, and what surprises me is the effect this has on my own teaching (*Rule* 65). Literature is grounded now in something other, in God, in the truth that is the referent for all that we study together at the seminary, no longer cast away into a vague, abstracted neverland where words have no meaning outside of them-selves and criticism amounts to showing what can be said and resaid about the nothing that is there. English studies has undercut its reason for being, but instead of escaping into professionalism and the confer-ences as many colleagues do, into the old dodge of research versus teach-ing, our real work versus the mere "service courses" we have to teach, I have through grace been afforded the experience of another kind of com-munity, another way of imagining who I am in a classroom.

Before Christmas I was showing *Hamlet* in the basement of Anselm Hall, standing in back with the remote control, freeze-framing scenes to give little lectures and appreciations. There were the swooping, prancing speeches and the dark foreboding and the rising and falling of the music, the dark, theatrical castle, and we were experiencing them all slowly, in careful, unfolding pieces. I had the sense of time having slowed. When I hit the pause button and started to enthuse again I felt all at once

suspended—in the play, in the idea of the play, explained and organized
and situated by it, intensely. Once in sixth grade I played Ebenezer
Scrooge in *A Christmas Carol*, bounding out on the stage in my costume
pajamas. The gym smelled of wood polish and aftershave, outside it was
snowing, and warm and safe in the circle of the lights, my friends and I
acted out our parts in our bumbling, earnest way. It was just like that in
the television room at Mount Angel. We were in the play. We were the
characters, too, speaking our parts, the heroes and the fools. The tragedy
of reading is when the reading is over, because outside of the play there
is only ceaseless flow. Outside there isn't exultation at the close, no community or actors, because life isn't a story in that way. All reading is an
act of longing and nostalgia. Except at the seminary. Except for
Christians. For the Christian the hope, the faith, the wild surmise, is that
at the heart of the ceaseless flow of things is a plot every bit as tragic and
beautiful as the plot of *Hamlet* or *A Christmas Carol*. There is suffering
and struggle but also at the end a resolution beyond words in which true
nobility and awareness are achieved and flights of angels sing us all to our
rest. What Christians believe in is a story, the Christmas story, of the
child born in the manger, the Easter story, of the man who is murdered
rising again. They believe *Hamlet* is true.

Looking out into the classroom I see an intensity on Michael's care-
worn face. He's caught, I see, he's inside the play, too, understanding it,
alive to it. He's leaning in towards me. He's looking up as if he wants to
say something but doesn't yet know what it is.

I let go of my teaching and get it back, smaller and deeply refresh-
ing. I give up my hope of finding salvation in the teaching of literature
and rediscover the solace and the challenge that teaching literature can
provide. Literature now is in the diaconal position, not an end in itself
but in right relation to something larger, and now it shines, it matters.
We can talk about our lives, without embarrassment. We can try to learn
how to live. We can read the great works of the past and the present for
what they might really teach us, what they might really offer us in our
hard, mutual work of learning how to lose.

## Poetry and Prayer

This is the first level of meaning in that moment of learning, in the pouring out of the poems, the level of transfiguration, of transformation and
resurrection through a giving up. The second is the level of poetry. The
second important element of the moment is that it is poetry pouring out
of me in the classroom, not theological treatises or moral certitude. It's
images, not propositions, and in this we return to the introduction, too,
to the idea of story, but from a different perspective.

The gift of commuting back and forth to a monastery for these years is not just to immerse me in the poetry of Christianity but to teach me that Christianity is poetic. Every weekday I am in the presence of fifty monks chanting the poetry of the Psalms and praying the stories of the gospel and celebrating the great dying of Jesus and the great rising from the dead through what the Benedictine Jean LeClercq calls the great "poem of the liturgy" (236), the acting out of the drama on the stage of the altar, the going through of what are only motions because only motions, only the physical and the experiential, can over time, through contact day-to-day, imbue us with a reality not otherwise accessible.[19] People want to argue about Christianity, for it or against it. People think of Christianity as a set of moral precepts to be taken or left from the start, black and white. But the Christianity I experience at the monastery and as a teacher and then a student at the seminary, while it respects the powers of reason and rational deduction, understands the moment of faith as a moment of joy and grief and abandon in the presence of a silence, a person. The Benedictine "burns with the desire," St. Bernard says, "not so much to know as to experience." What the Benedictine seeks and what any Christian seeks "fervor alone can teach; it can be learned only through experience" (LeClercq 5), and though there are other, later traditions, like scholasticism in the high Middle Ages, which proceed in more syllogistic and deductive ways, the Benedictine practice isn't simply a style or version of the Christian life but its first and truest expression. Its role in history has been to repeatedly call the church back to its source.

Its method is the method of *lectio divina*, of divine reading, a method of praying the Scriptures privately and slowly and with the commitment of the whole person which recognizes most of all that the language of the Bible, as LeClercq puts it, is "concrete, full of imagery, and consequently poetic in essence" (54–55), as is the eucharistic celebration that gives these poems their fullest and realest expression. The method has four distinct stages that in the spontaneous act of prayer and praise blend into a single movement:

*Lectio*: the slow reading aloud of the words of Scripture.

*Meditatio*: the thinking aloud about what the words might mean, free associating, very much as in freewriting, remaining open to whatever an image might invoke in memory or desire without censoring or second guessing.

*Oratio*: the translation of these free flowing thoughts and feelings in prayers and petitions, into statements and requests, much as in the editing of freewriting into a product for others to read.

*Contemplatio*: the waiting in silence and hope for whatever God might
say in reply, the listening, the watching.

This isn't a form of disputation, still less of logic. It's a way of guiding the
believer into the living heart of the stories, opening them up into the
present. The question isn't, did this really happen, but what does this
mean? Not, can we prove this, but what are these words saying at this
very moment? And they are saying something. The faith beneath the
method is the astonishing faith of the *meditatio* that somehow the words
on the page are the way God is speaking to us about our own lives, today,
at this hour; that whatever occurs to us in the uncensored act of thinking
and feeling is what God himself wants us to think and to feel. The world
is being created now and the garden laid out now and the Lord walking
in it in the cool of this day; the light is shining on the mountain and the
dove is descending not long ago but here in this instant in this act of
reading.

To pray in this way can be a labor, LeClercq explains, a difficult quest
full of hardship and emptiness and long, dreary days of nothing disclosed.
But now and then it opens up to "the sweetness of God," now and then
the sweetness of God seems to be pouring down on us, and the enthusiasm that rises up in us then can only "blossom in the form of poetry and
hymn"(5) as it blossoms in me sitting in the light of the leaves and the
trees, there in class at seminary, writing little poems instead of taking
down the notes on the board. My response to the growing sense of God's
presence in the world naturally blossoms into poetry and hymn because
it's through poetry and hymn that this intuition, this hope, has been sown
in me to begin with.

In *Professing Literature* Gerald Graff ridicules the American professors in the nineteenth and early twentieth century who made this connection between imagination and faith. He sees it as naïve. Such teachers
believed that literature could in some way foster a deeper spirituality in
their students, but for Graff this is a merely romantic notion, assuming
an emotional identification with the text that we now know, from our
postmodern perspective, is far trickier and more problematic. Emotional
identification can't really be taught, Graff says. It can't be explained. It
doesn't lend itself to principles of criticism that can be laid out and taken
up by others.[19]

But maybe there is such a thing in the teaching and learning of literature as a second, not a first naïveté, an entering into story that comes
from a deliberate and knowing leap, a leap that knows all about the trick-
iness and the problems. And maybe such a leap can be taught, but only
through the creating of a culture in which students come to understand
over time what can't be explained directly, only through ten weeks of
coming together with fifty other students and practicing in community a

*lectio* if not a *lectio divina*, repeated acts of *meditatio* somehow turned at the end into focused language addressing the teacher and each other if not God himself. Maybe school is such a culture, or can be, the place where students enter into a way of life, an organizing of their attention. A way.

For me, in any event, the connection suddenly becomes vivid and real. My experience at the seminary takes up and ennobles what I have always secretly loved about literature, what I first loved and have over time come to be embarrassed by and afraid to admit. That connection between poetry and faith reconverts me. "Poetry," Newman once wrote in a book review, "is the refuge of those who have not the Catholic Church," for "the Church herself is the most sacred of poets." She is "the poet of her children; full of music to soothe the sad and control the way-ward,—wonderful in story for the imagination of the romantic; rich in symbol and imagery, so that the gentle and delicate feelings, which will not bear words, may in silence intimate their presence or commune with themselves." Indeed, "her very being is poetry" (qtd. in Ker 322).

This is why I become a deacon. I feel called to be a deacon because I feel called to be a poet, as I think we are all called to be poets. I feel called to be a deacon because day to day the monastic life is not only immersing me in poetry but proclaiming that it's true. It's all true.

September 19, 1931, three in the morning. C. S. Lewis and J. R. R. Tolkien are strolling up and down the cloister of Magdelen College at Oxford, talking about the nature of Christian faith, a faith that Lewis is just on the verge of accepting after years of struggling through the questions logically and analytically, like Augustine, and like Augustine, without result. But "Jack" is still resisting, and after a long evening of brilliant talk "Tollers," a Catholic, is pressing his advantage into the early hours. What Lewis can't understand is how the life and death of a man who lived 2,000 years ago can help us here and now except as an inspiring example. Tolkien's stroke of genius is to point out that this is an imaginative failure on Lewis's part, a failure on the level of story and image. When Lewis reads stories about pagan heroes and the myths of other cultures he is moved by them. He feels "the myth as profound and suggestive of meanings beyond my grasp" as Lewis says in a letter describing this moment, "even tho' I could not say in cold prose 'what it meant'" (*Letters to Arthur Greeves* 426–28). Fine. So far so good. The problem, Tolkien says, is that Lewis doesn't respond to the Christian stories in the same way, with the same openness, but becomes all at once a critic and an empiricist. He sets his heart aside and starts taking the stories apart, skeptical and deconstructing.

The key is to understand that the Christian story is just like all the other stories. It is a story, an imaginative construction, and it needs to be accepted in exactly the same way, with exactly the same kind of imaginative openness, though with this crucial difference, this "tremendous difference": "*it really happened.*"[21]

And this is it. Before this moment in the fall, walking among the dark trees of the sleeping college, Lewis is not a Christian. After it, he is, as after my experience of the monastery and the seminary, slowly and gradually, still on again and off again, but more often than not, I am a Christian, too.

The crux of the argument in this letter, the pivot underneath this enormous shift, is that Christianity has a literary structure and requires a literary way of knowing, that "this Christian story is to be approached, in a sense, as I approach the other myths." It's a sudden insight into the priority of story that sounds much like Ricouer:

> The "doctrines" we *get out* of the true myth are of course *less* true: they are translations into our *concepts* and *ideas* of that wh. God has already expressed in a language more adequate, namely the actual incarnation, crucifixion, and resurrection.

By "truth" Lewis seems to be thinking in part of God as the storyteller and of the life of this man from Nazareth as his story—a life, not a declaration of ideas, a person in whom is embodied a truth that can only be embodied. In this sense any interpretation of that story is inevitably secondary, however important. The story itself is where the truth is embedded.

People want to make Lewis into the tweedy saint of religious conservatism. They want to make him into the master logician who defeats all the atheists, so they turn to the popular theology of his middle years, to books like *Mere Christianity* in which the Irish barrister side of Lewis is the strongest, the debater who sometimes bullied his students. But this isn't the real Lewis. "The imaginative man in me is older," he wrote to the Milton Society of America, "more continually operative, and in that sense more basic than either the religious writer or the critic" (undated 1954; *Letters* 443–44). His first response to his Christian conversion was to join with Tolkien and others in their group the "Inklings" in the writing of science fiction and adult fairy tales, producing his own Ransom Trilogy of stories about an English professor who becomes the Pendragon and leads the fight against the evil eldils. The idea was through story to "steal past" the "inhibitions" which "paralyze" us as we read the Bible and go to church, to "steal past those watchful dragons" of reason and doubt and to appeal to our deeper, truer longing for dimension and depth (*On Stories* 47).

His biographer A. N. Wilson tells us that later in life, after getting trounced in a debate by the Christian philosopher Elizabeth Anscomb,

Lewis turned his back on his apologetics, admitting what he had already suspected, that they were thin as theology and that his real talent was for narrative. He never wrote theology again, turning instead to the so-called children's books that became *The Chronicles of Narnia*.[22] Fairy tale, he realized, "was the genre best fitted for what I wanted to say," because what he wanted to say was the beauty and the power and the reality of Christ, the experience of him. What he wanted to write were stories that would "strip" the Bible of its "stained-glass and Sunday school associations," casting its truths into an imaginary world where "one could make them for the first time appear in their real potency" (*On Stories* 47). Lewis never lost his own appetite for fairy tale and children's books, especially the stories of George MacDonald, which he regarded as truly "devotional" books. The reading of fairy tale as the writing of fairy tale could be a kind of "*askesis*," or spiritual exercise, he says, perhaps because like *lectio divina* it exercises the imagination and the heart, not simply the mind, providing an experience for the reader, not a list of abstract truths (*On Stories* 39).

Lewis wrote fairy tales for the same reason that I find myself writing poems, for the same reason that a Benedictine commits his or her whole life to the singing of the great Hebrew hymns that are the Psalms, because we cannot "in cold prose" say of our faith "what it means," because only fairy tale or silly, little, childlike poems or the majestic simplicity of the Psalter can suggest all these meanings "beyond our grasp." This is just what Ricouer means when he insists that the symbol is "primary"; when he says that "symbols precede hermeneutics," that a symbol "presents its meaning in the opaque transparency of an enigma and not by translation" (16).

And somehow it's true. It's all true. All stories are true.

There's a fairy tale by Woody Allen, "The Kugelmass Episode," about a bald, Jewish man named Kugelmass who longs for better things. He meets a Jewish shaman who has a box. Walk into the box with your favorite book, the shaman says, and suddenly you're in the book, you're a character inside of it, living the lives the characters live. So Kugelmass, skeptical but ready for anything, walks into the box with Flaubert's *Madame Bovary*, and all over the country college students in comparative literature courses find this bald, Jewish guy making love to Emma Bovary, having an affair with the village doctor's wife. Kugelmass is thrilled at first, though in the end Emma escapes into our world and Kugelmass mistakenly ends up in an elementary Spanish text, pursued for eternity by huge Spanish verbs.

But that's just how it feels when I'm on the altar during Mass sometimes, standing behind and to the right of the priest, as if I've suddenly entered into the story, become a character in a play by Shakespeare, or a lyric by Frost, or a novel by Eliot. There's such intricacy and sequence to the order of the Mass. Everything makes sense and fits with everything else, everything means so much more than it says, there's such silence sometimes all around us. By the mystery of this water and wine, I pray, silently, as I prepare the gifts for the altar, pouring a drop of water into the chalice, by the mystery of this water and wine may we come to share in the divinity of Christ who humbled himself to share in our humanity. And all at once the language of that beautifully balanced and antithetical sentence seems true, it seems true, all of it's true, and I'm inside of that structure, I'm inside of that trope, disappeared into it as we all of us are disappeared into it, all of us in the congregation like Kugelmass, poor, misguided Kugelmass, but the story we've gotten inside of isn't a story of loss and betrayal but of loss and gain, the loss and the gain of everything, of the whole world.

"It is not difficult," Tolkien says in an essay on fairy tale, "to imagine the peculiar excitement and joy that one would feel, if a specially beautiful fairy story were found to be 'primarily' true, its narrative to be history, without thereby necessarily losing the mythical or allegorical significance that it has possessed":

> It is not difficult, for one is not called upon to try and conceive any-
> thing of a quality unknown. The joy would have exactly the same qual-
> ity, if not the same degree, as the joy which the "turn" in a fairy-story
> gives; such joy has the very taste of primary truth [. . .]. (84)

This is just what it means to be a Christian, Tolkien goes on to say, echoing his insight to Lewis that early September morning. The "turn" in a fairy tale is the turn when the disaster is averted, the hero saved, the happy ending achieved. It's the moment when we as the readers catch our breath, blinking back tears, and Tolkien believes, as Lewis believes, that this moment is a foreshadowing:

> The Christian joy, the Gloria, is of the same kind; but it is pre-emi-
> nently (infinitely, if our capacity were not finite) high and joyous.
> Because this story is supreme; and it is true. Art has been verified. God
> is the Lord of angels and of men—and of elves. Legend and History
> have met and fused. (84)

When I drive up to the seminary and have the odd sensation of having somehow driven into Narnia, into Middle Earth, it's not just the small scale that I'm experiencing, the sense of smallness and enclosure, not just the fields and the trees, it's the deep affinity between the culture of Christianity and the promise of the fairy tale. The music and the architecture and the statuary and the icons, the landscaping, the books in the library, the structure of the days and the rhythm of the liturgy, all of the life and the culture of the monastery is meant to infuse into the people who live there over time the growing conviction that they are in fact living inside a story, and that this story is preeminently and infinitely true, and that what's truest of all about this story is its happy ending, the happy ending beyond all other happy endings. The gospel is fairy tale, the greatest fairy tale of all.

## Into the Sea of Stories

In the light of these experiences, shaped and ordered by this culture, how can I when teaching the fifth book of Homer's *Odyssey*, Homer's great and founding fairy tale, this enormous epic story that is also one of the first narratives in our culture to enter into the realm of the fairy tale, of the supernatural—how can I when reading the *Odyssey* or a great story from any work of literature be anything other than deeply moved? How can my faith be anything other than opened up and confirmed? How can the line be anything but crossed?

The sun is streaming through the window, the students are listening and intent, and all at once the waves are "churned into chaos," the "heaving breakers roiled up," the raft is shattered in all the great, green surging of the sea, snapped and hurling, and Odysseus is fighting his way to the surface, "spewing bitter brine." "What a wretched death I'm doomed to die!" he cries out in the darkness, but even then survives, stripping away his heavy garments, naked, bone-weary, tossed about by the waves until finally he struggles through breakers and over rocks to the mouth of a river, miraculously, inspired by Athena, and heaves himself onto the shore of the Kingdom of Phaeacia (5.345–65).

That night Athena has come in a dream to the beautiful daughter of the king, Nausicaa, in her flowing robes, and moved by the vision the princess takes her maids to the river the next morning to wash the palace linen in the rocks and the pools. The water comes "bubbling up and rushing through," "clear and cool," and they plunge down into it, "one girl racing the next to see who will finish first" until they've rinsed off all the grime (6.95–105). The lovely young women are dancing the linen clean, playing over the rocks, and soon they are playing a game of ball, "white-armed Nausicaa" leading their singing, "outshining them all, though all are lovely," shining among her maids, "a virgin, still unwed," but self possessed and royal in bearing, when Odysseus rises up naked from the leaves where he is buried, "a terrible sight, all crusted, caked with brine." She stands her ground and takes his measure as the broken hero, still strategizing, but desperate, defeated, throws himself on her mercy (6.111–21, 6.151).

This is the story of dying to live, the one great story, this is my own story, of dying in depression and rising again, of flinging myself out into the wide waters, overwhelmed, of rescue and release, of cleansing, on the shore of the kingdom. And there are tears in my eyes, I am deeply moved as we talk about the story that day, because what the beautiful young white-limbed girl in her dignity and grace offers the beaten man is the hospitality of the kingdom, the full hospitality of that clean and ordered and sustaining place. "We live too far apart, out in the surging sea," she says, to deny any stranger what we ourselves most need (6.223). "Every stranger and beggar comes from Zeus" (6.227), and so she lays out a cloak and shirt and a golden flask of olive oil, and he bathes himself in the cleansing waters, scouring away "the brackish surf," and he comes up out of the waters transfigured, Athena "lavishing splendor over his head and shoulders, glistening in his glory, breathtaking," born again not just through the grace of the gods but through the courtesy and the culture of other people as full of dignity as he himself is full of dignity and power and restraint (6.260). Later there are gleaming halls and brimming bowls, ceremonies and games, a civility that Odysseus hasn't discovered any-where else in his voyages and that he will find missing in Ithaca when he returns.

This is how we are saved, I know, through grace and through culture. We must first be defeated, our magic and our power taken away, illusory anyway, before we can understand the vastness of the world and our need for each other, and this is Christ, this is the teaching on the mountain before the blinding light. And because of the choices I have made in the teaching of this class, because of the steps that I have already taken toward a more radical pedagogy, it's difficult for me to hold all this back in this moment, to restrain the joy I feel.

I have been using the popular anthropology of Joseph Campbell to explain the power of myth and story both simply and generically. Campbell, like Stafford, talks about the spiritual life in a way that doesn't scandalize my students or seem inappropriate in the classroom, though he is pushing the boundaries even so, simply by insisting that lit-erature must be about something, about the self, about what matters:

> Myths speak about the deep mystery of yourself and everything else. It is a mystery—tremendous, horrific, because it smashes all of your fixed notions of things, and at the same time utterly fascinating, because it's of your own nature and being. (45)

Or

Read myths. They teach you that you can turn inward, and you begin to get the message of the symbols. Read other people's myths, not those of your own religion, because you tend to interpret your own religion in terms of facts—but if you read the other ones, you begin to get the message. Myth helps you to put your mind in touch with this experience of being alive. (5)

This is reading for a moral purpose, reading to learn how to live, and that means learning how to lose, as Campbell knows. His language enables us to talk about the emptiness of our dreams of heroic power, of success understood not as myth, not as fairy tale, because myth and fairy tale always require suffering, but as fantasy without trial, character without conflict, the American dream not of gods but of gratification. Our respect for a reality beyond us, a reality that Campbell frankly calls spiritual, should humble us, it should "smash us," and out of that smashing should come civility, hospitality, communion:

If you realize what the real problem is—losing yourself, giving yourself to some higher end, or to another—you realize that this is itself the ultimate trial. When we quit thinking primarily about ourself and our self-preservation, we undergo a truly heroic transformation. (154–55)

These are values we can even act out in the act of reading, abandoning our presuppositions, suffering the confusions and misreadings that an ancient and complex text like the *Odyssey* inevitably leads to, remaining open and hospitable to the strangeness and otherness of this primal story.

I have asked the class to freewrite about a time when they were tossed by the waves, when they felt they were drowning and beaten and barely escaped, rescued maybe by others, even a beautiful young woman, and in freewriting itself we are abandoning ourselves to the waves. We are turning inward as Campbell in his role as shaman, as priest of high culture, as guru, instructs us to do, experiencing in the spontaneity and surprise of unedited writing some of the mystery and power of this underlying sea of story and image, this sea within us, too.

But as Lewis realizes the early morning of his conversion, as Tolkien knows all along, the great myths are not at odds with Christianity but contained within it. Christians have always taken the literature and culture of paganism and read it allegorically as prefiguring Christ, leading up to its full revelation as all things good and true lead up to that revelation. This is why Dante's hell and purgatory and heaven are full of monsters and people from classical literature, why Virgil is the one who serves as his guide in the first place. The early Christians, reading

allegorically, believed that Virgil had even foretold the coming of
Christ. Augustine, reading allegorically, takes the image of the Israelites
plundering Egypt as a symbol of this appropriation. Just as the Israelites
in their escape from the Pharaoh stop to carry away all the gold and silver and precious things of their oppressors, all they can fit into their sad-
dlebags, so Christian readers should feel free to help themselves to
whatever is useful in classical or any other kind of learning (*Teaching
Christianity* 160).

But here in this classroom, in this moment of the sun streaming
through the window, all these Nausicaas and Jennifers and Melissas sitting in their jeans and their sweatshirts, all these fine young men like
Telemachus, here in this classroom these analogies seem dangerous and
tricky. Because we are freewriting, because we are reading Campbell with
his urgings inward, because I am trying to teach literature not as form
apart from content, content apart from life, teaching not just reading but
a kind of disguised divine reading, teaching in a way that I realize is
increasingly Benedictine, concerned with fervor, not knowledge, experience, not fact—because I have learned from Elbow and Palmer and St.
Bernard how to establish a structure for teaching in which I can honor
my own inner nature, my own inner needs—because I have already been
moving in the direction of the spirit, my Christian faith keeps threatening to rush all the way in. Campbell has gotten a foot in the door. Elbow
has prepared the way.

The scandal in the minds of students would be the scandal of specificity, of the Christian claim, if I were to make it at that moment, that
Christ in particular is the way, the truth, and the life. But that's not really
the scandal at all. The scandal is already here, implicitly, in the acknowledgement of the self and the rejection of a false objectivity. Christianity,
in a sense, only fills in the gaps, and more and more, despite myself, it
keeps threatening to.

And finally this doesn't have to do most of all with theme or universal mythic patterns, dying to live or any other. It's not just a question of
Christian appropriation more generally but of the experience of literature
in particular—the experience of it, not the ideas of it. The moment in the
water with Odysseus and on the shore, begging for mercy at the foot of
that beautiful young woman, that moment is only the most intense and
beautiful of what becomes a string of moments. The feeling of joy and of
abandonment, of wildness, of mercy, keeps welling up in me.

It happens when I'm teaching the Raymond Carver story, "What We
Talk About When We Talk About Love," at the end, in the moving final
paragraph, when the sadness of the narrator and his despair well out of
him in a moment so deep and ambiguous it becomes a kind of hope:

> I could hear my heart beating. I could hear everyone's heart. I could
> hear the human noise we sat there making, not one of us moving, not
> even when the room went dark. (*The Story and its Writer* 126)

I feel Tolkien's turn here, the catch in the breath, even though in Carver's
spare and unsparing world there is little hope of the fairy tale's happy
ending, only experience of the fairy tale's suffering and challenge. There
is dying here but not dying to live, not resurrection, except perhaps in the
dramatic power of the writing itself. There's that sense of listening, of a
world outside more vast than we knew.

It happens at the beginning of another fairy tale, another parable,
this breaking down of the barriers, this blending and coming together:

> As Gregor Samsa awoke one morning from uneasy dreams he found
> himself transformed in his bed into a gigantic insect. He was lying on
> his hand, as it were armor-plated, back and when he lifted his head a
> little he could see his dome-like brown belly divided into stiff arched
> segments on top of which the bed quilt could hardly keep in position
> and was about to slide off completely. His numerous legs, which were
> pitifully thin compared to the rest of his bulk, waved helplessly before
> his eyes. (*The Story and its Writer* 439)

There is no hope in Kafka's great novella *The Metamorphosis*. The inex-
orable logic of the story moves poor Gregor towards humiliation and
death. But there is a matter-of-fact humor here, a resolute attention to
the actual details of this situation, a kind of realism in a way, and in that
there is delight. Somehow the tightness and determinism of the story
functions so economically and well that here, too, the language opens out
to a world, a mystery, we couldn't think about in this precision and depth
except in the reading of the story.

What I experience for the first time so blindingly that morning with
Odysseus and Nausicaa and Jennifer and Justin and Megan and Sean is
the necessary affinity of literature and faith. I experience what is in the
very nature, the very structure, of image and story, a connection to the
mystery, to the divine. "The virtues of art, like the virtues of faith,"
O'Connor says, "are such that they reach beyond the limitations of the
intellect, beyond any mere theory that a writer may entertain. If the novelist is doing what as an artist he is bound to do, he will inevitably suggest that image of ultimate reality as it can be glimpsed in some aspect of
the human situation" (158). This is what I experience that morning and
again and again, the reaching beyond the limitations of the intellect,
beyond theory, an effort that the novelist cannot avoid if she is faithful to
the writer's primary task of describing the way the world really is,

describing it in its particulars, details. These are the very details from which our abstractions are drawn; as O'Conner says:

> The novelist and the believer, when they are not the same man, yet have many traits in common—a distrust of the abstract, a respect for boundaries, a desire to penetrate the surface of reality and to find in each thing the spirit which makes it itself and holds the world together. (168)

It's especially difficult for a Christian to teach literature at a state university, especially ancient literature, especially the epics and the fairy tales.

It's not just that the convicted Christian believes the whole world to be charged with the grandeur of God; that, as Newman says in *The Idea of the University*, "all that exists is from Him," that "all that is true, all that is beautiful, all that is beneficent, be it great or small, be it perfect or fragmentary, natural as well as supernatural, moral as well as material, comes from him" (53, 54; 1.3.7). It's not just this logic of the incarnation, of sacramentalism, as O'Connor, too, understands, that every detail a poet or scientist can describe is spiritually significant because made by God and infused with his presence. It's not just that the convicted Christian believes reason to be the ally of faith, leading up to it, not contradicting it. It's not just that the convicted Christian is able to read all pagan literature and all art and all things altogether allegorically and in light of Christ, with Christ as the key, everything anticipating him, ordered by him.

It's that in some fundamental way literature in particular bears on the Christian experience. It's that story is a kind of Eucharist. It's that in some fundamental way all Christian experience is literary in its very nature—and so every literary expression is at least potentially Christian in its very nature. "Every symbol is finally a hierophany, a manifestation of the bond between man and the sacred," Ricouer says (356). Every symbol, from Odysseus in the sea to Carver looking out the kitchen window. Mystery gives rise to story gives rise to thought, and it's story first, story closest. Once that link is made, once that connection is established, the divine can't help but keep flooding in. If mystery gives rise to story, story is always connected to mystery, intrinsically. If mystery gives rise to story, story is always in some fundamental sense "spiritual" or "religious," even if we don't name this spiritual feeling or experience in a specifically religious way or would even want to.

This is especially true of the classics, since they are still closer to the source of the mystery than the stories that come later, almost unmediated, the culture's first, spontaneous response to the world as it really is before our analysis and layering and thinking. They are the culture's dreams, the culture's freewriting, capturing and preserving our first naïveté and so teaching them in a public classroom is always dangerous. There is always the danger that we may make contact with the original energy just behind the story.

When we do, we can't help but lose our intellectual detachment. When we do, we can't help but stop analyzing the gaps. We can't help but fall through them, all the way through them, if not back into a first naïveté at least into a second naïveté, a giving up of the self to the surge and swell of the story itself. If the symbols we are experiencing are "flush tight" with the mystery that Christianity names with Christ, as Shea puts it, even in the experience of the mystery itself, prior to that naming, available to other names, the Christian can't help but find the source of all joy and all life.

What makes great literature so Christian is its invocation of the sea. What makes great literature so Christian is exactly its refusal to name what can't be named.

We're right up against it. How can the mystery help but keep pouring in?

————

And if it's happening for me, internally, how can it help but happen for my students, too, at least some of them? How can at least some of my students not join me in the water, not plunge in, even if I haven't come out and asked them to, even if I have kept my own emotions hidden?

And they do. When I read their journals over the next few days I see that they do, a handful of them, that for some of the students in the class, that day in the water is a plunging in for them. A Christian student comes excitedly to my office, talking about how his faith has been deepened and informed by his reading of Homer. An atheist writes in his journal:

> *I was resisting you before, I was resisting this class. I just wanted to read for the form and the history of things and I thought you were really pushing things. Being fuzzy. But that day in class when we talked about Odysseus drowning I felt it, too. I was sort of drowning, too. That Campbell stuff suddenly really made sense and I started thinking about how school has seemed to me the last few years. How pointless it's been. And then that seemed like the ocean, that seemed like my drowning. I'm not saying this very well. I guess for the first time in a long time I felt like instead of just reading a story for school I was reading it for myself, it meant something to me. I'm not sure what to do with this, but there it is. (Now if only I knew some really beautiful princess I can ask out!)*

Perhaps it's because the *Odyssey* isn't an explicitly religious text that the student has been surprised into this openness and surrender. Perhaps the magic and the special effects have stolen past the "dragons" of doubt and suspicion that would still be standing guard if this had been a Biblical story, all too familiar. Campbell recommends that we study the myths of other traditions for just this reason, because then we can appreciate them as myths, not as truths in some unconsidered sense, because then we won't be struggling against the wrong questions and doubts, and perhaps this is why I have fallen through myself, this day, why I have made the turn into the fairy tale: because this is a fairy tale, not Scripture, not a Biblical text that in my anxiety about line-crossing I can't allow myself to experience fully or claim personally.

"My parents' divorce is my drowning, I guess," another student writes. "I've been drinking a lot lately and I think I've got a problem," another writes in class and shares with me later. Another: "I feel like the princess somehow. I know that sounds funny, but I do. Life has been so great since I came here that I feel like I'm dancing on the rocks."

Teachers shouldn't take credit for these breakthroughs, or blame. Sometimes a teacher has the privilege of being the one who opens a door for a student, a student who was ready for the door to be opened. Teachers are waiters, not the chef. Deacons.

And this is dangerous, powerful stuff. It's close to the source. It asks us to plunge in.

And there is freewriting. There is Campbell on myth.

———

It's the students who cross the line, too. It's the students, right there, in the classroom, in the journal, for just a moment.

## CHAPTER 4

# The *Confessions* as a Model for the Academic Life

My second experience of the congruence of faith and reason takes place the next term, in winter, when I'm teaching Augustine's *Confessions*. Teaching the *Odyssey* I had fallen in, experiencing the closeness of literature to the spiritual. What Augustine makes clear is that this plunging in and this immediacy of experience is what Christianity affirms, explicitly, what it describes as orthodoxy. Everything that Ricouer talks about—the primacy of the concrete, the multiplicity of interpretation, the notion of critical thinking and reading that I've been exploring so far—is exactly what Christianity professes, too. Truth is always incarnate for Augustine, always embodied, and such truth is forever beyond what we say about it. Our language is always inadequate, wonderfully so, blessedly so. This is the central dynamic in Augustine's thought and in all Christian thought, even if eventually it must lead us further, to the making of specific commitments.

And if this is true, Christianity and the university have the same agenda, at least at some primary level. If this is true, teaching is believing, because it's exactly this insistence on multiplicity that I've said defines the university, too.

Critical thinking is the work of the university. Christianity is grounded in just this kind of critical thinking. Therefore, Christianity does the work of the university.

To develop this syllogism I spend most of the chapter recreating our class discussion of the *Confessions*, using Augustine's conversion and his reading of the Bible to talk first not about the university but about faith itself, its necessary humility and playfulness. This is the harder and more controversial move, it seems to me, to establish the connection between Christianity and interpretive open-endedness. With that sense of the tradition in place, that understanding of orthodoxy, my concluding argument about education quickly follows, since I've already established in the first few chapters the university's own commitments to interpretation.

Where my reading of Augustine finally leads is to a figure and to an experience. The figure is the figure of Mary, the mother of God, who is also the mother of the reader and so in the end the mother of the university. The experience is an experience on the altar, a Sunday morning when the boundaries for a moment collapse again and I am discovered by one of my students, preaching in the Mass exactly what I professed in the classroom the week before.

## Confounded and Converted

The second term of the Literature of Western Civilization. A gray, winter day.

We are discussing Augustine's *Confessions*, this difficult fifth century book that students always resist and misunderstand, when finally these misconceptions and this resistance call us all to a new and deeper insight.

I write the word "Christian" on the board.

Free associate, I say. Write whatever words first come to mind, as quickly as you can, not censoring.

Here, God help us, are the first three phrases that students share: "close-minded," "judgmental," "exclusive." Here, God help us, is the sense that so many students and faculty have of Christian tradition, whether through ignorance or prejudice or lived experience, of a faith narrow and hurtful, of a faith so sure of itself as to lead right away to the judgment of others. Close-minded, judgmental, exclusive. Other hands pop up, other words, from students anxious to insert the positive and hint at their own faith: "truth," "the way," "confidence," "conviction." Security. Love. The Right. The Moral. But these phrases share in the same assumptions, are more faithful expressions of the same contemporary sense of the religious life, that to live it is to walk in certainty, that to follow God is to exist in a state of blessed and convicted stasis.

No one suggests the words and phrases that would naturally come to Augustine himself: humility, confusion, joy in complexity, awe before the greatness and subtlety of a God too loving to be reduced to any phrase at all. The way, yes, but the way of life, an ongoing life, a difficult life, a journey, a struggle.

A little later in our discussion of the *Confessions*, as Augustine's fifth century faith starts to come clearer, a twenty-first century student asks, plaintively, in her journal: "How can Augustine believe if he has so many questions?" The entry of another student implies resistance to what she is beginning to understand about the way that Augustine and the ancient Christians read the Bible:

> If the Bible is a literary collection of oral stories and personal accounts
> of a person's experience with God, then how can we be sure that we
> will give the correct meaning to any set of words or stories told?

This is a reasonable question, and the right one, from a post-modern, post-Enlightenment perspective, but one that implies the gulf between our imaginations and Augustine's, between what we take for granted and what the first Christians took as given. For many contemporary readers the goal is correct meaning, the assumption is that there is a correct meaning, the hope is for sureness and control of the text, and these are goals and assumptions we project onto Augustine as we project them onto Genesis and the Gospel of Mark.

Augustine's reasoning becomes more intricate and intense as the *Confessions* goes on, more heated and abstract, an abstractness that students find just as difficult and off-putting as his God-talk. The "drops of time" that have made the *Confessions* famous, the stealing of the pears or the conversion in the garden, are few and far between, but the abstractness of the style at this point mirrors the theme: that Augustine is looking for God in ideas, in propositions he can arrive at logically and demonstrate permanently. This is the attraction of Manicheanism, this bizarre and complex vision of God's luminous body and the forces of lightness and dark, a system we might think too odd to be compelling. But what it promises is a nearly scientific comprehensiveness and certainty, a rational explanation for the creation of the world and especially for the question that troubled Augustine most of all, the origin of evil. Easy, the Manicheans say, confident in the intricacies of their systems: God isn't responsible for evil and neither are we. Reality, all of it, comes down to substance, either the substance of good or the substance of evil. Where evil comes from is from the evil substance.

For a mind like Augustine's, longing for clarity and order, there is something reassuring in this breathtaking materialism. For the Manicheans, Augustine explains, "scientific knowledge" becomes "an integral part of the structure of the doctrine of piety" (95; 5.5), and it's this scientism, this claim to the explanation of all things, that holds Augustine for a time. It calms him. "I wanted to be just as certain about things which I could not see as I was certain that seven and three make ten" (116; 6.4), he says, a longing that Manicheanism satisfies, for a time, as it satisfies Augustine's intellectual vanity, his desire to win the public arguments and dazzle others in the subtlety of debate.

But Augustine has too much intellectual integrity to rest in the reductions and oversimplifications of such a system. Finally his searching brings him to the point where the intricacies begin to unravel, where reason only succeeds in deconstructing itself, as he dramatizes in the intensely abstract middle chapters of the *Confessions*, describing his last anguished years of philosophical and theological despair. He can't answer his own questions, he can't solve his own difficult puzzles, he cares so deeply about these irresolvable problems that by book VI he is finally on the verge of breakdown and depression, his mind become a "wasteland" (51; 2.10).

Sixteen centuries later, in a hot, stuffy classroom in Corvallis, Oregon, the rain starting to fall outside, I try to get my students to forgive Augustine his misogyny, to look past his disgust with the body and his obsession with sex, and most of all to see that right at the heart of the *Confessions*, here in the sixth book, Augustine arrives at an understanding of Christianity so opposite our own as to require from us a paradigm shift at least historical if not also personal:

> From now on, however, I began to prefer the Catholic faith. In requiring belief in what was not demonstrated [. . .] I felt that the Catholic faith showed more modesty and more honesty than did the Manichees, who made rash promises of certain knowledge. (117; 6.5)

This is Augustine's turning point. This is the point where he has given up his desire for a certainty as certain as seven plus three equals ten. This is the point where he acknowledges such scientism to be absurd, contrary to the very nature of religious experience. What the long dark night of intense reasoning has demonstrated is the vastness of God and so the limits of demonstration. What the long dark night has proven is the need for a further, different kind of knowing, the knowing of faith, a knowing that is not only content in the midst of confusion and uncertainty but that sees confusion and uncertainty as the very signs of authenticity and truth.

"So I was both confounded and converted," Augustine says of this breakthrough (116; 6.4), and for him these words are not opposed but mutually interdependent. Conversion requires confusion. Augustine is converted exactly *because* he is confounded, I say to the students that wintry day, surprised as I say it, galvanized, suddenly clear.

For Augustine, Christianity is contrary to what we think we know about it. For Augustine, Christianity means open, not closed. For Augustine, Christianity means modest, not arrogant. For Augustine, Christianity isn't a matter of finding the answers but a way of living with the questions, ever more deeply. For Augustine, this is Christian orthodoxy, at the source: *the embracing of complexity*. For Augustine, this is the plot of Christian autobiography: once I was found and now I am lost, once I was sure and now I am not, though that uncertainty is joyous now and convinced, grounded in what can't be named or reduced. What's uncertain isn't the reality of God but the validity of any single interpretation of that reality. What Augustine has surrendered is not his faith but his arrogant need for mastery. "I no longer desired to be more certain of you, only to stand more firmly in you" (160; 8.1).

The famous conversion scene in the garden, in the eighth book (174–183; 8.8–12), fulfills the insight of the sixth, an insight that Augustine falls away from and loses sight of and returns to again and again in the books that follow, until one afternoon, in Milan, beneath a fig tree, overwhelmed with emotion and losing control, he sits down and hears from somewhere close by the voice of a child, of a boy or of a girl, he doesn't know but of a child, a small child at play probably, chanting a rhyme or a playing a game: "take and read," is how he hears it. "Take and read." And finally and completely then he abandons reason as the measure of truth. Finally and completely he abandons his pretenses and pride and becomes then like a child himself, as helpless as a child, as spontaneous as a child, as aware all at once of the great forces and movements in and around him. And he stands now and he walks to the words of St. Paul, in a book nearby, and he decides then and there to let his eyes fall on whatever they will fall on, to take whatever passage comes to him, and to read it and to assume in reading it that whatever it says applies to him, is about his own particular moment, his own particular choices.

What's crucial in this act isn't the passage itself or the content of his interpretation but the way Augustine interprets, the way he lets the words move him on a level deeper than reason, deeper even than interpretation. It's his trust, his radical trust, that's important, his trust that in that particular moment God is taking hold of him and guiding him, and that he can lay down the burden of his philosophy and the burden of his rhetoric and the burden of his pride and simply play in the garden of the Lord's delight, in the garden of the word, freely and safely and with hope in the loveliness or justice of whatever he might infer, whatever might come to him. He stands and he reads and he weeps and that weeping is now the measure of his knowing. Weeping is now the way that he reads.

Reason is not unimportant in all this for it is largely through reason that Augustine has learned to read through the falseness of the grand philosophical claims.[23] But when reason finally reaches its limits, this other kind of knowing and seeing must take its place, a knowing in love, a knowing in faith and so a knowing never reductionist or arrogant, always humble before the mystery and complexity of things. "O highest and best, most beautiful. My God, my life, my holy sweetness,"

Augustine cries out again and again (19; 1.4), more as in a love letter than in a philosophical disquisition, more as in prayer, which is what the *Confessions* really is. Its abstract analysis is wrapped up from the beginning in one joyous outpouring of love for the God Augustine first accepts when he plays like a child in the garden, when he surrenders his will.

To be God at all God must be beyond all language and beyond all substance. This Augustine has deduced rationally, in the years of thinking and rethinking and thinking again. The Manicheans must be wrong, because as soon as God becomes substance he becomes measurable and knowable, and as soon as God becomes measurable he ceases to be God. That's the center of all theological analysis: that God exceeds our categories altogether and that any system which denies this must be false on the face of it: "Can there be anything capable of containing you? Can heaven and earth contain you, heaven and earth which you made and in which you made me?" (18; 1.2)

But from the beginning of the *Confessions* this isn't an idea that Augustine thinks about. It's a sweetness that he savors, it's a love that he feels, it's a reality that he again and again witnesses to in the apparent spontaneity of his prose as he paces back and forth, dictating to an amanuensis, the words tumbling out on the page in the ebb and flow of his own unfettered thinking. In the face of God's greatness, only spontaneity is possible. In the face of God's love, only love can be our response. In the face of this wordlessness, the only possible source of knowledge is lived and intuitive experience, is the heart: "O highest and best, most powerful, most all-powerful, most merciful and most just, most deeply hidden and most nearly present, most beautiful and most strong, constant yet incomprehensible. [. . .] My God, my Life, my holy sweetness, what does any man succeed in saying when he attempts to speak of you?" (19; 1.4)

The answer: nothing. No one can succeed in saying anything sufficient or definitive about God. Yet it's just this greatness that calls forth our creativity and our imagery and all our language. In the face of such beauty we must abandon propriety and abandon logic and let our hearts swell with what we long for and what we believe.

"The central truth, or mystery, of the Christian faith is primarily not a matter of words," Louth explains, "and therefore not ultimately of ideas or concepts, but a matter of fact, of reality. To be a Christian is not simply to believe something, to learn something, but to BE something, to experience something" (74). This is the passage that I was reading at Mount Angel, in the oak grove, the focal point of the intellectual joy that I described in chapter 1, and it's Louth's way of explaining exactly what Augustine experiences in the garden, the insight toward which all the rest of the *Confessions* is always tending. The movement is from one order of knowledge to another, a movement required by this reality that is being known, this multiple and inexplicable reality of God. As Augustine quotes from Isaiah, you *must believe in order to understand*. That's the key, that's the sequence. "Let me see you, Lord, by praying to you and let me pray believing in you" (17; 1.1). In the order of knowledge reason only exhausts us so that we can start over again from the point of prayer, fervent and desiring prayer. It's this that yields the only knowledge it's possible to have of God, relational knowledge, experiential knowledge—the knowledge that comes from "standing" in God, not from "certainty" about him.

It's this, too, that leads quite naturally to the role of the church as Augustine understands it in the *Confessions*, not as the proclaimer of laws and the repository of precepts but as "the community through belonging to which we come into touch with the Christian mystery," as Louth puts it (74). If the reality of God is something we can only experience, the church must enable us to have this experience. It must teach its truths and communicate its insights not by explicit commentary, rational disquisition, or long, deductive arguments but rather by creating a set of cultural practices in which people over time come to live the mystery. "We come back to the fact that Christianity is not a body of doctrine that can be specified in advance but a way of life and all that this implies," Louth says (86). This is the idea that Augustine experiences in the garden, when he abandons his effort to solve the theological problems on his own and to accept instead the teaching and the tradition of the church as it is contained in the writing of Scriptures and to accept as well the church's ways of reading and understanding those Scriptures. He gives himself up to the tradition, as he trusts himself, too, to his friend and companion in the garden, Alypius. Throughout the *Confessions* Augustine is gathering a community of believers and followers and setting up for them rules for reading and prayer because he knows that it's only in this way that he and the others can over time experience in their hearts the lived reality of the divine.

Faith is not a truth we possess but a journey we take. Faith is not an argument we prove but a life we live.

It's story.

## Reading the Bible, Reading Life

Story is the key to Augustine's thinking, as it is the key to Ricouer's—as it is the key, I have argued, for the university.

And what follows from the idea of story is the idea of reading, of interpretation, both of our lives and of the Bible. Because experience and the Scriptures are both narrative, are both story, they require a kind of interpretive finesse and awareness very like the finesse and awareness required by a university. That's what universities do, after all: they teach us how to read.

––––––

First, our lives.

For Augustine, God is not first to be found in books and ideas, though he is of course present there as he is present everywhere. God is not first to be found even in the trees and the stars, though of course these are his creations, informed by his love. God is not finally to be found outside at all but inside, in the heart, in the memory, in the person. This is Augustine's insight in the garden, that God is most present in the shape of our lives. "How then, Lord, do I seek you?" (229; 10.20). By telling my own story, by remembering my own experience.

This is the idea I touched on in the introduction, and here, in the *Confessions* itself, it comes clearly into focus. Because God has come into the world, the world is redeemed in all its particulars. Because God has come into the world in the story of a human being, the stories of all human beings are now infinitely meaningful. Because, as McClendon puts it in *Biography as Theology*, "Christian beliefs are not so many 'propositions' to be catalogued or juggled like truth-functions in a computer, but are living convictions which give shape to actual lives and actual communities," "the only relevant critical examination of Christian beliefs may be one that begins by attending to lived lives" (22).[22] Paul is the first to see this, to understand that God is in him, that the shape of the life of Christ is the shape of his own life, and Augustine carries this idea to its completion. God is present in his mother's womb and his mother's milk and in his own infant cries. God is present in his boyhood games and his boyhood urges and even most of all in boyhood failings and sins, in his ambition and pride and greed. "My very being is your gift." "You have made all things good" (39, 51; 1.20, 7.12). The incarnation now orders all the stages of the psyche, right down to the breaths we take and the dreams we dream.

God is so vast and infinite that there is nothing he doesn't fill, however small; yet the paradox of the incarnation is that it's now in these smallest of places that he is most visible. Or it's even more primary, goes even further back, to the creation itself, the moment celebrated in Genesis and that Augustine comes back to again and again in the *Confessions*, the moment of the *imago Dei* when the human person is made in the image and likeness of God, when in the smallness of the person all glory and honor is made to be reflected. The incarnation restores what was first intended, that we are by our very nature holy, in our very essence and our very selves:

> My pen's tongue will never have strength to declare all your exhorta-
> tions and your terrors, the consolations and the guidance. [. . .] And
> suppose I have the strength to declare all this in order, yet the drops
> of my time are too precious, and for long I have been full of a burning
> desire to *meditate in Thy law* and to confess to you both my knowledge
> and my lack of skill in it, the first beginnings of the light you shed on
> me and the remnants of my darkness, until my weakness be swallowed
> up in strength. (258; 11.2)

In the creative act of Genesis, restored and fulfilled by Christ, the infinite is made to reside in the finite, timelessness within time. The glory
of God is contained through grace in the very "drops of time" that make
up our lives, in those "precious" moments when in the particulars of
what we touch and taste and see—in the pear trees, in the sight of a beggar, in a garden by the sea—we glimpse what has made those particulars
and what shines through them forever. Our task then is to "meditate" on
such experiences just as we meditate on Scripture, and with just the same
conviction, that each moment and each text contains inexhaustible
meaning.

Liberty Lake. Very hot. A radio playing on the beach. A jet ski whining and racketing. But when I dive down into the water I am all at once
buoyant and clean. The light is shimmering, green and gold, and for a
moment I am suspended.

The stars coming up over the ridge in the Wallowa Mountains on
the west fork of the Lostine River. My head tilted back. And I feel my
eyes and heart going up to meet the stars, opening out into all that darkness, and then the insignificance we always feel before the night sky, the
sense of being flattened that somehow is also joyous, full, a completing.

Mary Rose needs a nap and her mother asks if I'll put her down. We
sit in her darkened room, in a rocking chair, and she puts her head on my
shoulder and crosses her little brown feet. Her breathing begins to slow.
Her little hands relax.

The Lord of all humbled himself even unto death, the Creator of the
universe became a person just like us, and because of that we are all
exalted forevermore. The Lord is the man who takes the child in his
arms, he is the father and the mother, and the Lord is the child, he is the
little girl, innocent and pure. He has made himself vulnerable. And
whenever we make ourselves vulnerable, too, I think then, whenever we
take someone else in our arms, he is present in the room, he is filling the
room.

Thus the crucial importance of memory and so of autobiography,
since it's only in memory, when these moments have passed and taken
shape in our minds, that we can begin to understand their depths. The

*Confessions* is a long act of re-collection, of re-membering, inspired by the recognition that memory is sacred. "I shall pass on, then," Augustine says, "as I ascend by degrees toward Him who made me. And I come to the fields and spacious palaces of memory, where lie the treasures of innumerable images of all kinds of things that have been brought in by the senses" (217; 10.8). This is where God is to be found, in the fields and palaces that lie within the mind itself, in those images of all that has happened to us. "How great, my God, is this force of memory, how exceedingly great! It is like a vast and boundless subterranean shrine" (219; 10.8). Just as in Scripture there is always more than one meaning, there are vast mysteries and depths, always more than whatever we might translate into a simple proposition, the "correct" meaning that contemporary students long for, so within ourselves is a mystery, a holy mystery, a boundless shrine. "Who has ever reached the bottom of it?" (219; 10.8).

Buechner explains this central Augustinian insight in contemporary terms. "If God speaks to us at all in this world, if God speaks anywhere," Buechner says, "it is into our personal lives that he speaks." We wake up in the morning and go about our work. We have lunch with a friend, we embrace our wife. Now and then someone we love dies or betrays us or we betray them, something extraordinary happens to shake us out of our complacencies, but always even the most ordinary of moments have for us a sweetness, a sadness, an elusive meaning. "Into the thick of it, or out of the thick of it, at moments of even the most humdrum of our days, God speaks" as if life itself is the great text to be read (*Sacred Journey* 1–2).

In this sense, Augustine and all the autobiographers are simply imitating the Bible, the primary narrative, the first stories that come out of the people as necessary response to the story of God in their lives. Genesis and Mark, as we have seen, show rather than tell, they give us people and places and actions in time, not abstract pronouncements and detached theology, and they do this for just the reason Buechner suggests: because they have to, because for them as for him the language of God himself is just as metaphorical and concrete and so just as elusive, just as open to interpretation.

———

The Bible simply mirrors life. It's hard to read because life is hard to read. Buechner again:

> God's words to us are always veiled, subtle, cryptic, so that it is left to
> us to delve their meaning, to fill in the vowels, for ourselves by means
> of all the faith and imagination we can muster. God speaks to us in
> such a way, presumably, not because he chooses to be obscure but
> because, unlike a dictionary word whose meaning is fixed, the mean-
> ing of an incarnate word is the meaning it has for the one it is spoken

to, the meaning that becomes clear and effective in our lives only when
we ferret it out for ourselves. (*Sacred Journey* 4)

Buechner's simile works both ways: just as life is like the Hebrew alphabet, the Hebrew alphabet is like life, full of gaps to be filled, necessarily,
unavoidably. A lived truth is never reducible. A lived truth is never single, and it's this kind of truth that the Bible instinctively captures.

Certainly this is Augustine's underlying assumption in his interpretations of Scripture, as it is the underlying assumption of the ancient
Christian world. What Augustine's faith and experience and long years of
reasoning naturally lead to is the rejection of the literal and the embracing of metaphor and multiplicity.

Early on, in his pride and his vanity, he found the Scriptures too halt-
ing and humble. "They seemed to me unworthy of comparison with the
grand style of Cicero." He "shrank from their modesty," his eye "was not
penetrating enough to see into their depths" (57; 3.5). To read the Bible
in its fullness humility is required, the humility of a child, but this is just
what Augustine in his lust for honors and success cannot at this stage
imagine. It's only later that he learns to penetrate these depths, after he
has been humbled by the failure of reason and come to see beyond fame
and reputation. He learns through his teacher St. Ambrose and the traditions of the church that he has once scorned, learns what we've already
seen is the great Christian technique for praying the Scriptures, *lectio divina*.

From Ambrose he learns "the rule to go by," that the letter kills but
the spirit gives life, that scripture is useless and even absurd if read literally, that only when we read beyond the details and look for "the spiritual
sense" does the Bible open out into worlds of meaning (116; 6.4).
"Meditation" on the words is the beginning of wisdom, the *meditatio* of
*lectio divina*, the stage of the discipline in which we assume that whatever
the text describes is in fact about our own given situation, our own lives,
not some merely historical event that took place countless years ago. The
question isn't what happened, but what does this mean, and it's a question that trusts in a thousand possible answers, varying moment to
moment and reader to reader. To practice *meditatio* is to practice a life-
long free association, an inventive and spontaneous looking through and
beyond, always open and tentative, always joyous and grateful before the
reality of a God who exceeds our notions as he of course exceeds all substance.

As the *Confessions* is one long act of re-collection, it is also one long
act of *lectio divina*, saturated with Scripture that Augustine knows so well
he has swallowed it, he has memorized it—*lectio* on two levels at once, in
both the constant act of meditation and in the next stage, *oratio*, the
translating of these reflections and these multiple readings into repeated

acts of prayer, of address to God, joyous or contrite or fearful or awed but always faithful, always inventive. The *Confessions* is a long conversation with God, a long petition, and in that petition what Augustine is always doing is reading his life through the text of the word, reading the word through the text of his life. All the autobiography is both meditation and prayer, *meditatio* and *oratio*, an unpacking of Genesis and the Psalms and the Prophets and the Gospels. All the Scripture is commentary on his own life story, its fountain and its frame.

In the last three chapters this ongoing meditation culminates in an inspired and wildly inventive allegorical interpretation of the first chapter of Genesis. Allegorical: the spiritual dimension of the text. Later in the Middle Ages allegorical reading develops into a four stage interpretive key, the academic parallel of *lectio*: the literal meaning, or what the words of the text actually mean; the allegorical or spiritual meaning; the moral meaning, or the implications for how we should behave and live with each other; and finally what the church called the "anagogical" meaning, that which has to do with heaven or hell, that which has to do with our ultimate salvation. The four levels are everywhere in the literate world, in every monastery and every library right up to Dante and beyond—Dante who wrote an important letter on the four levels, taking them for granted and making them the basis for the architecture of the *Divine Comedy*. Jerusalem, let's say. Literally: the city of the Jews. Allegorically: the church of Christ. Morally: the human soul. Anagogically: heaven.

Though the technique isn't yet this developed or systematic for Augustine, his allegorical reading of Genesis proceeds from the same assumptions, scornful of merely literal meaning, convinced that there exists a whole range of spiritual meanings—and beyond those levels, a love and a presence, the creative principle himself. Of course the first chapter of Genesis can't be read as science or history, Augustine says, sixteen centuries ago, taking that for granted as the truest part of the tradition has always taken it for granted. It doesn't make sense if we do. It's nonsensical, contradictory. Of course we must take historical and cultural context into account, not mistaking the divine message for its human medium—this sixteen centuries ago, this from a man close to the source of Scripture itself. To do otherwise "is to judge merely out of man's judgment and to measure the whole moral structure of the human race by one's own particular and partial standard of morality" (61; 3.7).

Of course Scripture has more than one meaning. Of course. Always. "Can you not see how foolish it is out of all that abundance of perfectly true meanings which can be extracted from those words rashly to assert that one particular meaning was the one which Moses had chiefly in mind?" (307; 12.25) The very theme of Genesis is the abundance of God's mercy, the overflowing creativity and abundance of God. How can we assume that the human speech he inspires could be any less generous, less full, less rich? To pretend otherwise is to be guilty of the sin of pride, the sin of the Manichean bishop Faustus, for example, whose "presumption" that he knows the single truth about creation is by its nature "sacrilegious" (95; 5.5). It's to be arrogant. It's to be in error about the facts, since the facts are wild, the facts are joyous, the facts are beyond all our counting.

To pretend otherwise is to violate the very charity at the heart of the Gospels and at the heart of the faith. To pretend otherwise is to be guilty of a "pernicious quarrelsomeness" which "offends charity herself, for whose sake he, whose words we are trying to explain, said everything that he did say" (308; 12.25). Later, in his clear and systematic treatment of Biblical exegesis in *Teaching Christianity*, drawing on what Jesus calls "the greatest" commandments (Mark 12.28–34), Augustine condenses this last point into a single, operative rule for the reading of Scripture: though Scripture requires a range of meanings, any interpretation "contrary to love," to the love of God and the love of neighbor, is wrong and to be rejected (115–224). Love is the interpretive limit. Love is the limit of orthodoxy and what orthodoxy exists to guarantee.

And so the spirit that moves upon the waters is the Holy Spirit, and the water in which Odysseus bobs for twenty days is the depth of our nature, and the forming of the earth and of the seas and the ordering of all things becomes the redemptive work of Christ and the Spirit raising us up out of sin into health and abundance and fruitfulness towards the firmament of heaven which is at once intellect and spirit, and the Bible itself and even the leviathans are allegorical, even the great whales are symbolic, of the ignorant and the infidel and all who must still be redeemed from the waters, for all these, all these, are "allegories for the movement of the mind" (334; 13.21). It's an imaginative reading, full of delight in the depths of meaning and full of generosity and tolerance towards other interpreters. "How amazing is the profundity of your utterances!" Augustine exclaims. "One cannot look into them without awe and trembling—awe of greatness, trembling of love" (294; 12.14).

And given that love and trembling, what harm can come if we disagree? Given that love and trembling, "what harm can it do" if my "view"of what is meant is "different from someone else's view"? (300; 12.18). All is well here, in this genesis of meaning, all is well as long as love is observed and love is respected, here in this "true diversity of opinions" (313; 12.30), here in this "figurative" universe (339; 13.24), this wildly symbolic cosmos, along this "allegorical way" (341; 13.25), where all that is just and true is forever "allegorically intimated" (348; 13.34). "Let all of us who seek the truth and speak the truth that is in these words love one another." Let all of us be "reverent" as we read, and what reverence requires is love for "a third or a fourth truth" or indeed any other truth at all, for all the truths that different minds can see, as of course "different minds" will "see different things" (313; 12.32).

"See, Lord my God, how much I have written on these few words! Really how much! What strength of ours, what length of time would be enough to comment in this way on all your scriptures!" (314; 12.32)

And this is the most disarming thing of all, Augustine's combination of unabashed enthusiasm and genuine humility, his self-awareness, his humor. "I see it in a way," he says of one of his ideas, "but I do not know how to express it" (263; 11.8). Later: "who can easily grasp this in his mind?" (323; 13.11). And: "I am asking questions, Father, not making statements" (270; 11.17). And: "I would rather say 'I don't know' when I don't know than make a kind of reply which brings ridicule on someone who has asked a deep question" (266; 11.12). This is a man whose "soul is on fire to solve a very complicated enigma" (274; 11.22) and who shares this fire in what begins to seem like an unrestrained freewriting, a record of his mind at the moment of his thinking and feeling. "Press forward, my mind! Go forward with all your strength" (279; 11.27), as if the writing of the book is a journey, is a process happening in the now of composition itself, nothing censored or taken back, each stage captured on the page.

It's an exuberance and spontaneity that comes both from joy in God's greatness and a healthy sense of his own human limitations, as he suggests, somewhat wryly, at the beginning of the twelfth book, catching his breath before plunging back in: "the poverty of human understanding shows an exuberance of words, since inquiry has more to say than discovery, asking takes longer than obtaining, and the hand that knocks does more work than the hand that receives" (285; 12.1).

This is a Christianity radically different from the kind my students assume, radically different in form as it is radically different in content—not a sermon but a searching, not a series of answers but an outpouring of questions, and an outpouring that issues not from anger and disgust but from joy, not from absolutist conviction but from an ecstatic humility, an awe-inspired rush of hope and trembling. This is a notion of the Bible radically different from the one my students bring to the *Confessions*, a notion in which multiplicity and uncertainty are to be celebrated, not repressed or contained. This is a radically different image of what faith is about, of faith as a stream, with all the playfulness and abundance of a stream, not a fixed set of truths to grasp once and for all:

> A spring shut in a small place has a more plentiful supply of water and distributes its flow to more streams over a greater area of ground than does any single stream, however far it goes, which is derived from that

spring. It is the same with the writing of him who dispenses your word. This writing will do good to many who will preach and comment upon it, and from a narrow measure of speech it will spread and overflow into streams of liquid truth, and from these, as they wind away in lengthier stretches of language, each man may on these subjects draw what truth he can—one man one truth, one another. (308–9; 12.27)

Pluralism, diversity, overflow and abundance—seen as necessary, as inevitable, as both the condition and the result of reading an ancient myth that in the twenty-first century inspires just the intolerance and the narrow-mindedness that so many students rightly associate with Christianity. Augustine sees the Bible as so many in the ancient world saw it, not just as a stream but as a forest—not a machine, not even a garden, but a forest. "It was not for nothing that you willed that so many pages should be filled with the writing of such dark secrets," he says, "nor are these forests without their stags which shelter there and range and walk, feeding, lying down, and chewing the cud"—chewing as in ruminating, as in turning an idea over and over, slowly, deliberately, meditating (258; 11.2).

## A Brief History of Orthodoxy

None of this finesse and awareness would be important, of course, if Augustine were exceptional. None of this would matter if he were not orthodox. But he is. The *Confessions* is important, and it's important because it's representative, because its assumptions are the assumptions of the whole tradition, its method the defining method.

Louth put it this way in his description of the patristic mind in *Discerning the Mystery*, the mind that produced and canonized the New Testament and first taught us how to read it:

> It is important to realize this: that the traditional doctrine of the multiple sense of Scripture, with its use of allegory, is essentially an attempt to respond to the *mira profunditas* of Scripture, seen as the indispensable witness to the mystery of Christ. [. . .] *Mira profunditas*: a sense of the depth and richness of Scripture, a richness derived from the mystery to which it is the introduction, of which it is the unfolding. A depth, a complexity, a *difficulty*. (112)

For centuries the reading of the Bible takes place in this context, with this spirit, complexity and difficulty seen as necessary, multiple interpretation seen as reverent, as a witness to the mystery hinted at by the words of the inspired text.[25] St. Benedict makes *lectio divina* and allegorical interpretation of this sort the basis of the monastic life that anchors and then preserves western culture, that gives rise to the university, that I experience myself in my commuting to Mount Angel. "What page, what passage of the inspired books of the Old and New Testaments is not the truest guide for human life?" he asks in his *Rule*, then requires his monks to spend hours of each day reading between the lines of scripture for the truths it implies for their own spiritual struggles (95). St. Ephrem the Deacon, calling Christ the "Lord of Symbols," instructs every reader in tolerance and open-mindedness:

> Who is capable of comprehending the extent of what is to be discovered in a single utterance of Yours? For we leave behind in it far more than we take from it, like thirsty people drinking from a fountain. The facets of His word are more numerous than the faces of those who learn from it. God depicted His word with many beauties, so that each of those who learn from it can examine that aspect of it which he likes. And God has hidden within His word all sorts of treasures, so that each of us can be enriched by it from whatever aspect he meditates on. [. . .] Anyone who encounters Scripture should not suppose that the single one of its riches that he has found is the only one to exist; rather, he should realize that he himself is capable of discovering that one out of the many riches which exist in it. Nor, because Scripture has enriched him should the reader impoverish it. Rather, if the reader is incapable of finding more, let him acknowledge Scripture's magnitude. (qtd. in Brock 50–51)

Openness. Tolerance. The celebration of depth and subtlety.

What gives this way of thinking authority is that it stands at the source of the Christian tradition, is closer to the mind of Christ himself than the fundamentalist and rigorist distortions that come so much later, in modernism. What gives this way of thinking authority is that it forms and guides the reading of the Bible for a millennium and more.

For all the ways it seems to dominate our popular discussion of Scripture and religion, for believers and nonbelievers both, fundamentalism is not central to the tradition. The questions that my students ask simply are not asked until the Renaissance and Enlightenment, when science and doubt begin to change our worldview. As Karen Armstrong has demonstrated in *The Battle for God*, her study of the history of fundamentalism, the obsession with historical accuracy and single meaning is possible only in modernism, only as response to the rise of science, a response that is in itself oddly scientific. Born into a culture created by Newton and Hobbes, our students are rational in a way that Augustine and the Fathers and the Jews before them are not. For all their logical fallacies, for all their resistance to sustained philosophical discourse, for all their longing for easy answers, our students are propositional and idea-driven, as abstract as any Enlightenment philosopher.

Yet, on another level, these literal-minded students are in the minority, despite their apparent influence. Though we would never know it from *Time* or *60 Minutes*, the majority of Christians and Jews alive today do not read the Bible literally, but instead try to return to this original mythic, imaginative, allegorical response, reading as literate and informed postmoderns, but at the level of what Ricouer calls "second naïveté." It's not just that mature believers recognize the silliness and limitation of literal interpretation, but that they're *believers*: believers in a God who by definition exists beyond substance and so beyond reduction to even the historical and cultural background recovered by contemporary Biblical studies, however important and necessary that recovery has been. Mature Christians and Jews reject literalism exactly because they believe. "The unbeliever thinks he really knows all about God," Walter Kasper says. "The believer, on the other hand, knows that he cannot provide himself with answers and that the answer which God gives is a message about an abiding mystery" (129). Or as Hans Urs von Balthasar explains this central belief, applying it directly to the Bible: "The idea that one has understood a passage of scripture finally and completely and has drawn out all that God meant in it is equivalent to denying that it is the word of God and inspired by him" (21).

Karl Barth would agree—Barth the father of postmodern Protestant and Evangelical theology. "The word of God on the lips of a man is an impossibility," he says. "It does not happen; no one will ever accomplish it or see it accomplished" (124).

This is what I know that traditional and contemporary theology holds to be true about the church itself, and theology itself, about all that we say of the "organized religion" my students so resist and think they need none of. Most of them last thought about religion in fourth grade Sunday school if they have thought about it at all, and somehow they seem to assume that it's not possible to think about religion in sophisticated and adult terms, that all thinking about religion has remained there in the church basement, among the paste and the construction paper and the soft-focus calendars, to be rejected or embraced. But that's not so. The same openness and awareness of complexity that characterizes Biblical interpretation defines the church's long thinking about its own identity. *Lex orandi, lex credendi* is the ancient Latin phrase for its deepest intuition: the order of worship determines the order of faith. First the experience of faith in all its complexity and richness, then the interpretations and the analyses that, however important and necessary, are always secondary, always far less than what they try to explain or point to.

Buechner explains this idea in a wonderful passage, affirming his own faith as a Christian. "At its heart," Buechner says, "religion is mystical":

> Moses with his flocks in Midian, Buddha under the Bo trees, Jesus up to his knees in the waters of the Jordan: each of them responds to something for which words like shalom, oneness, God even are only pallid, alphabetic souvenirs, "I have seen things," Aquinas told a friend, "that make all my writing seem like straw." Religion as institution, as ethics, as dogma, as social action—all this comes later and in the long run counts for less. Religions start, as Frost said poems do, with a lump in the throat, to put it mildly, or with the bush going up in flames, the rain of flowers, the dove coming down out of the sky. (*Alphabet of Grace* 74)

Institution and ethics and dogma and social action are all necessary and important but in the long run count for less, because religion starts as poems do, religion is poetry, religion begins and ends not in straw but in the rain of flowers. This is C. S. Lewis, too, on the night of his conversion, aware that the "doctrines" that we "get out of the true myth are of course less true than the myth itself," as he puts it in his letter to Arthur Greeves, that they are "translations into our concepts and ideas of that which God has already expressed in a language more adequate, namely the actual incarnation, crucifixion, and resurrection." This is Flannery O'Connor, rich in her experience of the "mystery from which we draw our abstractions," a mystery that the novelist as the gospel writer can never escape or oversimplify. This is Ricouer: Mystery gives rise to story gives rise to thought.

You must believe in order to understand.

This is the insight underlying Lewis and O'Connor and Buechner's sense of the literary quality of Christian faith, what LeClercq calls its "poetic essence" (55). This is the fundamental nature of the experience that gives rise to the literary or poetic nature of Benedictine monasticism, with its grounding in the chanting of the Psalms and the imaginative reflection on Scripture and the living of a prayerful life day to day—all that sense of the affinities of literature and faith that we touched on earlier, here taken and named as central to what it means to be Christian.

Even Cardinal Newman, writing in the difficult nineteenth century, when the church was in its most reactionary phase, for all his defense of orthodoxy and denouncing of what he calls "liberalism," for all his defense of the authority of the Catholic Church, defines that authority as grounded in the recognition of God's loving otherness. The church, he says in his *Apologia*, is the "expression in human language of truths to which the human mind is unequal" (44), an insight recovered and made plainer in Vatican II's *Lumen Gentium*, where the church is defined as "the sacrament of salvation"—a sacrament, a concrete vehicle for expressing the divine, which like all concrete vehicles is not the divine itself, is a mixing of the merely human and so the flawed with glimpses and intuitions about what redeems the human.

Friedrich von Hügel's later summary of faith, in the early twentieth century, echoes Augustine's conversion experience in the fifth:

> Never try to get things too clear. Religion can't be clear. In this mixed-up life there is always an element of unclearness. [. . .] How can it be otherwise if Christianity is our ideal? [. . .] If I could understand religion as I understand that two and two make four, it would not be worth understanding. Religion can't be clear if it is worth having. To me, if I can see things through and through, I get uneasy—I feel it's a fake. I know I have left something out, I've made some mistake. (8)

Augustine's equation is seven plus three, not two plus two, but the point is the same, that in Christianity by its nature there can be no exactness in some mathematical or measurable sense. In Christianity there is only the certainty of lived experience, which is always mixed-up, always containing "an element of tragedy."[26]

———

Jacob runs away from the brother he has wronged, hiding in a strange and stony place. He lies down to sleep with a rock for a pillow and all at once dreams of a shining ladder and of the angels walking up and down the ladder and of a promise made, a promise beyond all hope and expectation. "Surely the Lord was in this place and I did not know it!" he says, and here the story is really about reading (Gen. 28.16). God is revealing himself to Jacob in the text of that stony place and in the text of Jacob's own life, but not in any way that is clear or helpful, as Jacob spends the next twenty-one years struggling and suffering anyway, at the hands of Laban. Coming back in the end he has another theophany, and this, too, is finally about reading. It is dark and Jacob is afraid that his cheated brother is camped against him with his armies, so he retires to the far side of the river Jabbok where out of the darkness a strange man appears and challenges him to a wrestling match that lasts throughout the night. No one wins, Jacob is hurt, limping away in the morning light, but once again, after the fact, after he has had the experience, not before, Jacob realizes that he has been in the presence of God—not a God who makes things easy, not a God who clarifies anything at all. To be called is to be called into greater complexity and messiness than before. Eventually the man who is so marked by this experience as to be renamed, to be called Israel, he who wrestled with God himself, becomes the befuddled old father deceived by his sons as he deceived his own father years before.

In her reflection on the book of Genesis, *In the Beginning*, Armstrong calls the story of Jacob at the Jabbok an "emblem of the painful effort that the Bible so often demands of its readers." Speaking from within the Judeo-Christian tradition, summarizing and embodying it, Armstrong explains that believers for centuries have turned to their holy books "not to acquire information but to have an experience." Believers for centuries have known that "the true meaning of scripture can never be wholly comprised in a literal reading of the text, since that text points beyond itself to a reality which cannot adequately be expressed in words and concepts." This is what the wrestling at the Jabbok embodies. We can read it as implying a nonliteral and non-reductionist way of reading because this reading is in keeping with the people's actual experience of God, the experience that their stories reflect: "The sacred was too great a reality to be contained within a purely human definition or system of thought," Armstrong says. "Thus, the people of Israel would have only fleeting and frequently ambiguous glimpses of the divine." Thus they understood what the image of the wrestling match suggests, that not even their religious heroes could achieve enlightenment "effortlessly or with the calm serenity of the Buddha" (4–5).

In the same way the miracles and the healings and the teachings of Jesus in the Gospel of Mark lead not to conviction and certainty but to questions, amazement, fear, even offense and rejection, rejection so severe that finally he is killed, nailed to a cross. Jesus multiplies the fishes and the loaves and feeds the glad ten thousand, then walks on the water, steps over the waves—this is the text to be read, two miracles, two special effects—but even the disciples who have eaten and slept with this man and again and again listened to his private teachings and most intimate explanations simply don't get it, they don't get it at all: "And they were utterly astounded, for they did not understand [. . .] but their hearts were hardened" (Mark 6:51–52). But in a way, too, this difficulty and failure in understanding on the part of the disciples is an appropriate response, an index to the subtlety and obscurity and radicalism of the message. Of course they don't get it. When it's not too dazzling and spectacular to take in, it's too subtle to infer, as in the indirectness of the parables. And when not too subtle to infer, the message is too radical to accept. Even when the disciples and the others do finally get the point, they reject it, outraged and threatened. Jesus is walking through a wheat field on the Sabbath and stoops to pick the grain, offending the Jewish prohibitions against doing work on the day of rest. "Have you never read," he asks the rigorist Pharisees, "have you never read" in the story of David how he once broke into the sacred bread and ate of it himself in his hunger? Do you only read on the surface, in other words, do you only read literally, do you only look at the letter and not the spirit? (2:25)

All these interpretive and theological issues come to their climax on the mountain of the transfiguration when Jesus is bathed in the dazzling light, so panicking poor Peter that all he can think of is to build three booths. All he can think of in the face of such glory is somehow to capture it, institutionalize it, own it and sell tickets to it, but of course, as Mark insists, "he did not know what to say, for they were terrified" (8:6). Anyone who imagines Christianity as justifying complacency and self-righteousness and religious chauvinism hasn't read the story of the terrifying and glorious light within which Jesus is revealed as who he really is. Or they have read it, and like Peter have shrunk away. It's entirely human to abandon and repress the wildness and power of such a moment, to substitute for it a golden calf.

We can only sympathize with Peter, finally, for he quite rightly embodies the challenge of reading a text this difficult and unexpected. In the great speech right before his transformation on the mountain, Jesus has explained that he must die and that the disciples must die as well, die to themselves, surrender their will and desire for control. But it's too much, reverses too dramatically what Peter and the others expect and hope for. The Messiah is to be a king of power and a king of status, not a man who gives up all his power and gives up all his fame to die like a criminal, horribly. It's too much. Not only has God hidden himself in the incarnation, obscured his infinite capacity in the mere flesh and blood of a human life, but now he has taken that obscuring to its infinite extreme, becoming so concrete and so human as to die. Death is the ultimate concreteness, the ultimate self-emptying, all glory obscured in the details of negation.

But part of what Peter has to learn is that his interpretation here is wrong, as all interpretations are finally wrong or finally secondary, less than what they point to. In fact, the dying to self that Jesus asks of Peter and the other disciples can be seen as an interpretive demand, as a model for how texts and lives should be read: openly, humbly, without giving in to the desire for a single, controlling, fixed, comforting meaning. It's our own interpretations we are to die to, whatever else, our own language.

———

Cape Look Out, weaving in and out of cool old growth forest and suddenly the ocean shining all around me, the ocean widening and widening, as far as I can see, vast and shining and empty.

The wine on the altar the color of hay, of the fields and the trees looking down from the hill at Mount Angel. I am serving with the monks at the monastic Mass, standing on the altar. Sunlight through the doorway. The vestments hanging from my shoulders, green and brown, heavy as two strong hands.

I arrive at the hospital a minute late. The body, though warm, is twisted and shrunk, blood still drying around the mouth, eyes rolled back. I hurry in to comfort the grieving wife as best I can, and then I turn, and leaning against the rail, make the sign of the cross in the air above the corpse.

Why do I believe? I believe for the reasons Buechner believes, "because certain uncertain things have happened," because of beauty, because of glimpses and moments and hope. I believe even in the absence of such things, "without the miracles I have prayed for then," when "none of the questions that I have come with are answered except as the silence is the answer" (*Alphabet of Grace* 49, 45).

Why do I believe? I'll first have to tell you a story, I'll first have to tell you the things I have heard and the things I have seen. My wife in her bathrobe, playing solitaire on the basement computer. Maggie practicing Mozart on her French horn, the beautiful, swelling music pouring out of a room so strewn with dirty clothes she can barely get across it. Later I might use the language of tradition and faith to explain these moments— and I think they can explain these moments, at least a little; they can help me to tell you what I think they could mean—but in the end it's the stories themselves that remain, the light on the water, the dead man's eyes. In the end it's the sight and the sound and the touch of things that seems real and irreducible to me, and the best I can do is tell you that. The best I can do is tell you that yes, these things certainly happened, whatever they might mean. They really did.

The student chapel in college, when I was an undergraduate, bare empty space, nothing but carpet, sunlight coming through the dusty windows. I am reading Wordsworth, the page of my *Norton Anthology* open to "Michael," and as the sun falls on that plain and spare and moving language I feel something gathering inside me, some confidence or longing or hope, coming together and rising.

The day at Mount Angel when the poems start pouring out, unexpected, useless, free. The plunging into the sea of stories, Odysseus naked and tossed in the waves, thrown up on shore at the mercy of the beautiful young maid. And the sun is shining through my windows and my students are looking up at me, listening hard.

My son on the sidelines giving himself up to the game so completely. The ball falling and falling into the empty net.

## Teaching as Believing

We come back, then, to the theme of education, to the relationship of faith and the university.

In light of our reading of Augustine and of the tradition, that relationship suddenly gets more complicated.

On one level the scandal is merely personal, since in teaching Augustine that gray winter day I am teaching what I myself believe. Augustine's longing for God is my longing. Augustine's sense of God's presence is my own sense of his presence. Augustine's conviction that reason is limited is my own conviction. Faculty are supposed to be objective, of course, faculty are supposed to be detached, but I'm not, not that day. I'm professing what I most dearly love, what I hope beyond hope is true.

But something complicates the scandal, there's a tremendous irony, because in professing what I believe in that moment I am also professing what the university believes.

My argument has been that the metaphor and density of the Christian classics lend themselves especially well to the critical thinking that the university is all about. Now that argument expands: that the central theme of these works, their consistent and explicit point, is the need for exactly such critical thinking and intellectual humility in the face of God's enormous mercy. Suddenly Augustine names everything we've been talking about as Christian, now identifies all the previous chapters as making up one essential stage in the way of faith.

If this is what Christianity is really all about, if this is really orthodoxy, the aims and methods of faith are very close to the aims and methods of the university.

---

An image.

Every Wednesday when I was doing a communion service on campus, I kept the Eucharist in my briefcase, safe in its pyx, hidden among my books and papers and thermos, taking it out now and then only as a specimen, an example of point of view, one among many. But these are consecrated hosts, they are the blessed body, they contain and enact the dying of Christ and the rising of Christ, the paradox of loss that leads to recovery, and teaching Augustine that gray winter day I feel this paradox breaking out and expanding, becoming the whole truth, even in the classroom, not an option but a lens, not a specimen but an engine, a key.

A figure: the figure of Mary, in the Gospel of Luke, Mary the ideal reader, Mary the figure of the intellectual, the only one who seems to get it, the one who does what Peter and the others fail to do, who dies to her self and so lives. Mary the deacon, Mary the mother of deacons, Mary the mother of diaconal knowing.

The angel Gabriel first makes an announcement to Zechariah, that he will be the father of John the Baptist, but his response is to ask, "How can I know this is so," the emphasis on the word "know," *gnosis*, implying the desire to master the message, shrink it to something manageable (1:18). Zechariah is more like Coleridge than Shakespeare in Keats's famous comparison, irritably reaching after fact and certainty, and that reaching so irritates the angel that he strikes Zechariah dumb.

Mary's response to the angel when he comes to her, when he announces that she will be the mother of God himself, Mary's response is very different, and not just because she says "Here I am, the servant of the Lord" (1:38), not because she's passive, a doormat, mindless. On the contrary, Mary was "much perplexed by his words and pondered what sort of greeting this might be" (1:29). She "treasured all these things and pondered them in her heart" (2:19). Mary's response is ongoing, reflective, active, engaged, much more like Ricouer's "second naïveté" than a first, simple, unreasoning naïveté, a choice, not an acquiescence, and one that must be made in the face of continuing doubts and questions.

One of the verbs for "pondered" here is from the Greek *sumballo*, from the words for throw, *ballo*, and union, *sum*.[26] To ponder in this sense is to throw together. It's to juggle. It's an active keeping of different ideas in the air, in motion, not a mere tossing, not a gentle dropping, but a throwing, active and vigorous and involving the coordination of lots of different elements. It means: "to combine, to converse, consult, dispute (mentally), to consider, to confer, encounter, meet with, ponder," far richer connotations than the English "ponder" can evoke. The irony is that it's Zechariah the priest, the man in the sanctuary, who doesn't get it. It's Mary, a woman barred from the sacred things, denied the scrolls, who embodies here not only the Christian ideal of reading, but the Hebrew ideal of the student of the Torah, studying and meditating and pondering in the way celebrated by the Psalms, not the righteous man but the righteous woman who mumbles and coos the words of the law day and night. In this oral culture to read well means in part to internalize the heard text through constant memorization so that in the end the words are taken into the body, eaten the way Ezekiel swallows the scroll. Mary has done more than eaten the words. She is pregnant with them. The implication is of commitment, alertness, suffering. It's of process—the process that both Gadamer and Ricouer describe, the hermeneutics of suffering, then of wager, of leaping into the tradition with the full autonomy of independent thought.

What's negative about this capability is that Mary can obey the angel and live her life without having understood the paradoxes of Gabriel's announcements. What's remarkable about her acceptance of God's will is that it comes in the midst of confusions and struggling. Even years later, when she and her husband discover Jesus discoursing with the rabbis in the temple, they "did not understand what he said to them" (2:50). Even for Mary the mystery of the incarnation is hidden, obscured in the growing up of this otherwise ordinary boy just as it was first obscured in her womb, and she must keep reading the boy, studying him. It's not obvious. In a sense Mary is always doing what she does those frantic few days in the temple, searching for Christ, searching for Jesus, searching in just the sense of *darash* and *midrash*, reading between the lines. The life of Jesus is "a sign to be opposed," as the prophet Simeon says, a sign opposed exactly because it is so difficult to interpret, so hard to accept (2:33).

What organizes and sustains this life of searching are the traditions of Judaism, the living in accord with the daily and seasonal demands of the faith, going up to Jerusalem for the Passover, doing "everything required by the law of the Lord" (2:24). Zechariah's tongue is finally loosened only at the liturgy of his son's circumcision and naming. Culture is the hermeneutic in the end, as Louth insists. Mary searches for Jesus in the temple, in an institution, because it's only in institutions, with other people, through history, that we can ever hope to grasp the meaning of the stories we have been born into.

Zechariah's great hymn of praise, the *Benedictus*, affirms that there is a "way of peace," a way much like "the road" or "way" that the disciples travel in the Emmaus story, the story that ends the Gospel of Luke as Mary's story begins it (1:68–79). The echo seems deliberate. The Annunciation and the Emmaus story frame the Gospel of Luke as if in one overarching *inclusio*, as if Luke is deliberately calling our attention to the issue of interpretation, calling our attention to the way in which the gospel should be read. The very day of the resurrection, two unknowing disciples walk down a road outside Jerusalem, tired and discouraged and confused, the dust on their sandals, their mouths dry, when a stranger falls in alongside them, walking along through the same landscape and breathing the same air, asking questions. It is only gradually, as the stranger begins to interpret the Scriptures, that the hearts of the disciples begin to "burn," that little by little they warm to the man they have come across, until all at once, at the breaking of the bread, they recognize the presence of Christ in their midst. Then he vanishes (24:13–35).

Revelation is often not like the angels but subtle, fleeting, a blink of an eye, a certain angle of vision. This is the nature of the Emmaus experience, just as it is the nature of all the post-resurrection experiences, a quality of the fleeting, the limnal, the indirect. To know such an experience is not to possess it once and for all but live with it, over time. To know such an experience requires us to walk down the road of custom and tradition acted out most of all by the Eucharist, the symbolic meal that the Emmaus story clearly represents. They know him, we are told, only in "the breaking of the bread" (24:35), only in the celebration of a ritual that carries on day-to-day the teaching of Christ, carries it on concretely, humanly, as action not as concept, as an event to be experienced again and again, over time. It is through liturgy that the church preserves what Basil call the "unwritten teachings . . . unintentionally transmitted by custom," the silent truths protected by the "use" of the "unperverted churches" as they worship over the years. The truth is always "silent." It can't be spoken, only experienced (98–102).

Orthodoxy itself isn't a set of contents to be enunciated and then assented to. It is a process. As Kasper puts it, orthodoxy "is not a fixed standpoint—it is a way, the way which the church takes, and which the person takes with the church" (103). It is the road to Emmaus, the road that Mary is the first to walk down.

It's Mary who stays in the mind of the church as the ideal of the reader, coming down through the centuries in paintings and icons and songs and poems as our model of reception, of self-emptying and openness. In the icons the angel is always coming in from the left, Mary always reeling back slightly, in alarm or surprise. Later in the Middle Ages and the Renaissance, the painters show her with a book in her lap, reading. In its meditations on Mary over the centuries the church comes to see its own identity. This is a central idea in Newman's thought, in fact, Mary the icon of what he most believes as both a Christian and an intellectual. As he puts it before his conversion, in a sermon addressed to the university community at Oxford, Mary is the symbol "not only of the faith of the unlearned, but of the doctors of the Church also, who have to investigate, and weigh, and define, as well as profess the Gospel." She

> is our pattern of Faith, both in the reception and in the study of Divine Truth. She does not think it enough to accept, she dwells upon it; not enough to possess, she uses it; not enough to assent, she developes it; not enough to submit to Reason, she reasons upon it; not indeed reasoning first, and believing afterwards, with Zechariah, yet first believing without reasoning, next from love and reverence, reasoning after believing. (*University Sermons* 312–13)

Story is first, as belief is first, all our abstractions and interpretations coming later, all of them evolving and changing as the mystery presents itself to us in ever new forms and ways. Humility then combines with strength, the strength of active and sustained and uncompromising reflection. Reason is all the more important and necessary when it's seen as secondary, because its work is never finished. It must always continue.

A Sunday morning. The nine o'clock Mass.

I worry so much about the boundaries between the academic and the religious life, between university and church. I feel such tension sometimes as I try to move back and forth from one world to another. But for a moment that Sunday the boundaries again fall away and there is one world after all. There are no lines to cross, or the lines seem far away, or the crossing seems spacious and wide, and what I'm preaching to the congregation, standing in my alb and my stole, is exactly what I was lecturing about in class a few days earlier, no different in content at all.

The gospel text is Luke's account of the Annunciation, when the angel appears to Mary.

Mary is one tough and realistic young woman.

She knows that to believe in God is to come into contact with a mystery so great it overwhelms us. She knows that to believe in God is to be troubled, it's to wonder. She's the mother of those who are troubled, the mother of those who wonder.

A strange man, an angel, has just promised her pregnancy without sex and a child without marriage. The angel has just promised her something completely unbelievable. Of course she's going to be deeply "perplexed" by the angel's words. Of course she's going to "ponder what sort of greeting this might be," as Luke puts it in this great story of the Annunciation. We're dealing with an angel here, not the UPS man. We're dealing with mysteries.

And for me this is profoundly reassuring. A lot of us are under great pressure, a lot of us are despairing, a lot of us can't understand why things happen the way they do, and Mary is the best model of all for how we should handle this.

The story of the Annunciation, of course, is always read during Advent, and during Advent we're supposed to be at peace with the world. It's time for warm moments by the fire, laughter in the malls. So why does an airplane go down? Why does a child die? Why does a family pull apart? Divorce and cancer and just the slow progress of the years—what do they mean? Even our happiness is inexplicable, in its suddenness, its brightness. Sometimes our flashes of joy are so brief it's hard to credit them. And what can they mean when there's so much suffering in the world? How can they be valid in the context of so much suffering?

This is what Mary is wondering, too, I think, and what she never figures out because it can't be figured out. This is what I wonder about every day, as I know we all do, too, and it's terribly important that we not feel somehow un-Christian when we do this, as if we're betraying our faith.

The story of the Annunciation describes the exact moment of the Incarnation, the exact moment when everything begins, everything becomes possible, and it's a moment when nothing is clear, nothing makes sense. The Lord is with you, the Angel says, just then, that very second.

To be troubled is to be Christian. To be troubled is to be in relation with God.

I go on to talk about Augustine and to share the discussion in the Literature of Western Civilization class, alluding, too, to von Hügel and, indirectly, to the idea of *lex orandi, lex credendi*. After quoting the pivotal passage in book 6 of the *Confessions*, where Augustine accepts Catholicism because it doesn't promise "certain knowledge," I conclude:

> von Hügel must have this passage in mind when he celebrates what can never be clear. We must always have it in mind. It's the key to faith. It's Mary's intuition: that so much is unexplained and that we have to live with that and let it overshadow us and take it into ourselves, on faith, never knowing because it can't finally be known.
>
> And then all joy is possible. What's so magnificent about Mary is that she says yes to God even when she doesn't have everything figured out. She takes an enormous risk, she opens herself up to the mystery there in front of her, overshadowing her, and suddenly it's inside her, leaping up, and she is full of grace, she is alive with faith that can't ever be put into words.
>
> This is the sequence. It's not, you understand, therefore you believe; but, life is a mystery and you say yes to it in all its complexity. And then: the Lord is with you.
>
> As Augustine puts it earlier, he'd much rather that we find God in our uncertainty than in our certainty to miss him.
>
> Nothing is more important than that we free ourselves of a false idea of faith, one that no one can really hold to for long because it's so unrealistic and silly. What Christianity really promises is so much deeper and sweeter and more various. What Christianity really promises is so much truer, so true that it can't be reduced to Augustine's 7 plus 3 or von Hügel's 2 plus 2. You can't be argued into it. You've got to be overshadowed, you've got to feel the presence of the Lord both so vast and so subtle all you can do is take it into yourself.

Of course the style of the homily is different from the style of a lecture, less detailed, more direct. And of course in the largest and most obvious way the aims of the homily are different from the aims of the class. A preacher urges the congregation to believe and to act on that belief in their lives. A university class on Augustine, like a class on the Bible, sets out to do something quite different, at least most generally, at least on one level. It doesn't ask the students to believe but to believe that Augustine did, that the gospel writers did, in these ways, in these terms. A university class shares an interpretation of a content, of a historical process, of historical facts: these people believed these things.

But the Augustine homily raises a complicated issue, brings the paradox out in the open. There is nonetheless a conjunction here, a conjunction that can't be evaded simply by claiming it to be private, and the students sense this, as they always do. Students always sense when a teacher isn't being objective, when a teacher has an agenda, as teachers always have and always should have. Teaching isn't preaching, but neither is it detached.

One of the students from the Augustine class comes to hear me preach that Sunday. She is sitting in the congregation with a friend, curious, probably, to see what a professor would say in such a different setting. She's newly converted to a nondenominational group on campus. She has no experience with Catholicism. And she's outraged, as taken aback as Mary, though far from seeing me as an angel or accepting what I announce:

> *I was so shocked and upset when I heard you in church saying exactly the same things you'd been saying to us in class. What gives you the right to be preaching to us in a class this way, without warning us that this is what you're doing? You're not supposed to do that! You're supposed to keep your own beliefs out of teaching and not force us to believe as you do.*

Katie is right in this e-mail: I'm *not* just identifying a bias when I teach Augustine in the Literature of Western Civilization. I'm *not* just showing how I think. I am trying through example and analysis to encourage my students to think in a certain way themselves, I am urging on them values that are also Christians values, I am trying to convert them into reading in ways that Christians also read—not to become Christian but to take from Christianity its humility and precision.

Because what seems clear this day in the classroom teaching Augustine is that humility and precision are exactly what a public university should be teaching, exactly what it's about. This humility and precision are exactly the basis of the intellectual method that state universities can and do and should promote, not objectively, not as a mere option among others, but as value and obligation and good.[28]

Mary is the figure not just of the reader of the Bible but of the reader of anything, of the intellectual, embodying all the virtues of ecological thinking. Her capacity to dwell and use and develop and reason, in

Newman's words, is just the capacity universities are designed to teach. "To combine and converse and dispute and encounter and meet with"—the meaning of the word "ponder"—is just what English Departments and all departments do every day. The task of the university is always to counter the kind of foolish, dangerous two-dimensionality behind much fundamentalism in our culture today—behind much racism, sexism—behind all the isms—and for this Mary is a powerful model. The pondering and treasuring and juggling that she does wouldn't be necessary at all if the message were self-evident or a guarantee of bliss forevermore, and that's Luke's point, too. By placing this story where he does he is suggesting from the outset that we are to read the gospel with far more struggle and engagement and uncertainty than many contemporary readers ever imagine is necessary. So should we read everything else, so universities exist to teach us.

"Once I was found and now I am lost" is the plot of university education even as it is the plot of Christian autobiography. What a liberal arts education is designed to do is complicate and slow and mess things up enough that charity and courtesy and process and revision become the basis of method.

In *The Soul of the American University*, George Marsden tells the story of how the American university began in an assumed alliance of Protestant values and democratic aims—an alliance problematic and doomed from the start. The religious element of the mix was soon absorbed into the political and tamed by it, lost, become now a way to exclude and homogenize, the holy *really* flattened and reduced, a cover for the xenophobic. This is not the kind of relation I mean. What I experience now and then in my teaching is more basic, more fundamental, not American or democratic but essential to all genuine critical thinking, all mature intellectual work, all response to the world—fundamental to the real and original work of the university, which is to find the truth. This is the truth, the truth that Christianity sees: the world is mystery. This is the method, the method that Christianity creates: to read that mystery over time, again and again, in all humility.

Augustine's forest of meanings is the forest of Leopold's deep ecological concern, is the Drift Creek Wilderness, is the forest of all meaning at the university, intricate and interrelated, systems within systems in which the tiniest details matter.

"What we need," Ricouer says again, declaring, as a Christian himself, what can be taken as the aims of the university, "is an interpretation that respects the original enigma of the symbols, that lets itself be taught by them, but that, beginning from there, promotes the meaning, forms the meaning in the full responsibility of thought" (349–50). A university should respect the original enigma behind the symbols and promote free and responsible and competing interpretations of that enigma.

Christianity is not the only way to accomplish this end. Many religious and philosophical traditions approach it. Students need not convert in order to succeed in the university, only respect and incorporate the values underneath Christian methods of reading as they are underneath other methods as well.

But Christianity is one of those traditions, one of those methods, entirely congruent with the professed aims of the university, aims not in the least objective but rightly insisting on commitments carried out with a certain broad charity. What we could wish for our students of whatever faith or variety of doubt is just what the Biblical writers attain: a concreteness, a multiplicity. We could do no better than to hold up as a model Augustine's *Confessions*, for its passion and its drive for connection, for its grounding in the person, for its combining of the personal and the intellectual, for its impatience with the superficial and the partial, for its love of truth even and especially when it is so very difficult to find.

# PART THREE

# The Way of Faith

CHAPTER 5

# Moving Beyond the University

Chapters 1 and 2 were grounded in Newman's momentary concession that a "line" exists between the way of the university and the way of faith. The last two chapters have been grounded in his rejection of that idea. God is too big, God is everywhere, he says, overflowing, and so nothing is free of his presence and his urgings and his structures, not even the work of a chemist or a linguist.

But in the end, there is a line after all. In the end Newman makes his most important point, that intellect alone is never enough and so the university is never enough. Though the university is not at odds with faith, it can't save us:

> Knowledge is one thing, virtue another; good sense is not conscience, refinement is not humility, nor is largeness and justness of view faith. [. . .] It is well to have a cultivated intellect, a delicate taste, a candid, equitable mind, a noble and courteous bearing in the conduct of life— these are the connatural qualities of a large knowledge; they are the objects of the University; I am advocating, I shall illustrate and insist upon them; but still, I repeat, they are no guarantee for sanctity or even for conscientiousness. (89; 1.5.9)

In this central passage from *The Idea of the University*, there is distinction after distinction, boundary after boundary, and it's the same boundary that I have been trying to describe. Liberal education is a good thing. It cultivates a discerning intellect and a delicate taste, and intellect and taste are good and necessary. "I am advocating, I shall illustrate and insist upon them," Newman says. But they are not virtues, in themselves. They do not lead to salvation, necessarily. However important the university is as training ground and preparation and foundation, "liberal education makes not the Christian, not the Catholic, but the gentleman."

Ricouer would say that the purpose of the university is to point out the provisional nature of our interpretations. But finally: we have to choose. We have to name our experience in a specific way—we all do, whether we admit it or not—and as Christians we name our experience Christ, and as Christians we believe that this choice and this name are a response to a reality.

Or the cross. Because the beams of faith and the university are broad and wide, their intersection is broad and wide. The *Odyssey* exists in that intersection and the *Confessions* exists in that intersection and from within that intersection a critique can be made that might help to reform the university. But ultimately that vertical beam continues past the borders of the classroom and extends out of sight. The vertical beam of faith is a road, it is a way, and it arrives at somewhere in particular. It is the road to Emmaus, and it ends at a table in the evening where two friends and a stranger sit down to break bread. Then the stranger is revealed, and vanishes (Luke 24:13-35).

The next two chapters explore the creative tension between faith and the university, returning to the theory of education in the second chapter, now with more nuance and qualification, and to my own experience as a believer, at the seminary and in my everyday life. They also carry forward my discussion of what orthodoxy means in Augustine and in the whole tradition. I begin in this chapter with a representative story, which then gives rise to a sequence of related claims, which then leads to the argument of the final chapter, to the central paradox of the book: that Christianity can contribute to the university only by staying apart from it.

The story is about my crossing of a street. It is also about the cross itself, as all stories are.

## Teaching Good Friday

It's Good Friday, the day that we crucified the Lord, and I have returned for a moment to the Gospel of Mark and his description of the crucifixion, though it is spring in the Literature of Western Civilization and we have gone on to read Tolstoy and Kafka and the moderns. Spring fever has broken out and there have been problems lately with attendance and sloppy work. Several new students have joined the class, students with an intellectual chip on their shoulder or who seem to specialize in a kind of detached, postmodern cool.

Some of the journal entries have been recalcitrant, resisting. The new students seem to see me as overenthusiastic. "During this term," Melissa writes, "we have talked a lot about Christianity but not about any of the reasons that some people might feel uncomfortable with Christianity." For Melissa, a sympathetic treatment of the Christian tradition is suspect, given her own experience growing up. She sees me deliberately "overlooking" a set of very important issues. "Unfortunately I, like a lot of people, have had an unsavory experience with people professing to be Christians." This is the atmosphere in the class lately, and it's made me wary.

I try to begin.

The soldiers mock Jesus, weaving for him a crown of thorns. Hail, King of the Jews, they cry out, the name a joke, a jeer. As he hangs on the cross he is mockingly named again, by the people and the chief priests— "Let the Messiah come down from the cross" (15:32)—and what they mean of course is that Jesus is not the Messiah. They are naming him as a fake, a pretender, merely human after all. Later, as Jesus cries out, quoting the great psalm of lament, Psalm 22—My God, my God why have you forsaken me—the bystanders shift their interpretation. They misinterpret, in fact, thinking that maybe Jesus is asking for Elijah the prophet to come down and rescue him, that perhaps there will be a display of power after all. But it doesn't happen. Though the curtain splits in two when Jesus breathes his last, he breathes his last. He dies. There is no display of power, there is only self-emptying, radical self-emptying. There is only silence. It's only the centurion, as we have seen, who in a sense gets it right, looking up at Jesus and naming him as Mark seems to want us to name him: surely this man was the Son of God.

But look, I say. Mark observes his great authorial silence at the most important moment of all. Here is the cross, on a hill, here are the soldiers and the people and the chief priests and scribes standing around it and interpreting it, providing for us a number of possible names for it, and Mark doesn't intervene. He doesn't tell us explicitly how he wants us to understand this image, this silence, except perhaps in the carefully structured sequence that leads to the words of the centurion. But this is showing, not telling, literary technique, not moralizing. Mark is imitating Jesus himself in this terrible and overpowering scene that we remember on Good Friday each year. Mark is imitating Jesus who says nothing except once to cry out in pain and questioning, Jesus who except for that cry is entirely silent, entirely undefended, who offers his body to be looked at and read. Mark honors this silence with his own, not telling us which name we must choose. The effect, I say, is to put all of us as readers, at this moment, in the same position as the people standing around the cross in the story. We are confronted by the cross. We must name it.

"Well, all I see when I see the cross is oppression and hypocrisy." This from a student in the front row.

"All I see is the Inquisition, all I see are the Crusades," another says.

"I just can't get past all those people knocking on my doors all the time," another joins in, "all those people asking if Jesus Christ is my personal savior."

A ripple of laughter.

Someone in the back is reading the student newspaper.

Another student walks in late, carrying a skateboard.

It's Good Friday, this is the story of the crucifixion, I can't read it without being moved, and to have that emotion countered with a kind of jokey indifference seems like a criticism of the emotion itself. A slap. A put down.

But I try one more time to rise above the mood and open up the discussion. "OK, OK, that's of course valid in many ways. Christianity has done a lot of bad things and our memory of those things is part of the baggage we bring to the reading of this scene. Of course. That's part of why we read, to become aware of those assumptions and frames."

"But look. Let's try to 'forget' those assumptions for a minute, in the way that David Tracy suggests. Let's try to set them aside and look at the scene fresh, as if we've never read it before. Let's try to enter into Mark's authorial silence."

"What's so moving for me in the scene is how it forces us into acts of interpretation, whatever they are. Here's the mystery, here's the cross. It's right there, on the hill, and we have to be related to it. We are related to it. That's what John Shea means, I think, when he says that 'we are all inescapably related to mystery.' Don't even think of it in Christian terms. Think just of mystery giving rise to story giving rise to thought. We are all related to that mystery, whatever our stories, whatever our names for it."

"I'm not related to mystery," Tina says. "I'm not related at all."

And that's it. The floor drops away. My mouth is dry, my knees are weak, the moment becomes among other things a moment of public shame—irrationally, since that handful of students is simply being casual and small. But I have been worked up, I have been identifying with the material in very personal ways, and in the face of the class's amused indifference I can't help but feel that maybe I have lost control. The mechanisms of shame are deep and mysterious. For whatever reason the period becomes one of those that Palmer in *The Courage to Teach* encourages us to describe, a day that I wish I had never been born. The floor drops away, my emotions rise, and all I do the rest of the fifty minutes is talk, lecturing on the history of interpretation.

---

Let this moment stand, as a composite, of many such experiences, not just with students but with colleagues as well, moments when resistance doesn't clarify my thoughts but confuses them, moments when my best intentions are stymied and opposed, moments when I come home from the university beaten and drained, feeling like a fool, tired of being the token Christian. "I look out of myself into the world," Newman says in the *Apologia*, "and there I see a sight which fills me with unspeakable distress." That's how it sometimes feels, on the bad days. "The world seems simply to give the lie to that great truth, of which my whole being is so full" (260).

I feel anger, too, when the shame begins to fade, and with it the clarity that can come from anger. Christianity is the source of good things, too. It gives us Dante, it gives us the civil rights movement, it gives us the university itself, it gives us the literary theory governing the very things we are doing in the classroom that day. The Christian tradition is a rich and complex tradition, full of everything human, both suspect and noble, but when the average student comes into contact with Christian institutions she applies to them a skepticism far more thorough and dismissive than she applies to any other.[29] Students willingly and rightly accept the committed feminism of their other professors. They willingly and rightly accept the committed environmentalism of their other professors. They willingly and rightly respect the gender of their professors in women's studies and the race of their professors in ethnic studies, realizing, as they should, that who we are in our bodies and our lives is everywhere connected to what we think and what we know. But when it comes to Christianity, when it comes to a Christian professor teaching a Christian text, when it comes to any contact with Christian ideas, suddenly my students and even many of my colleagues devolve into old-fashioned Enlightenment rationalists, suspicious of bias, on the lookout for any trace of commitment.

But if this is my anger, a kind of intellectual anger, if this is the critique that emerges when the shame has evaporated, it is not what defines my reactions that Friday or most Fridays. The experience that I am describing is just that, an experience, a matter not of ideas but of something felt, and what I feel most of all on many Fridays isn't a desire to debate or reform but a desire to flee, to escape, to find refuge. Anger isn't the dominant feeling. It's exhaustion—and then, rising up out of that, a longing, a desire, a thirst. "As the deer longs for flowing streams," the Psalmist says, "so my soul longs for you, O God." "My soul thirsts for God, / for the living God" (Psalm 42).

There are days in my teaching when I can confidently confess my Christianity as a way of demonstrating the situatedness of all reading. There are days when my faith seems congruent with the aims of the university, when there is overlap and intersection. But there are moments of tension and loss as well, moments when the university swamps and wounds and defeats me, as it swamps and wounds us all, I think— moments when it flattens me, moments when it bores me—moments when I am sure in my hurt and my longing that the university is not enough, it is not where I belong, it is not my home.

So I cross the line.

I walk out the door of the classroom and the doors of the brick building that English shares with psychology and off across campus through the leafy quads and the crowds of students and across Monroe, the strip of pizza joints and coffee shops that defines the border between campus and town, past the fraternities and the apartments and the old houses, until a few blocks further up I reach the church—I reach St. Mary's—and crossing the threshold find myself home.

---

It's Good Friday and I am the deacon, standing on the altar, holding up a large wooden cross, an hour after my disastrous class. I've had to hurry to make it, cutting across the lawns and the parking lots, throwing on an alb before processing up with the priest. The first readings were read and I proclaimed the gospel, the passion according to John, John's version of the story that Mark tells with such spareness, and now I am standing with the priest supporting a large wooden cross as the people file up the center aisle, genuflecting before it or touching it or kissing it. The cross bumps and shifts with the pressure of each contact: a little girl in a pink t-shirt, kissing it near the bottom, an old woman in a walker reaching out with her hand, a man wrapping both arms around the vertical beam.

The cross is made of two large 6 x 12's of oak. It must weigh a hundred pounds. The priest stands on one side and I stand on the other, both of us supporting it from behind, lifting up our arms. Mine have grown numb. My left hand pushes against the horizontal beam, my right against the vertical. My back spasms from the weight.

The church is silent except for the chanting of the choir. I've been standing for half an hour now as hundreds of people wait their turn, kneel, cross themselves, reach out. The silence settles inside of me. Conviction deepens again. Joy.

The cross that I am holding up isn't merely an example for me now, it isn't merely an option, it isn't merely a token, it isn't merely a marker in some critical thinking exercise. I'm not stepping aside from it and explaining its function and history and meaning, pointing out the gaps to be filled and interpretations to be made. I am venerating it. I am professing it. I am claiming it, with longing and hope and faith and love, embracing it myself, as truth and light and the meaning of things, and I do this out of need, my own need. I am praying, humbling myself before it, standing behind it, and it's this cross, this particular cross in this exact moment that I am supporting, steadying for the people to touch—not a cross on a page, not the idea of a cross, not the idea of symbol itself in all its varieties and cultural manifestations. This cross, these two oaken beams. This weight. This joy.

Because we don't just die. We live. We don't just interpret, we believe, in particular, here and now.

In the class we had removed all the names, we had exposed the names as interpretations among others, possibilities always suspect, in order to get as close as we could to the original complexity underneath, the mystery, the reality that exceeds us. But now I have put the name back, reinstated the suspended meaning, and it's single, it's real. This cross. This heavy wooden cross. "There is no way to gloss over this specification," O'Connor says. Christians don't just believe, she says. They believe in a person. They believe in the infinite narrowing itself down to a particular point, a particular body, a particular moment. The Christian God, O'Connor says,

> is an unlimited God and one who has revealed himself specifically. It is one who became man and rose from the dead. It is one who confounds the senses and the sensibilities, one known early on as a stumbling block. There is no way to gloss over this specification or to make it more acceptable to modern thought. This God is the object of ultimate concern and he has a name. (161)

We move from a first naïveté and innocence and ignorance into a difficult stage of analysis and unmasking, of realizing that what we first thought was true is contested and constructed. But then we make a leap. We make a wager. We give in, we let go, and we reach another stage, a higher one, the one that Ricouer calls the stage of second naïveté, where in spite and even because of all the suffering and analysis that we have endured we believe anyway, we believe again, we enter into the realm of joy and conviction, knowing it now not as fact but as choice, as risk, as faith. As beyond us. But we are there again, in faith. We are there again but more deeply, more fully.

When I read the gospel aloud Good Friday or any day, I'm not interpreting it, I'm proclaiming it. I process in with it, make the sign of the cross over it before I read it, kiss the page when I'm finished. And it's not the words on the page but the words in the air that are proclaimed, and they are alive, happening now. And I believe them, I enter into them fully, as I've done before, as I've done many times before—as I did at the seminary, in the oak grove reading Louth; as I did at exit 244, beneath

the apple trees with my son—which is why I have an interpretive position to begin with, why I have a point of view that I can identify in the
first chapter and fall into in the third. I don't arrive at this position after
or outside class, I come to class with it already in place and work to keep
it suspended, to take it off and hang it up, one garment among the others. It's always already there. mystery gives rise to story and story gives
rise to thought and I am at the stage of thought now, as I hold up the
cross and the people come forward. I have chosen a "thought." I have
recommitted myself yet again to the very idea that in class I unmasked. I
can feel it in my hands, in the numbing of my arms.

There are many voices here but they are either silent or chanting the
same song. There are many people here but they are all streaming to the
cross. The church is an enclosed space, bounded and safe, but once inside
it we seem to open and expand, moving ever outward.

But there's more involved in this moment than escape from the
tumult. What is gained from surrender goes deeper than peace. A world
is gained, a truth. What proceeds from that peace is an openness to a
reality beyond all others. When we surrender our will and our reason,
when we do what the cross itself invites us to do and die to ourselves, to
our own ideas, our own language, our own striving, when we weep in the
garden and listen to the voices of the children—take and read, take and
read—suddenly the mystery itself can come rushing in, can overwhelm us
fully, can reveal itself. When we give in and let go suddenly we become
aware again of the very mystery that started the whole interpretive
sequence from story to thought, the mystery we have lost sight of in the
midst of our analysis and rethinking. But now it's here again, breaking
through, at just the moment of our interpretive failure, just the moment
of our exhaustion. What the cross embodies isn't just the crucifixion but
the resurrection, and we experience that resurrection now, internally,
personally, emotionally. "How glad I was to give up the things I had been
so afraid to lose," Augustine says in the *Confessions*, later, when he has
made his turn:

> For you cast them out from me, you true and supreme sweetness; you
> cast them out from me and you entered in to me to take their place,
> sweeter than all pleasure, but not to flesh and blood; brighter than all
> light, but more inward than all hidden depths; higher than all honor,
> but not to those who are high in themselves. Now my mind was free
> of those gnawing cares that came from ambition and the desire for
> gain [. . .] and now I was talking to you easily and simply, my bright-
> ness and my riches and my health, my Lord God. (184–85; 9.1)

We go through the stages of the sequence, the steps of the cycle, and suddenly, at the end of it, we make the radical shift into joy. And from that

joy we read backwards now through the steps we have taken. We turn the sequence upside down and start over again, from joy. The world makes sense. A new kind of knowledge has been granted, a knowledge that can't be gained through effort of will and that can't be explained in words.

Yes, Lord, I believe.

"I no longer desired to be more certain of you," Augustine says after his conversion, "but only to stand more firmly in you" (160; 8.1).

We cross the line, we cross campus and Monroe street, we cross the threshold of the church and so escape from the urge for certainty, the constant drive for answers and proofs, from the uncertainty and the multiplicity and the endless alternative readings and we leap, we make what Ricouer calls the "transcendental deduction"—we abandon the fruitless search for answers and all at once God in his sweetness takes the place of that searching, God himself, knowing us, searching for us—and now we are standing firmly, firmly in God, we are standing behind the cross, the two 6 x 12 beams, our arms growing numb, tears in our eyes, because it's true, it's all true, and it's true here, it's true now, it's true in this way.

Here I stand I can do no other, Luther said.

*Here* I stand: at St. Mary's, on a Friday, a Good Friday, the rain falling on the roof.

And it's I who is standing, me, this professor of English, this deacon, five foot seven, hair graying.

And I am *standing*: not thinking, not abstracting, not analyzing, but standing with my own two feet on the frayed red carpet of this church and no other.

I can do no other. I have made this choice—me, for myself—I can't speak for others, I can't judge what others have done or should do—I'm too busy holding up this cross to judge anyone else, I'm too occupied with praying and with the joy I so seldom feel and never feel for very long but am feeling here and now, the joy that comes through the pain of the crucifixion, the triumph that comes after the jeering, that joy comes flooding through me as it so seldom does but is now, here in this place.

We are not the chief priests and the elders. We are not the jeering crowds. We are the centurion, standing at the foot of the cross, looking up at Jesus of Nazareth.

Surely this man was the Son of God.

Surely. This man.

## That There is a Line

My Good Friday experience, in both parts, can be taken as an emblem of the right relation between the university and the church, a way of

clarifying and extending my discussion of Gadamer and Ricouer at the
end of chapter two. Monroe Street is the line that neither should cross—
even on the good days, even on the days of overlap and intersection when
all has gone as well as it can.

The university shows the gaps to be filled, the church fills them. The
university shows the process, the church moves through the process to its
final stage. The university shows the options, the church chooses one.
The university uncovers the fact of interpretation, the church chooses its
interpretation all over again.

And if not the church, if not faith of some sort, Jewish or Muslim or
Buddhist or Hindu, it's other "thoughts" or ideologies or positions or
commitment that supervise the move beyond analysis and reading to
action in the world. Atheism is such a commitment, such a name.
Agnosticism is such a name. Marxism, Freudianism, any variety of postmodernism or feminism or any "ism" whatsoever, any version of an
understanding of ultimate concern, whether that involves believing or
disbelieving in the possibility of a God—these are all the choices and acts
and namings that have to take place on the other side of Monroe Street.

It's not that the university should pretend to a false objectivity. On
the contrary. The way we honor the line is by continually pointing out
that we've crossed it. The way we honor the line is by repeatedly showing *how* we've crossed it and *why* we've crossed it and that we're crossing
it even now. It's by confessing to all our frames of reference, all of us,
together, the more the better. The way to avoid dogma is to multiply
them, to get them all out in the open. As James Kincaid puts it, speaking
of English studies, "we need to teach not the texts themselves but how
we situate ourselves in reference to those texts." We teach any subject by
discussing our various and competing assumptions, showing that these
assumptions are themselves "constructions" and that there is consider-
able debate among them. We teach any subject, he says, by showing that
our assumptions are not themselves "innocent" but "value-laden, interested, ideological" (qtd. in Graff 262). What Ricouer says about the
ethics of the interpreter applies to the university as well: to be honest we
must make presuppositions explicit and state them as beliefs.

The job of the university is to be both plural and generic. Any move
to the specific is a move that has to take place across the boundary. And
this is true even on a good day. Even when a class goes well, even when
the students aren't jeering and resisting, the most that should happen
within that room is a consideration of the line and an awareness of the
various ways that exist to cross it. My exhaustion and hurt on Good
Friday only make more obvious what is always true, that as Moberly puts
it, the duty of the university is not to inculcate a particular position but
to help others in forming one. To quote Ricouer again, in full:

> A philosophy that starts from the fullness of language is a philosophy
> with presuppositions. To be honest, it must make its presuppositions
> explicit, state them as beliefs, wager on the beliefs, and try to make the
> wager pay off in understanding. (357)

Even on a good day the work of the university stops right at the stage of
the wager. Even on a good day the best that I can offer in the classroom
is the cross as one more piece of cultural information and one more kind
of critical analysis, one option among the others.

––––––

Here I've shown my students the magnificent defeat, the greatest
sadness as the way to the greatest joy that has ever been known—here
I've shown them the heartbreaking courage and beauty of the cross—and
they nod and yawn and put it up on the shelf, right between Freud and
Foucault. How can that be?

I will admit that one of my emotions in the Good Friday experience
is the drive to convert, to pull the different fields of the field distribution
model into the one truth, the one way, the one field, the field of the Lord.
Like Newman there is a strong impulse in me to argue that theology
should be allowed on campus because it's true. It's the truth. It's all true.
And my desire to convert in this sense comes as much out of love and
concern as out of anger. If I've found the truth, shouldn't I want to share
it? If I care about Will and Katie and Tina and the others, shouldn't I
want to help them?

But this is just the impulse that I have to resist within the confines of
the university, at least as I know it here in the twenty-first century, in my
own experience. Corvallis isn't Dublin. It's not the Catholic Church but
the Morrell Act that has brought my university into being. The impulse
to convert is an impulse that I can follow only on the other side of
Monroe Street—and that my faith itself forbids me to follow except with
charity and humility, an awareness of what Tracy calls the "intrinsic inadequacy" of any theology, including that of my own tradition. Theology
at best is only "relatively adequate," he says (22), as any interpretation is
only relatively adequate, and most days this is enough, and it has to be.
This is all we have.

Of course, it's not that simple. The whole point of hermeneutics is
that the interpretive sequence isn't neatly linear. It's a cycle, always going
on. We reach the end of one sequence and arrive at a judgment, then the
sequence begins all over again with that judgment in place as a filter or
lens. Because experience is never "without presuppositions," as Ricouer
puts it, subjective values can never be kept out of the university, nicely
assigned to the other side of the divide.

Moreover, there are clearly certain values that the university
does offer as more than mere options. There are certain values that

it endorses, that it espouses, and it should: respect for others, acceptance of diversity, attention to detail, precision of proof, the need for documentation. The intellectual humility that we considered in the second chapter is both a precondition for the interpretation of texts and a consequence of interpretation.

But these are basic, foundational values that all people can share, regardless of faith or variety of doubt, intellectual or civic virtues that people from all traditions can hold in common. In a state university made possible by the Morrell Act, the exchange of ideas is bound by the first amendment. In a state university as in any public institution religious belief should neither be coerced nor prohibited. Individuals are allowed free expression of particular positions as long as they adhere to certain core values, certain generic principles of inclusion and respect. It's not that the institution is assumed to be objective but that it attempts to be democratic, and to be democratic it asks for agreement on the fewest and most generic values possible, the lowest common denominator of subjectively held beliefs.

Newman himself acknowledges this line between the generic and the particular, even in his ideal Catholic university. It's the line between reason and faith. The purpose of a university is to create what Newman calls, in a happy phrase, "intellectual culture." The purpose of a university, any university, is to "cultivate the public mind," giving the student "a clear conscious view of his own opinions and judgments, a truth in developing them, an eloquence in expressing them, and a force in urging them." The university doesn't seek to impose particular opinions or judgments, not at this level, but to provide the intellectual tools necessary for seeing and expressing opinion and judgment generally. "It teaches us to see things as they are, to get right to the point, to disentangle a skein of thought, to detect what is sophistical, and to discard what is irrelevant" (125–26; 1.7.10). These capacities and skills may be called "virtues of the Intellect," virtues that are very good to possess, that have a "social and political usefulness" (127; 1.7.10). But they are primary virtues, not secondary, virtues of critical thinking, and whether they "be viewed within or outside the Church," they "do not necessarily take cognizance of the Creed" (129; 1.8.1). We may acquire these virtues and not become Christian, just as we may freewrite without becoming Christian or read Mary Oliver without becoming Christian or learn to lose in all the ways I described in chapter 3 without taking the next specific step of embracing the cross on Good Friday.

The university doesn't ask for the wager. It doesn't ask for the transcendental deduction. It asks for certain initial understandings and agreements and for the rest is always in the act of unmasking itself. Beyond the level of the intellectual virtues, "what is essential to honest thinking is that presuppositions be uncovered," as Moberly puts it (64), and that's what as faculty we are always trying to do, uncovering our presuppositions, me as a Christian, my colleague as a feminist, another colleague as a Marxist, another colleague as a scientist—for science, too, is never innocent or pure, as scientists themselves are often the first to admit. Science, too, is situated, dependent upon metaphor, always, at its best, conscious of the limits of the language it uses, always suspicious of its own bias, continually testing and retesting. All our interpretations, in every field, must "respect the original enigma," in Ricouer's phrase. Chapel isn't obligatory and neither is consciousness-raising. All that is required at the university is courtesy, respect, and coherent discourse based on proper evidence.

Responding to the impulse to convert our students would be like eating of the tree of the knowledge of good and evil. It's prohibited. The line we shouldn't cross is around that tree—just as, from the point of view of the church, the line is around the tree seen as a symbol of a mystery that can never be understood or reduced.

———

It's of course true that the university is sometimes inconsistent and hypocritical in its treatment of Christianity, allowing every demonstration of bias except that of faith. Feminism is sometimes presented as truth, without self-consciousness or humility, faith dismissed as stupidly subjective. This is true in society at large, where as Stephen Carter has argued the legal system has so misinterpreted the original intentions of the founders as to exclude from the public square nothing but the religious argument. Religion has become the one great exception—wrongly, Carter says. The first amendment bans the imposition of religious belief, not the expression of it:

> The religion clauses of the First Amendment were crafted to permit maximum freedom to the religious. In modern, religiously pluralistic America [. . .] this means that the government should neither force people into sectarian religious observances [. . .] nor favor some religions over others. [. . .] It does not mean, however, that people whose motivations are religious are banned from trying to influence government, nor that the government is banned from listening to them. (105–6)

To honor the Constitution, we should foster what Carter calls genuine "epistemic diversity," where all ways of knowing are allowed to speak. "What is needed [. . .] is a willingness to listen, not because the speaker has the right voice but because the speaker has the right to speak," and if this is true in the public square, it is even more true in the public university. Of course we shouldn't try to convert our students, Moberly agrees, but neither should our conviction be suppressed. Students shouldn't be made Christian, but they should be able to hear the Christian challenge (110, 111).

There's no danger of Christianity once again regaining control of the discussion. Its days of domination are long gone. Christianity is merely one voice in the forest of voices—a voice that perhaps has too often earned the resistance it sometimes faces, too often been guilty of the stereotypes, but a voice that by logic and reason and fairness alone should be included along with the rest.[30]

---

But finally this isn't the interesting argument. This isn't the important point, partly because except now and then in moments of social awkwardness, Christian professors at state universities in fact do have the freedom to join in the forest of voices, do have the freedom to demonstrate their own commitments—at least I do, in my teaching if not in the grants and fellowships that I am eligible for. We all benefit from what Graff calls the "field distribution model," the "systematic nonrelationship" built into the way that professors are hired and courses offered. Because we don't create a curriculum on shared assumptions or articulated differences, all of us are free to do what we want within the certain broad limits, even the Christians. Departments become malls and we can all set up shop. Within the curriculum itself at least I am allowed to demonstrate my Christian values just as my feminist colleagues are allowed to voice theirs, all of us distributed across the curriculum, each of us left to our own devices.

Christianity used to war against academic freedom. Now as a Christian I benefit from that freedom in fact if not always in tone or atmosphere or social welcoming. Christianity used to tyrannize but has now become another minority. There is no center. We are all on the periphery. The Newman Center Mass is allowed to take place at the Memorial Union as are meetings of any other registered student group. The Mass is said alongside discussions of the retirement system or the gay/lesbian alliance. Christianity isn't singled out.

What's really interesting and important is not that Christians have the right to speak but that this right is limited. What's really interesting and important is that there is a line, the line does exist, for Christians as for everyone else. Yes, I was angry and hurt on Good Friday, but I was right to walk across campus and into the church. Yes, I was within my constitutional rights to declare in class that I am a Christian and that I read from a Christian perspective, but it was necessary for me to cross Monroe Street before offering my prayer and praise. It's one thing to say, I believe, another to say, this is true; it's one thing to teach and another to preach—even though teaching always has an element of preaching. And that distinction is important not just from a constitutional perspective or from the perspective of the university but from the Christian perspective itself. I honor it not only because I respect the democratic principles and practical realities of the state university where I teach but because this line, this line between reason and faith, is fundamental to my life as a Christian.

O'Connor puts it starkly. "It would be foolish to say there is no conflict between these two sets of eyes. There is a conflict, and it is a conflict which we escape at our peril" (180).

A conflict, not just a line. A tension.

———

I intended the moments teaching the *Odyssey* and the *Confessions* in chapters 3 and 4 to be provocative, to suggest unusual and misunderstood connections. But maybe these stories are not so provocative after all. Maybe in the end there's nothing really scandalous about these experiences of overlap and intersection.

The university in the West has Christian foundations, as I've already outlined. It comes, quite literally, *ex corde ecclesiae*, "out of the heart of the church," beginning in the monasteries and the cathedral schools, and even centuries later, on the secular mega campus, it's not so surprising that I might as a Christian sense the spiritual structure underneath. The green lawns and the leafy quads are what remain of the monastic enclosure. The faculty are heirs of the monks, though long since free of even cap and gown, the last vestige of the habit. The gathering of students into a single place Monday, Wednesday, Friday can be seen as not at all unlike the gathering of people for the Mass or the Liturgy of the Hours—the university as fostering a way of life, a culture, that enables the student to learn through experience, over time, what can't be learned all at once and discursively.

As a Christian professor I am in the ironic position of being able to understand very well the roots of what goes on inside this now secular enclosure: the practice of critical thinking, the practice of certain habits of attention and analysis, the practice of precision and humility before the complexity of things. *Lectio divina* has become mere *lectio*, but reading is still reading. It's merely truncated, not different in kind.

The Christian foundations of reading explain the resonances I might feel teaching literature as well. From the monasteries of Europe through the American universities of the early twentieth century, religion and literature have always been understood to share a common base, to draw on some common source of intuition and imagination. That we have since abandoned the particular Christian naming of this experience doesn't change the experience of the source. I am tapping into that source whenever I learn how to lose or plunge into the sea of stories.

Even in the moment of being confounded and converted, in the moment teaching Augustine when I might seem to come closest to crossing the line, I remain on this side of it. My identifications are implicit, my emotions private. It was Augustine claiming Christ as the way, the truth, the light, not me, at least not in the classroom. My speculations about a Marian method of understanding the university are just that, speculations, and I didn't make them then and there, in that secular setting. What upset the student who complained was my preaching, not my teaching, but that preaching took place where it ought to take place, in a church. The only values that I urged on my students that day in class and that I should ever urge on them are the more general virtues—the intellectual and civic virtues—that all people in a democratic society can share. Christianity may be one of their sources, Christianity at its root may share in these values, but in a state institution, quite properly, those values cannot be claimed as exclusively Christian.

But that's just the point. In the twenty-first century these congruencies can exist only at the level of foundations. They can exist only underneath. As soon as I name my thinking as Christian, as soon as I profess a particular faith and tradition, I cross a line that however fuzzy and paradoxical nonetheless exists. It's a line that changes over time. In a democratic society it's a line that changes as the makeup of the culture changes, since what's generally accepted for a Christian majority is quite different from what's true in a pluralistic democracy. But the scandal is still the same. The scandal isn't the scandal of intersection or overlap. It's the scandal of specificity, of just exactly what we determine to be on one side of the line and what on the other.

And this is just what I have to do. I have to name my thinking as Christian. I have to name what I love as Christ. The tension occurs at just this point. The line gets crossed just here, when we make a choice, when we commit ourselves, and it's an important line, a necessary line. O'Connor is speaking as a Catholic when she insists that we pay attention to it, drawing on a long tradition beginning at least with Augustine's great *City of God*, his description of the Celestial City and the merely earthly one, the first built around love of God, the second around love of self. It's not just in the twenty-first century after all that the cities are seen as distinct. The Celestial is always understood as far higher. We can improve the earthly city by acting in faith and love and humility towards others, the City of Man can benefit from those who belong to the City of God, but even at its best the earthly city is limited, it is bound. "Peace in this life [. . .] is such that it should be called a solace of our misery rather than an enjoyment of blessedness" (476). Christians are always in "exile" on earth, they are always on "pilgrimage," because what they seek and what they long for exists only in God and on the last days, beyond whatever we might accomplish through reason and justice and our own creative work.

We can learn from the "heathens." We should learn all we can, Augustine says in *Teaching Christianity*. Their teachings "contain liberal disciplines which are [. . .] suited to the service of the truth, as well as a number of most useful ethical principles" (160). But these disciplines are partial. These principles only go so far. When as Christians we take advantage of the secular world we are like the ancient Hebrews plundering the silver and gold of their captors on their way out of Egypt. The silver and gold are valuable, we are glad to have them, but we're still on the run, we're still escaping, crossing the line of the city walls and running out into the wilderness to find our own homeland, however distant. We have to leave.

In his dialogue with Beatrice at the top of the *Purgatorio*, Dante has to stop and express his bewilderment. Why do her words "fly so high" that he can't "follow their intent?"

> "They fly so high," she said, "that you may know
> what school you followed, and how far behind
> the truth I speak its feeble doctrines go;
>
> and see that man's ways, even at his best,
> are far from God's as earth is from the heaven
> whose swiftest wheel turns above all the rest. (33.81–90)

"Doctrines" are "feeble," "far behind the truth." Virgil has been able to get the pilgrim only so far, Virgil as culture, Virgil as human art and science—only to the top of the Earthly Paradise, "as far as reason sees." Then he fades from sight, he disappears, and only Beatrice as the emblem of faith can take Dante the rest of the way, into heaven. This is the line. Virgil is the dean of the College, Beatrice the pastor of the Church. The university is purgatory. It can at best achieve only the Earthly Paradise. Heaven must wait, on the other side, attainable only through grace.

This is why Newman argues that even a Christian university trains gentle-people, not Christians. He understands the line that faith requires. God is present in all things in nature and in every part of the human self so it is true that there is nothing in the university that does not in some way involve or tend toward him at root and at base. This is why whenever I make real and genuine contact with the essence of a literary text or an idea in the classroom I will as a Christian inevitably make contact with the Lord our God.

And yet only partially. Nature and self are not enough. Reason, properly pursued, should lead right up to the necessity of Christian faith, but not necessarily. Reason is one thing, faith another. Reason is not at odds with faith, only insufficient without it. "It does not supply religious motives; it is not the cause or proper antecedent of any thing supernatural; it is not meritorious of heavenly aid or reward" (131; 1.8.3). Reason is in its ordinary operations "independent," not necessarily requiring "external authority" (128; 1.8.2). Viewed in itself, "however near it comes to Catholicism, it is of course simply distinct from it" (128; 1.8.2). It is a base, not a completed structure; a start, not a finish. It is generic, not specific. It helps supervise the work of identifying the wager—it doesn't make it.

"We attain to heaven by using this world well, though it is to pass away; we perfect our nature, not by undoing it, but by adding to it what is more than nature, and directing it towards aims higher than its own" (91; 1.5.10). What I can experience in the intellectual exchange in a classroom is nature, filled with God; what I experience when I cross the line is more than nature, is nature added to, explicitly put into relation with what is higher, nature named, and that name committed to.

The danger occurs—just the danger that O'Connor sees—when we forget this relation, this diaconal relation. What Newman here calls "liberal knowledge," the proper sphere of the university, while good in its place, "has a special tendency [. . .] to impress us with a mere philosophical theory of life and conduct, in place of revelation." It has a tendency to pride, to see itself not as means but end. "Knowledge, viewed as knowledge, exerts a subtle influence in throwing us back on ourselves, and making us our own center, and our minds the measure of all things" (150–51; 1.9.2). This is the danger of intellectualism, the special danger of the university, and we can't let it happen. "Taken by themselves," the methods of the intellect "but seem what they are not," Newman says to conclude the passage that began this chapter. "They look like virtue at a distance," and so it is that reason and method are "popularly accused of pretence and hypocrisy." It's not "from their own fault, but because their professors and admirers persist in taking them for what they are not and are officious in arrogating for them a praise to which they have no claim." Thus, "knowledge is one thing, virtue another; good sense is not conscience, refinement is not humility, nor is largeness and justness of view faith." Reason in itself is no "guarantee of sanctity" (89; 1.5.9). To forget this is to commit the sin of idolatry, the sin of pride—the sin that Dante himself is guilty of, according to Beatrice, the reason for the tongue lashing that she gives him right there in the Earthly Paradise. You've mistaken your desire, she tells him. You've mistaken the earthly for what it can only lead to and represent.

Newman understands. The Church may make use of liberal education—Christ may be present in all aspects of that education—but at the

same time, this education is "absolutely distinct" from faith itself (91;
1.5.9).

## That We Are Always Crossing the Line

But the argument isn't just that the line exists. The argument is that we
have to cross it. The argument is that we have to cross it and that we long
to cross it and that we are always crossing it anyway, whether we know it
or not.

Even on the days of coherence and joy, critical thinking is only part
of the Christian experience, a preliminary stage, a step towards something greater by far. "Beyond the desert of criticism," Ricouer says, "we
wish to be called again" (349). Beyond analysis we wish to believe,
beyond the obscure we wish for the clear, beyond the generic we wish for
the particular. We can't stay in the water forever, bobbing with Odysseus
on the beauty of the waves. We must reach shore, we must find land, we
must beg the beautiful princess for garments and meats and a roof over
our heads. We are inextricably bound to the particular.

"We may not know very much," as W. H. Auden once put it, "but we
do know *something*, and while we must always be prepared to change our
minds, we must act as best we can in light of what we do know" (17–18).

Let me return to the further point that I raised in the second chapter, that though symbol is primary, interpretation is of great importance.
"Everything has already been said enigmatically" in the story itself, as
Ricouer explains. All the meaning is there, not bound except to the
details themselves, multiple and open-ended, and we can never forget
this. But at the same time "it is always necessary to begin everything and
to begin it again in the dimension of thinking" (349). We have to make
sense of what the story means and to do that we have to give it particular language, particular meanings.

There is a way of understanding symbols which, "in a sense, remains
within the symbolic mode," content to display all the "multiple and inexhaustible intentions of each symbol." This is the way of understanding
that defines the critical reading of the first and second chapters and that
finally defines the work of the university. But we can't rest in that,
according to Ricouer. We can't be content with that, for "there the question of truth is unceasingly eluded." There we look at symbols merely as
symbols, keeping "truth at a distance," never having to ask "what do I
make of these symbolic meanings?" There we can avoid responsibility,
though not for long, since even when we claim to be escaping the
demands of interpretation, we are caught inside of them. The level of
analysis is always only an "intermediate stage" on the way to what ideally
should be "a passionate, though critical, relation to the truth value of

each symbol"—a relation consciously chosen and explicitly shared (353–54). Newman is blunt in the *Apologia*. There is intellectual and moral "cowardice" in not finding a "basis" for belief and in not "avowing that basis" (75).

––––––

A student brings me an advertisement to explain her faith position. A beautiful young woman floats in the air of a gray, futuristic room, a smile on her face, arms spread out like wings. A silver teapot is rising from a weightless table. On the right a television set is rising, too—a Sharp—even as it displays a picture of an astronaut spacewalking above a curve of earth. "No boundaries," the ad says. No boundaries, and that's what the student wants to proclaim, against my efforts to show her inevitable relation to the interpretive cycle, her responsibility to detail. I don't have to choose, she says. I'm free.

But the woman is floating inside a room, contained by four walls, and if she's weightless, she's presumably in space herself, in orbit, blasted there by a rocket and maintained there by supplies of oxygen and water and food. It must cost millions of dollars a day and involve around the clock ground crews just to keep her flying around the room like that, smiling. If she thinks she has no boundaries she should try opening an window.

A cartoon. Two fish in a bowl. The larger one says to the smaller one: "You can be anything you want to be—no limits." It's crucial. It's unavoidable. We can't live without making the move to the level of thought, which is to say the level of choice, even practically, day to day. Without the tiny choices and commitments that we make day to day we wouldn't be able to get up in the morning or out the door. To engage in interpretation is to free ourselves not from those commitments but from the illusion that we haven't made them.

Another day in class I ask why it's permissible to display a VISA advertisement on the bulletin board in the classroom—it's right there, on the wall—but not a crucifix. Why is it fitting and proper to invite people to apply for a credit card in this public space but not to seek the solace and challenge of the cross? "VISA doesn't have the history that Christianity does," Melissa writes, going on to talk about the church's long record of oppression and exclusion and hypocrisy. Yes. But nothing more is said about VISA, nothing more is said about the claim that VISA is without history. That notion is taken for granted, which only shows the success of advertising. Like the people selling us SUVs, the people selling credit cards want us to believe that we can outrun civilization exactly so that civilization can overrun us—but only one version of civilization, the commercial version, the version of the global economy.

––––––

"To grant a primary role to symbol in all discourse," Tracy says, continuing Ricouer's analysis, "is not necessarily to disparage the need for concepts."[31] To rediscover the complexity of language "is not to disparage efforts at second-order thought." In fact, without second-order thought we can't understand the role of symbol. It's a second-order thought, an interpretation, that defines the primacy of the symbol in the first place, that keeps reminding us, in explicit and clear and propositional terms, that the explicit and the clear and the propositional are always limited and provisional. Not only do "we enrich all thought by the use of concepts faithful to the originating symbols," as Tracy puts it, "we often need that second order language of concepts in order to understand first order discourse itself" (31).

Accepting the importance of interpretation in this way isn't just a matter of hermeneutics but of ethics. To avoid dogmatism and delusion we have to open up our interpretations and see them for what they are. But then, when that opening up is finished, it's crucial that we adopt those interpretations again. Pluralism is our goal. We must arrive at an understanding that allows us to be open and accepting of a variety of points of view, not complacent or unjust. But "whenever any affirmation of pluralism [. . .] becomes simply a passive response to more and more possibilities, none of which shall ever be practiced, then pluralism demands suspicion." Diversity is to be celebrated. But to do nothing more than celebrate diversity is to be disingenuous. It's too easy. It's the "perfect ideology for the modern bourgeois mind," Tracy says, alluding to Simone de Beauvoir, for it "masks a congenial confusion in which one tries to enjoy the pleasures of difference without ever committing oneself to any particular vision of resistance and hope" (90).

An appreciation of pluralism is only a stage, and it has to lead to choices, to practice. "Any worthy affirmation of plurality is the beginning, but never the end, of a responsibly pluralistic attitude. There must be other criteria besides those of possibility and openness. There must be criteria to assess the coherence or incoherence of any possibility with what we otherwise know or, more likely, believe to be the case" (91).

After all, however humble and self-aware, the "thoughts" that make up religious faiths are always claims to truth. They are always saying, yes, we know that the mystery is bigger than this claim we are making, but we do believe this claim to be in some way true. It's the best we can do, and we have to do something. To understand a religious tradition or any tradition—and to understand ourselves—we are "bound to struggle with the fact that its claim to truth is part of its meaning" (98).

An essay needs a thesis statement, one idea out of all the possible ideas. Otherwise the details have no meaning. Showing isn't all there is, even in fiction. All fiction writers, as O'Connor says, write out of some sense of the world, some moral and interpretive framework. For the Catholic writer that framework is the death and resurrection of Christ.

Now, the writer doesn't repress complexity in the interests of this "fixed dogma," merely illustrating the preexisting idea. The writer is always seeking to make contact with the mysterious reality beneath this dogma, the reality that gives rise to it. We might even take the novel in this sense as a model of what the university does, too—that like the novel, the university is devoted to describing the concrete details of the world the way it really is, even when somehow they don't fit the pre-existing framework and even especially then. But the dogma still exists, shaping what the writer describes. And more than that, dogma is part of the writer's obligation. Good fiction, O'Connor insists, doesn't just dramatize a "feeling." It "tells the intelligent reader whether this feeling is adequate or inadequate, whether it is moral or immoral, whether it is good or evil" (156). A story has an ethical purpose, in other words, even if that purpose can't be summarized simply or piously or reduced to fewer words than the words of the story itself.

Showing itself is telling. The arrangement of the words matters. What image is used and what image isn't tells the reader much about the writer's view of the world. To pretend otherwise is to indulge in what Graff dismissively calls the practice of "limited liability" (229–30). If we say that an image can't be paraphrased—if we say that a work of art is beyond politics and theme and discussable meaning—we are not liable for our interpretation. We don't have to debate it. We can stay out of the fray, but only by ignoring what is always true, for academic critics as for the general reader: that we read not just for story but for meaning, not just for drama but for instruction.

I can't stay floating in the water forever, plunged in the sea of stories, and in fact, I can revel in the water, I can plunge into the sea of stories one day in the classroom and find there Christ, find there in some basic and foundational way the sea of the Lord, only because I bring to that sea the assumptions I made before, at the end of another, earlier interpretive cycle. These assumptions are part of the vertical beam prior to class, underneath it to begin with, and it's because I've gone through the cycle before that I am able to identify my floating as Christian.

I weep in the garden or the oak grove, in the Drift Creek Wilderness, I reach the end of my rope, I have read all that I can read and thought all I can think and I break down, exhausted. Then I hear the voices of children, then I hear the invitation: take and read. Make the leap, make the wager, and when I do I realize that this is what I have so longed for, this is what I have sought: the truth of this leap, the security of this leap, the coherence of this leap. "O Lord, late it was that I loved you, beauty so ancient and so new" (*Confessions* 235; 10.27).

This is why we make the move from analysis to thought: out of longing.

———

The university is a culture. It organizes a set of cultural practices that enables students to experience over time what can only be experienced over time, not spelled out up front once and for all. In this sense it is just like the church as Louth describes it: an organizing of experiences to communicate what can only be experienced. But much of the culture of the university is the culture of death, the culture that shocks me when I first return from the seminary and that shocks me still. It is the earthly city, not the celestial one. The cultural practices that determine the life of the university and so the idea that is finally passed on to the students often seem to be governed more by market forces than by detachment and reason. Too often it's not Enlightenment ideals that seem to be at work in the university, for all the lip service that is paid to them. It's the global economy. Part of what the distribution model of the faculty and curriculum reflects is not devotion to order and coherence but surrender to the random forces of the market, faculty reduced to the grant money they can haul in or the numbers on their student evaluations, students reduced to the tuition they pay and their grade point averages.

What institutional practice celebrates at the state university is more and more the economy, not the *economia*. It's product, not person, and it's what wears me down as it wears us all down, on Good Friday and any Friday. This is how the university has crossed the line, and this is why I cross that line in the opposite direction, why I run across campus to make the Good Friday liturgy, so that I can escape from this diminishment and demeaning, so that I can escape from what Augustine calls this "hellish river of custom" into a culture more nourishing and humane.

The culture of the church is a human culture, flawed as any other, as I have already admitted—as we all must admit, sadly, inevitably. In that sense the church is the earthly city, too. But in the church we flawed human beings are organized not around the idea of self love but around the love of others and the love of God. The cultural practices that create the life of faith are intended to value rather than sell the self exactly by putting that self in relation to something greater. We are gathered in Eucharist around the great thing of Christ's body, all of us equal in relation to each other. Silence replaces noise. Genuflecting replaces self display, and we are free of the buying and selling.

I am no longer afraid, Augustine says, of "these professors of literature," these "buyers and sellers of literary knowledge" (31; 1.13). What does it matter now what we might lose or gain in acts of display? "Is not all this mere smoke and wind" (35; 1.17) Augustine asks, and there's such freedom in this question, the freedom that Thomas Merton feels centuries later when he escapes from the competition and ambition of the New York literary world and decides to become a monk. How freeing it is, he says, no longer to worry about what other people think of you! (388)

We have to cross the line into cultural practices that can either enslave or free us. That's the choice. The choice isn't between freedom and institution but between one institution and another.

There's a quality almost of game in this risk taking and giving in, as if we've simply acceded to a set of conventions or rules. C. S. Lewis talks about the benefits that can come from this kind of surrender to religious tradition, benefits of clarity and freedom. Writing to a woman on the subject of prayer, he advises giving in to the rote and established. The problem with meditative prayer is that it requires us to do two things at once, to invent our own rules while at the same time trying to follow them, to think about praying while at the same time praying. But with rote prayer the rules are already there. We can let go. We can pray. "The rigid form really sets our devotions free" (*Letters* 420). This is much like what Frost says about the advantages of following conventional poetic forms, that as writers we can concentrate on hitting the ball over the net, not on inventing the game. It's much the reverse of my experience in a men's group years ago where we spent so much time trying to figure out what combination of Native American or Taizé or Buddhist or ecological or drum-beating worship to do that we hardly had time to pray.

Newman makes this notion of formal surrender one justification for church dogma. The problem is that "we cannot restrain the rovings of the intellect or silence its clamorous demand for a formal statement concerning the Object of our worship." Better then to make that formal statement, to get it over with, so that the mind can rest and get on with worship and prayer. "Intellectual representation should ever be subordinate to the cultivation of religious affections," Newman insists (*Arians of the Fourth Century* 145–46). But that's just why dogma is so valuable and why we need to obey it. It frees us by giving us boundary. We no longer have to worry about where that boundary is but can live inside it. "The Lord is my chosen portion and my cup," the psalmist says in Psalm 16. "You hold my lot. / The boundary lines have fallen for me in pleasant places; / I have a goodly heritage."

This is what I feel as I stand behind the cross in my alb and my stole, the peace of boundaries, the peace of centeredness, the peace of coherence. The cross I am supporting organizes all that is around it, draws everything and everyone to it, and that's such a relief. The fighting and the searching and the arguing over terms have ceased. There is a blessed silence, a blessed order. There is the "enlargement" that comes from the intellectual work of the university, Newman says in *The Idea of the University*. There is the intellectual enlargement that can disturb and upset and even take our breath away, it's so confusing and challenging and new. But there's another kind of enlargement, "the enlargement not of tumult but of peace," and this is the enlargement of the church, of faith (97; 1.6.4). The world inside the boundaries is larger than the world outside, and that opening, that enlarging, comes from the assurance of love and of order and of hope.

This is why I cross the line, why we all cross the line: to be bounded, to be enlarged.

## That We Are Called to Cross the Line

But there's more. Crossing the line is more than a matter of arbitrarily accepting conventions in the interests of order. Something exists on the other side. Someone.

We can't reach this place or this person on our own. All that our interpretive efforts can finally reveal to us is their own futility, their own circularity. We are as trapped in language as the smiling young woman is trapped in her shiny gray room. But something happens when we admit this. Someone comes. When we drop our guard and drop our defenses and accede for a while to what seem like arbitrary rules, all at once the barriers fall away and we can see the mystery, the God, who has always been there calling us.

Only God can penetrate that shiny gray room. Only grace can break the hermeneutic circle. Only God can cross the line—the image of the cross is the image of the timeless breaking into time, the infinite breaking into the finite, the divine breaking into the human.

Why do we cross the line? Because we are called.

We long to be called, Ricouer says. And we are.

Dante breaks down in the midpoint of his life and wanders the dark wood, and he must, before Beatrice can send Virgil and the journey begins. But Dante's most important act is to fail. It's to get lost. Beatrice is the one who starts the journey on its way and she is the one at the other end of it, showered with a thousand flowers, radiant beyond all light.

"If we are to hold our paradoxes together," Palmer says, "our own love is absolutely necessary—and yet our own love is never enough. In a time of tension, we must endure with whatever love we can muster until that very tension draws a larger love into the scene" (*Courage* 85). The university creates the paradox and the tension. Faith is the acceptance of the larger love that these tensions draw near. This is what Tracy calls "truth as manifestation" (28)—not truth as human construction, not truth as human delusion or wish fulfillment, but truth as manifested,

really and in fact, however hard to interpret. Our hope is granted by a
reality that is other and that is not a product of our imagination. Our
hope arises from belief in grace.

This is why we cross the line, because hope is better than fear, life
better than death, person better than mindless force. We cross the line
because transcendence is the only way we can free ourselves, as Palmer
says, from mere objectivism on the one hand and subjectivism on the
other. As Tracy puts it, "the postmodern subject now knows that any
route to reality must pass through the radical plurality of our differential
languages and the ambiguity of our histories." This is the truth. This is
what we all know and can't escape. But what now? "After such knowledge, what identity, what coherence, for what self?" Because this is the
self's most urgent need, what it can't live without, identity, coherence
(81). And this is where theology makes its contribution, where religion
enters in. Because it acknowledges and even celebrates this understanding of a rough and ambiguous reality. Because it knows that its own for-
mulations can attain at most a relative adequacy always being undone,
always falling apart. But then it does something more. It goes further. It
offers hope. It moves beyond the postmodern to the level of action based
on hope.

Because believing theology can in humility and love trust in a reality
beyond its own musings, it can "envision some believable hope" that no
other system of thought can offer us (89). It can "reveal various possibilities for human freedom" (84).

But it's not finally theology that does this revealing. It's God himself.
The issue isn't that we know but that we are known, not that we long, but
that someone longs for us.

I am praying. I am trying *lectio divina* and I'm at the second stage, the
stage of *meditatio*, when as in freewriting I let the words and images tum-
ble through my mind, unedited. I let the words of Scripture invoke in me
whatever memories and desires. They all come flowing out of me,
unchecked, all my longing and my hope.

But it's not enough. I need to focus the stream. I need to find among
all this welter the one thing, the center, what I most need, and then translate that into a prayer, focus the longing into a point, petition—this is
*oratio*, the third stage: a telling, a thought, an interpretation that is really
a longing, that is really a hope beyond hope. Oh Lord, come to me. Oh
Lord, have mercy on me. This is my thesis statement: my own need. And
then I wait in expectation for the final stage of the process, the stage of
waiting and listening for what only God can say, what only God can do.
I wait and listen for the Lord. And when He comes, when he answers,
when he comes in his love and his tenderness I move past concepts again,
I move past names. I move past interpretation that can be put into words

and enter again into a vastness, but not a welter, a joy, a coherence. From showing to telling to beyond telling again. I am at the stage of second naïveté. And what I see, in those brief moments in my life when this happens, these fleeting moments, is sad beyond all sadness and beautiful beyond all beauty. And yet I see it. It has come to me.

In the second chapter of Genesis the greatness and beauty of this God who makes the stars walks in the garden in the cool of the day. The Creator of the universe in all his power and vastness narrows himself down in some unexplained way to a being who can walk in a garden, and he has to, at least for our sakes. What the God of the Jews understands is that communication is only possible in the particular, especially between the infinite and the finite. Human beings cannot possibly grasp the greatness of the truth that is manifested unless it is manifested, concretely, in burning ladders or burning bushes or strangers wrestling us in the night not by any river, not by all rivers, but by the river Jabbok, that night among all others, in the life of that person, Jacob, about whom the story in its details is told and retold. Finally this need of God's to make himself as clear as it is possible to be clear climaxes in the incarnation itself, God not just expressing himself through the ordinary but become the ordinary, become human, bounded in a human body that cannot only stand on the ground but be hung on a cross. All reality narrows to a point because it's only at that point that we bounded human beings can possibly even glimpse all that's beyond it. "The sacred takes contingent forms," Ricouer explains, "precisely because it is floating"—the sacred doesn't wish to escape the boundaries, doesn't wish to float weightless with the teapot and the television, but out of love and desire for us seeks out those boundaries in order to make his claims on us. And these claims, in turn, as Tracy says, can be interpreted "only by finite and contingent members of particular societies," people who are never weightless after all but inevitably grounded (86).

Expression requires form. Expression is always incarnated or it remains mere thought or impulse, unintelligible because uncommunicated. I can't simply think "I love you." I can't simply think or feel my commitment or affection, keeping it in my head and my heart, at least not if I want to stay married or in a friendship. For the love to be real it has to be expressed concretely, through the sending of flowers or the doing of dishes, through the embrace of arms, real arms, through the speaking of particular words that hang in the air, moments of sound, then pass away. Tracy says that in a classic text a universal truth is embodied in a concrete form, and it has to be that way. That's the only way that we can grasp the concrete, not just in a religious classic but in our own lives. There is no escape from interpretation, there is no escape from history. Even silence is a statement. Even passivity is an act.[32]

The way to understand the necessary particulars of a religious tradition is to see them as the particular expression of God seeking us out in love and our own particular expression of thanks and praise in response. We are given a gift—not the idea of a gift but an actual gift, in a package, wrapped up. We respond with thanks, not the idea of thanks but the fact of it, in words and music and candles and heavy wooden crosses, two oaken beams, 6 x 12. We don't say to our spouse or our child: I thought of you on your birthday. We throw a party, with balloons.

The Holiness Code of Leviticus—all those intricate distinctions about what to eat and wear and how to move about the day, so foreign and odd to many of us now—all those distinctions are exactly the right response to a love beyond all detail. What they attest to is the very nature of that mystery, that this mystery and love are expressed, have taken hold in the world, and that we then must do the same. God is in every detail, every detail is the expression of his love. So we must reply, with our bodies, in our routines. Perhaps this is the intuition, too, in Homer's apparent obsession with the details of ritual sacrifice and hospitality, the shape of the bowls and the proportions of the bull as it is sliced. The spiritual requires form.

## Dogma and the Particular

Two parallel ideas are implicit in what I've been saying.

First, Christianity isn't exclusive or dogmatic, but that is its dogma. That's its interpretation—a specific interpretation with its own limits and demands. It excludes things: mean-spiritedness, small-mindedness, intolerance. It requires a very particular discipline and a very particular humility. Aquinas says that all his ideas in the end are straw. Barth says that the Gods will laugh at his theology. All great religions testify to plurality, repeatedly asserting the limits of all knowledge including their own, continually resisting refusals to face plurality. This is just what we saw in the last chapter, in the teaching of Augustine's *Confessions*, the spaciousness and generosity of orthodoxy, how it doesn't depend on easy answers, doesn't amount to 7 plus 3 equals 10. Yet, as Tracy says, "even this startling possibility can only be understood by us if we will risk interpreting it" (86), that is, if we risk seeing it as a claim to truth. Theology is only relatively adequate, yes, but that's the idea, the startling, the challenging, the demanding idea.

"The main concern of theology," Louth says, "is not so much to elucidate anything as to prevent us, the Church, from dissolving the mystery that lies at the heart of the faith—dissolving it, or missing it altogether, by failing truly to engage with it" (71). Dogma exists to prevent dogmatism. Doctrine exists to establish boundaries so broad that what is most excluded is the effort to exclude, the effort to reduce. This is what all the heresies have sought to do, to reduce the mystery of Jesus Christ, from one end or the other, to flatten the vertical beam or raise the horizontal, to reduce the man to a God or the God to a man rather than keeping that paradox and mystery intact. To say that Jesus isn't God is to reduce him to what can be measured and understood. It's to refuse the mystery. To say that Jesus isn't man is to reduce him to a mere abstraction, to exclude him from the garden, to refuse the demands of the messy and messed up particular. As Louth sees it, "the fundamental thing that Christian theology can contribute, as one way of pursuing knowledge, to all other ways of pursuing knowledge," is a resistance to the "natural craving of the human spirit for a clear, transparent and definite system" (146).

This is the definiteness of Christianity, that it refuses the definite, heroically and repeatedly. In Jesus Christ God empties himself completely and radically in ways we still don't understand and never will. Jesus is the Son of God because *he doesn't* come down from the cross. Christianity offers an alternative form of knowledge by "keeping open access to the tradition which is the vantage point from which we can behold the mystery of God, which has been revealed in Christ" (146).

So this is the first main idea. The second is just as paradoxical: Christianity isn't exclusive but it is particular. It believes absolutely in its own revelation even as it remains open to the grace of God working in ways beyond it.

I am in love with my wife but I don't believe everyone should be in love with my wife. I live in this house but I don't believe everyone should live in this house. And this is true in still more profound and comprehensive ways in religious faith. Christianity offers an alternative form of knowledge by offering a particular vantage point for that knowledge, the vantage point of Jesus Christ. Louth can say in one sentence that Christianity resists the definite and in the next that this resistance to the definite is definitely revealed in Jesus Christ. There is no contradiction. This is the paradox of the incarnation.

James Fowler approaches this paradox through a discussion of the stages of religious faith. People in the earlier stages tend to see faith in terms of black and white: I am right and you are wrong, I am in possession of the truth and you are going to hell. But in the fifth stage, what Fowler calls "conjunctive faith," we are open to the possibility of other interpretations and other religious traditions, realizing that we don't have all the answers and that there may be validity of other traditions. And yet "this position implies no lack of commitment to one's own truth tradition. Nor does it mean a wishy washy neutrality." Rather, "conjunctive faith's radical openness to the truth stems precisely from its confidence in the reality mediated by its own tradition and in the awareness that that reality overspills its mediation." The person at this stage trusts her own experience of the truth, she believes in it, but she also assumes that other perspectives can "augment and correct aspects of each other, in a mutual movement toward the real and the true" (186–87).

This is also true in the next and highest realm, the "universalist," the realm of the saints and the great religious leaders who in the midst of their humility and openness put their lives at risk in acts of radical resistance, acts grounded in particular religious traditions. Here, too, the idea rests on a premise that Fowler calls "the absoluteness of the particular." The assumption is that through the details of a particular tradition what is revealed is really and truly the absolute, as much of the absolute as we can glimpse. But if the absolute is revealed in those particulars, it is revealed not only there. The very nature of the absolute requires us to understand that "the divine character can come to expression in different forms and in different contexts, with each of these instances bearing the full weight of ultimacy" (207). The very nature of the absolute is that it exceeds all categories and so can fill all categories. The very concreteness of our religious experiences should suggest that other kinds of concreteness are possible. Diversity of expression is a very feature of the mystery.

Part of the validity of Christianity is what it shares with the other great myths from the *Odyssey* through the myths of the East and of aboriginal cultures everywhere. There are deep underlying structures. This is part of the shock for students of coming upon the gospel story in the Literature of Western Civilization after reading the story of Odysseus: that Jesus is enacting the same fundamental shift, that he goes on the same journey, that Christianity is not in a sense unique, that it is in a sense just as mythic as the other myths. Yes, of course.

But there's no need to panic. The validity of other traditions isn't up to us to decide and doesn't finally matter anyway. All we know is that this path leads to the mystery, this particular path, this Christian path. Paul Tillich is making the same point when he cautions us against comparing "your religion and our religion, your rites and our rites, your prophets and our prophets":

> All this is of no avail. We want only to show you something we have seen and to tell you something we have heard [. . .] that here and there in the world and now and then in ourselves is a New Creation, usually hidden, but sometimes manifest, and certainly manifest in Jesus who is called the Christ. (17–18)

In a way the idea is simply that God is beyond all our categories. In a way the idea is close to Palmer's notion in *To Know as We Are Known* that faith in "the personal truth" embodied by Jesus is not "divisive and discriminatory" but "ultimately capacious": "it is not necessary to accept Jesus as Lord and Savior in order to find in him a paradigm of personal truth" (50). But more than "paradigm" finally. Reality, not model. Reality, not example. The New Creation that Tillich celebrates is "certainly manifest in Jesus who is called the Christ"—*certainly*, absolutely, without doubt, whatever the status of other faiths and traditions.[33]

It's almost as if in the presence of this concrete and capacious reality we're too occupied with our own joy. We're too happy, we're too full. In a way we're too satisfied personally and selfishly to look around and notice what anyone else is doing, though in another way it's just at this moment that we feel our deepest solidarity with others, our deepest sympathy, our deepest compassion.

We no longer desire to be more certain of God, only to stand more firmly in him. And we are standing in him. We are standing at the foot of the cross, we are standing behind it, holding it up with our hands. We are standing at the empty tomb, astonished. He is not here, he is not here, the angel says: not in the tomb of our limiting ideas, not in the rock of our traditions. That's their glory and their use. They are empty, blessedly empty, for Christ is now risen and spread through all the universe, in and of everything that is.

Some things are simply true. However we come to believe, however difficult it is to express our belief, always and in the end we do come to believe that certain things are true. We die. We need others. God comes breaking through. God comes breaking in.

## Jesus and the Scholar

A scholar of the law approaches Jesus in the Gospel of Luke and asks what he must do to attain eternal life (Luke 10:25-37).[34] This is a test of reading. This is a test of interpretation. "What is written in the law," Jesus asks him. "How do you read it?" The scholar replies, as Jesus expects him to, with the right answers, a recitation of the Shema, the summary of what all the Holiness Code and all the Pentateuch finally add up to: "You shall love the Lord, your God with all your heart, with all your being, with all your strength, and with all your mind, and your neighbor as yourself." This isn't a narrow statement but neither is it ambiguous. It doesn't reduce the mystery to a set of petty religious practices but neither is it vague or hard to understand. It doesn't show, it tells, simply, directly, compactly: less than everything isn't enough; we must love with our whole being, our whole heart, our whole mind. We must love others and we must love ourselves even as we love God.

The scholar, though, wants to push Jesus a little more—wants, in fact, to narrow the teaching down as much possible, to insist that doctrine be made smaller than it really is and so easier. "Who is my neighbor?" he asks, assuming, it seems, that Jesus as a Jew will suggest that not everyone is. A Jew is a Jew and others are not and what the scholar seems to want Jesus to say is that we should love only our own kind, only those within our doctrine and our dogma, only those with all our heart and mind.

It's now that Luke describes Jesus telling one of his most famous parables, one found only in Luke, the parable of the Good Samaritan. Jesus shows rather than tells. He isn't direct. He doesn't come out and say what he means explicitly, and like all parables the parable he tells opens up a gap to be filled. It opens up an interpretive indeterminancy so rich and deep that we can read this parable over and over again and get from it something new, something that connects to our lives in new and more challenging ways. And yet the showing is simple and direct, the story is told in an earthy, fable-like language every child can understand, and the moral that has to come from it, the central meaning, whatever other personal significance we might find in it, the moral is unmistakable and never changing: we must do likewise.

A man is suffering by the road and a priest walks by and then a Levite. They're right to pass by in a way, since if they touched the bleeding man they would be ritually impure and so unable to perform their duties in the temple. Only a Samaritan, one of the despised Samaritans, stops and nurses the wounds and takes care of the suffering man.

Who was the neighbor here? Jesus asks.

The scholar doesn't hesitate and neither can we, ritual impurity aside: the Samaritan.

Eighty percent of the Bible may be narrative, not propositional. It may show far more than it tells, and that showing may involve us in a range of possible interpretations, repeatedly. But that twenty percent of propositional statements is infinitely important and necessarily related to the stories because it repeatedly insists on compassion and inclusiveness as response to the infinite mercy of God. What the propositional language of the Bible does is repeatedly refuse to reduce the mystery to mere ritual detail. Love widely. Love completely.

Mark's version of this same pericope leaves out the parable of the Good Samaritan but makes the same point, in even more emphatic terms, as here it is Jesus himself who gives the proper answer. "There is no other commandment greater than these," to love God and neighbor, Jesus says (Mark 12:31). The fact that Mark's treatment of the story is different than Luke's—the fact of this interpretive complexity—doesn't change the underlying meaning, and indeed the underlying meaning is that we shouldn't lose sight of what's central, in reading or in the moral life. We shouldn't get lost in the details. We shouldn't mistake all the tiny ritual practices for what they are designed to express, we shouldn't make everything equally important, we shouldn't be "dogmatic" at all in the negative sense of that term but as "radically undogmatic" as the truly learned person in Gadamer's theory of education.

This is the very passage that Augustine in *Teaching Christianity* translates into his principle for reading the Bible (124). Any interpretation of Scripture, he says, that is contrary to this "twin love of God and neighbor" is false and in error. Yes the Bible allows and requires multiple interpretations—that's one of the clear and definite understandings we should have of what Scripture means: it is a reservoir that can never be emptied. But there are other limits, too, outer, broader limits, and these are the limits of love. Make no mistake about this, Augustine says. The simpler, clearer parts of Scripture should serve as guides and keys to understanding the many more obscure parts, and this teaching of love is the simplest and most fundamental of all.

Mark is like O'Connor's Catholic fiction writer in this sense, too, not just in his spareness and brevity. Though he doesn't reduce his narrative to a dogma, though he seeks to show the mystery beneath the dogma, though he couldn't have put his meaning in anything other than the words of the story he actually wrote, still he is guided by a doctrine, a doctrine that must be much like this, the doctrine of love, that must have existed in the believing community in which Mark lived and grew before composing the gospel in the first place. That community existed for at least a generation before he wrote the story down, grounded in the oral stories and teachings of Jesus and particularly in basic protocreeds or statements of faith known as *kerygma* statements—proclamations—short, fluid summaries of what the faith is about, what's central to it. We can see these in Paul, for example, writing in his letters probably a decade before Mark:

> I handed on to you as of first importance what I in turn had received: that Christ died for our sins in accordance with the scriptures, and that he appeared to Cephas, then to the twelve. Then he appeared to more than five hundred brothers and sisters at one time, most of whom are still alive, though some have died. (1 Cor 15:3-6)

Something is handed on, handed down, and what that is isn't hard to memorize and recite and hand on again. There are many similar statements in Paul and in Acts and in the Gospels, so similar in structure that they must pre-exist the stories themselves. They are narrative themselves, really, more showing than telling: Jesus died and rose and appeared. But in this crystallized narrative is a telling beyond all telling, that Jesus is the one, the Messiah—even if that word in its theological complexities isn't fully understood, even if Paul and the others couldn't have said in exact terms what we now might understand it to mean. The hope was clear and that hope was an interpretation, a definitive interpretation. Jesus, the Lord! And it must guide the composition of Mark as it must guide the composition of the other gospels, shaping what these writers in their genius can contact through story at some deeper level still.

You must take up your cross, Jesus says in the center of the story, on the mountain, in the midst of all the details and the blinding light. If you want to follow me, you must give up your life.

You must cross the line.

But it's not an abstract line that we cross, and we don't cross it for the sake of an idea. It's not an idea we are following. It's a person, a particular person, and the decision to follow that person comes with specific ethical and moral and practical consequences including, most of all, suffering. If we choose to follow this concrete reality, we, too, must be concrete. We must humble ourselves as he humbled himself, we must submit to the messy reality of things as they really are, even to the point of dying.

Why would I follow this person? Why would I cross that line?

Because of a love so generous as to include even me, a love entirely generous, entirely unearned. Because of a love so beyond the humility of interpretation that interpretation doesn't matter. Because of a love that I nonetheless can touch, nonetheless can feel, nonetheless can call by name even as he calls me by name.

Because this is all I long for, this limit, this love.

CHAPTER 6

# Living the Difference

In the last chapter, I put on the alb that I took off in the second when I returned to the university from the seminary, the alb the color of the oak grove, of the grass by Amos's grave. I put it on in the church, across Monroe Street, but I put it on, and though I'm looking back at the university from the other side of the street, from inside the Eucharist, this is exactly the right vantage point. It's from here that I can make my final argument.

In the last chapter, I showed that there is a line. In this chapter, I show that it's good: that the only way for Christians to contribute to the university is from the other side. The conjunctions that I experience teaching Homer and Augustine are so rich and deep they seem to provide all we need for a critique of higher education. But they don't. The critique depends even more on difference. As Christians we must remain prophetic, we must remain in the wilderness, because it's only in the wilderness that we find our strength—though the paradox deepens, because it's only by returning to the university and entering more fully into its life that we can continue dying to self in the way Christians must always be dying.

We don't just cross the line once. We cross it all the time. And we don't just cross it one way, but back and forth, every day, and it's in this sense that I call on Newman again, not just in *The Idea of the University* but also in his *Apologia*, the story of his own circuitous journey. It's in Newman's career, as well as in Tracy's hermeneutics and Carter's analysis of the first amendment, that I find support for celebrating the creative tension between faith and the world. It's in the cross, the cross that I am steadying on Good Friday, even as it steadies me.

## Faith and the University

The knowledge attainable on the other side of the line between reason and faith is far deeper than what the university can promise. The education possible is far richer. What Dante sees as Beatrice escorts him into heaven is a universe wonderfully and gloriously ever clearer and more coherent. You must believe in order to understand. Belief quickens understanding and extends it. Our inquiries now begin from knowledge of the truth that God is good and that all is ordered as it should be, and this truth sets us free. We don't have to worry about it anymore. We can stop expending our energies on the question of whether God exists—he does—and can turn our attention now to the details, the intricate and beautiful and mysterious details.

When I lead the Bible study at the Newman Center, a Tuesday evening of reading and praying the Scriptures with believing students, our discussions are often more intellectually rigorous and satisfying than the discussions I've tried to facilitate at the university during the day. I usually say things, about the Bible and about faith, too many things usually. I talk too much. But the most valuable part of each evening is the time we spend in silence, in the *meditatio* stage of *lectio divina*, 10 or 15 minutes journaling or closing our eyes, with music in the background, letting the words of the Sunday readings trigger emotions and memories and longings inside of us. We can go much further, then, when the discussion resumes. We have accepted first principles, we can stop haggling and positioning and seeking advantage or resisting authority. In the silence we have heard ourselves think. Now we can hear each other.

One night we were talking about the parable in Matthew of the wise virgins, how they patiently wait for the bridegroom to return, flasks full of oil for the lamps, and I got all excited and talked and talked about Matthew's community and the second coming and how we should read apocalyptic language as metaphor, not prediction. "Look! Here is the bridegroom! Let us go out to meet him" (25:1-13). I'd really prepared for this. But thankfully the spirit was too strong for me to put it out with all that language, because at the end, when I'd finally stopped, people started saying the most insightful and beautiful things. One of the people there was a woman named Jane, a very wise woman, and in the silence I finally allowed to happen she said, very quietly, very thoughtfully: you know, the wise virgins have to wait for the master, too. They don't control what he does. Their wisdom is beside the point.

And I felt this tingle when she said it. I felt the Spirit moving, it was such a good thing to say. It's all gift, it's all given. Trim your lamps, bring your oil, but wait in joy and expectation, because the master is coming. The master has come. The master is here.

"The Catholic writer," O'Connor says, "will feel life from the stand-point of the central Christian mystery: that it has, for all its horror, been found by God to be worth dying for." The Catholic writer writes from the position of "fixed dogma." "But this should enlarge, not narrow, his field of vision" (146). I think of the fountain at Mount Angel, the year I taught at the seminary, rising and falling in the window outside our class-room. I think of the faces of David and Michael and José the day I was teaching *Hamlet*, and how the language of the play seemed to grow crys-talline, brilliant. We could see right through it, to everything.

We need both our eyes to see clearly and well, the eyes of the intel-lect and the eyes of the heart. We need to shout across our *corpus callo-sum*, as Thomas puts it in "The Tucson Zoo" (7), across both the left and the right side of our brains, joining them together. We can't know a thing until we have loved it.

---

But if the knowledge on the other side of the line of faith is greater than what the university can promise, that knowledge can enrich the uni-versity. We can return to the university and argue from what we've dis-covered. It's our responsibility and our need. Odysseus leaves the world of the ordinary and experiences the world of the extraordinary, is hum-bled and enchanted and taught the mystery of things, and then he returns—he is the hero exactly because he returns, not remaining in retreat, not remaining in a solitary state of spiritual enlightenment but sacrificing his own peace and communion to plunge back into the con-flicts and struggles and intricate demands of his kingdom in Ithaca. The hero must return, if not to slay the suitors, to preach what he has learned about the foolishness and vanity of the world and the freedom and blessedness that can come from dying to it. Augustine leaves the world of the university but then returns to write the *Confessions*; St. Benedict leaves the university but returns to write *The Rule*.

Claims can be made about this world, from the other side, more clearly than before, and despite popular misconception, this isn't a con-stitutional problem. As Carter explains in *The Culture of Disbelief*, his study of the first amendment, "there's nothing wrong when a religious group presses its moral claims in the public square," as long as we are arguing *from* our faith rather than *for* it. The distinction is "between the religious motivation for a moral position that is otherwise within the power of the state to pursue and the religious motivation for a moral position that simply involves the oppression of members of other, less politically powerful faiths" (91). There's a difference between arguing "for official recognition of the exclusivity of one's faith" (91) and arguing, for example, against the war in Iraq. Religion can't be the object of a claim, but it can be the source, in the public university as in the public square, at least if we accept Carter's call for true "epistemic diversity," true acceptance of a variety of premises, drawn from a variety of ways of knowing.

Thus even in America, even now, as Christians we can return from our sanctuary and argue against both atheists and fundamentalists at the university. We can try to convert them both, not to Christianity but to a more literate and intellectually mature understanding of religious thought and so of their own lives, whatever their points of view, calling them from the lower realms of Fowler's hierarchy—the realms that as black and white thinkers they both still occupy—to the higher realms of conjunctive and universalist understanding, intellectually if not morally and personally. We are all of us in some way connected to the great sadness and great joy of the world, however we choose to name it; we all do choose to name it, to interpret it, and that interpretation involves specific commitments, commitments involving other people; for commitment and community to be valid they must not be exclusive, complacent or contrary to the doctrine of love; for commitment and community to be valid they must in some way describe and enact a dying to self; for commitment and community to be valid they must in some way involve a critical awareness of the mystery beyond the commitment and the community. These are the understandings that we can argue for, for atheists as for Christians as for Muslims as for Marxists as for anyone. These are the attitudes that we want to foster—fundamentally ecological attitudes, since they involve intellectual humility and awareness of relationship and responsibility, the attitudes of Mary, of Annunciation. Wherever people place themselves within this dynamic, we can argue that this is the dynamic, the dynamic that describes the lives they actually have to live.

To experience such attitudes and possibilities, in addition to whatever else they do, students need to read classic texts like the Bible and Dante and to risk a genuine encounter with these texts. Even at a state university. Especially there. Students should read these books and they should read them personally, with engagement, not neutrally or at a distance as if the ideas and situations being described don't matter or apply. They do matter and they do apply and to deny this is to fail to tell the truth. Even at a secular university, Tracy says, "we must allow for a genuine conversation" with the classics, a conversation in which the student really listens, a conversation in which the student doesn't assume that she already understands and can dismiss what the text might have to say. The texts are other and they may change us. We must be led with Dante to the edge of the Earthly Paradise if we are to confront these most fundamental questions of all. We may decide not to follow him into the realms of light, we may not even believe those realms exist, but unless we travel to the edge, unless we genuinely risk the encounter with the text, we won't be able to consider the questions at all, questions that must be considered. "The religious classics can [. . .] become for nonbelieving interpreters testimonies to resistance and hope," of any sort, even if the student chooses not to enter into their strategies and rewards (88).

This is how the classics challenge fundamentalists, since both fundamentalists and atheists alike resist the challenge of the other. "All methods of reductionism," Tracy explains, "whether by believers or nonbelievers, are grounded in [. . .] the belief that so secure is their present knowledge of truth and possibility that the religious classics can at best be peculiar expressions of more of the same." If they are "other," if they are "alien," they must clearly be untrue (100). But they are not untrue, only complicated, only hard. All our complacencies are at risk when confronted with the radical uncertainty of genuine, mature faith, faith too aware of complexity to be dismissed as naïve by an atheist, faith too aware of mystery to be thoughtlessly accepted by the fundamentalists.

This is the engaged and risky kind of reading that Palmer recommends in *The Courage to Teach*, a return to a form of *lectio divina*, though a general and democratic one, since it assumes, with Palmer, that there is something fundamentally spiritual to all education, spiritual in the sense that it must be concerned with ultimate questions, that it must move beyond objectivism, that it must understand and honor the necessary connection between knower and known, heart and head. In this sense, all "knowing, teaching, and learning are grounded in sacred soil" (111). By "spiritual" Palmer means "the diverse ways we answer the heart's longing to be connected with the largeness of life" (5). By spiritual he means that we must as teachers and students acknowledge the deepest mystery of our self, our "identity," and all that honors and conforms to this mystery, what he calls "integrity." Education must necessarily include consideration of identity and integrity, Palmer argues, as it must necessarily consider the presence of the sacred, of the transcendent beauty and challenge of the world outside of us, the "grace of great things," a phrase he borrows from Rilke (107).

As Christians we can cross the line to argue for this kind of generic spirituality—argue for it in a way that by definition is open to all other religious traditions and varieties of doubt, that simply tries to define the terms for the choices that later have to be made, freely and without complacency or false certainty—*lectio* that leads not to *oratio* but to provisional understandings of the nature of experience, directed not towards a particular construction of God or even towards a sense of God at all. We can cross the line and join with others to argue that the whole university, in all disciplines, become what Palmer beautifully calls "the community of truth," displaying those values of humility and openness and commitment: inviting diversity because diversity is demanded by the "manifold mysteries of great things"; embracing ambiguity because we understand "the inadequacy of our concepts to embrace the vastness of great things"; welcoming creative conflict because conflict corrects "our biases and prejudices about the nature of great things"; practicing honesty because lying "betrays the truth of great things"; experiencing humility because "humility is the only lens through which great things can be seen" and the only posture possible once we have seen them; becoming free people because "tyranny in any form can be overcome only by the grace of great things" (108). "Great things" can mean the complexity of a subject matter, the intricacy of the natural world, the sweep of history, the challenges of community—it can mean anything that is beyond us and to which we have a responsibility, which is to say, all things; which is to say, both nature and society.[34]

With Palmer we can join in arguing for this fuller and deeper understanding of education, an understanding that actively resists the reductionism and false scientism of so much educational practice today, a scientism contrary even to the field distribution model, even the model of the global economy. With Palmer we can argue that the self should be divided no more, the self of the teacher and the self of the student, and that this wholeness and this unity require new ways of understanding the profession and new ways of teaching in the classroom. Teaching should be more personal and engaged, more interactive, more open-ended. The moments of joy and connection that I have described now become normative. I no longer describe them simply as my own experience—gifts, not products of my own exceptional practice; unearned, surprising—I now argue for them. I now argue for ways of creating the space in which this community of truth that has now and then graced me can be actively and continually practiced. This is Palmer's definition of what it means to teach: "to create a space in which the community of truth can be practiced" (90). Teaching should be evaluated in different and more authentic ways and made to matter just as much as publication. Publication should change, a range of kinds of writing come to be regarded as valid, not just articles but essays, not just scientific or social scientific ways of knowing—though those are valued, too—but the humanistic, the creative, the narrative, the storytelling.

Augustine, too, railed against the vanity and triviality of the profession of letters in the fifth century, centuries before Palmer. He was taught to follow the wanderings of Aeneas without understanding his own wanderings; he was taught the agreed upon rules of style and usage, not what is true and worthy and important. The curtains at the doors of Schools of Literature in the ancient world hung "rather as a covering for error than a mark of the distinction of some special kind of knowledge," he says (31; 1.13). They teach pride, not wisdom, and this is wrong. "A thing is not necessarily true for being expressed eloquently" (97; 5.6). As Christians we can cross the line and make this argument again, actively resisting the hyperprofessionalism and hyperspecialization of English studies. The Johns Hopkins model of professionalism that was imported from Germany and came to dominate the American University in the nineteenth century is only one model of what English studies might be, only one chapter in a long history. It doesn't have to dominate. It replaced a more spiritual model, based on the nineteenth century romantic sense that literature can help us get in touch with our reservoirs of feeling and imagination, and this model can be recovered again, in a more sophisticated and self-aware and inclusive way, by postmodernism itself. English studies can be understood as the creating of a culture in which students over time come to experience deeper spiritual values.[36]

We can cross the line. We can cross the line and argue from our particular and engaged Christian perspective for the dignity of the person over and against the dehumanizing pressures of the market. The Beatitudes can give us a source for making the more general argument that competitiveness is not the only value, that meekness and mourning seen from one point of view are just the ecological values that we most need—that what both Alter and Leopold call "intellectual humility" is more than anything else what the world requires at this time of enormous environmental and social crisis, as I suggested in the first and second chapters. "Blessed are the poor in spirit [. . .] Blessed are those who mourn [. . .] Blessed are the meek [. . .] Blessed are the merciful [. . .]" (Matt 5:1-11). To hold up the Beatitudes against the mission statement of any public or private university in this country, with their emphasis on success, on power, is to see again how radically countercultural the gospel really is. Grief should be the goal of education, at least one of them, and we can argue for this. We can argue for compassion. We can argue for justice. We can argue against oppression. This is the role that the American Catholic Bishops have envisioned for Catholic campus ministry: "to help higher education attain its lofty goal of developing a culture in which human beings can realize their full potential." The market forces work against this. The market forces reject the "dignity of the person" in the urge for profit. In resisting this dehumanizing force, "the church joins its voice with others in promoting the ideal of educating the whole person" (4).

People grounded in other traditions and ways of knowing can make these same arguments. These are not exclusively Christian arguments, they do not demand a Christian position. As the bishops say, the church "joins its voice with others." But Christianity has both the right and the obligation to do this, to return from its humbling and its joy, drawing on its particular sources of insight and strength, and to become a part of this larger community of truth arguing for educational reform. "When the quest for wisdom is forgotten or diminished," the bishops proclaim, "the Church must keep the ideal alive for the good of society" (9).

## The Call to Humility

Even more importantly, in the midst of all this, exactly because it is a faith, exactly because it explicitly and publicly argues for faith, Christianity is uniquely situated to call the university to remember its own mission. It is uniquely situated to call the university to intellectual humility.

The postmodern university professes to be postmodern, to embrace the rough knowledge, the discontinuous and shifting and located, to resist any efforts at oversimplification and ease and cultural chauvinism. But Christianity has always known this roughness, always celebrated this mystery, always advertised this truth beyond mere reason. It lights candles, it plays music, it processes up to the altar of this embodied, incarnated, irreducible truth. It holds it up for all to see. It holds up the cross. The only difference between Philip Morris and the Apostle Philip in this sense—and it's a big difference, the crucial difference—is that the apostle is honest about his intentions. He doesn't hide them. "Do you know what you are reading," he asks the Ethiopian, then, with the man's permission, proceeds to interpret that text from an undisguised, enthusiastically professed subjectivity, the subjectivity of Christ. Here, he says, this is how we read it: from Christ (Acts 8:26-40).

Christianity is so obviously biased and situated and committed that it best represents what is less obviously true for every other position. As Tracy puts it, "religion, as the most pluralistic, ambiguous, and important reality of all, is the most difficult and thereby the best test of any theory of interpretation" (x).[37]

The problem with the university is that it tends to keep its faiths hidden, allowing even its anti-absolutism to become absolutist, postmodernism itself become a dogma that prevents any other considerations. Method becomes an end in itself, as if there is only method, no ends at all. Moberly identified this problem with great clarity in 1949, attacking what he calls "camouflaged partisanship" in the academy (56), the most dangerous kind of all. The most dangerous kind of presupposition is the kind you don't know you have, or that you pretend you don't, and this is as true in the university now as it was right after World War II. Globalism has only deepened the blindness:

> Whether neutrality is desirable or not [. . .] when probed it is found to
> be a sham. It turns out to cover an uncritical acceptance of the com-
> mon assumptions of the day or those of some particular social or pro-
> fessional stratum. In other words, so-called academic objectivity is a
> fraud; and the fraud is none the less disastrous and reprehensible
> because its perpetrators are commonly also its victims and deceive
> themselves as successfully as they deceive others. (54)

The university isn't supposed to cross the line but it does, all the time.
Because the church has already crossed the line, without question, with
all drama and liturgy, the church can look back and argue that the university has, too, and should admit it. It can say to the university, don't
pretend you're not professing values, don't pretend to be objective.
Acknowledge your biases, at least. The university's attitude about faith is
the best test case, in fact, because it's here that the unacknowledged bias
is most obvious. Faith isn't objective, the university says, in the act of
proclaiming its own faith. Nothing is beyond point of view, the university says—except, apparently, the university.

This is what Carter means when he says that "all deeply held beliefs
should be seen as religious beliefs" (218). This is what I think I help
accomplish simply by being a professor who is also a deacon, a seeing of
all beliefs as analogous to the religious, as not objective, as not necessary
but chosen. My alb calls attention to the caps and gowns of my colleagues, their own professions of faith—not to deprive them of these professions, but, in a kind of reverse of the Emperor's new clothes, to show
that they are there after all, that the Emperor is never really naked.[38]

Noah Porter, the president of Yale, made this point nearly a hundred
years before Moberly. "The question," he says, "is not whether the college shall, or shall not, teach theology, but what theology it shall teach,—
theology according to Comte and Spencer, or according to Bacon and
Christ, theology according to Moses and Paul, or according to Buckle
and Draper" (qtd. in Marsden 127). We have only to substitute names
like Foucault or Derrida to make exactly the same case, though the
names of Jesus and Paul and Moses remain the same. The university is
always implicitly trying to become the church. The church, by being the
church, publicly resists this tendency. The university is always implicitly
trying to turn reason into a faith. The church, by publicly identifying
faith as faith, resists this unacknowledged conversion.

This is Newman's argument for including theology in the university
curriculum. It prevents the other disciplines from usurping their place,
helping to keep them from following the natural impulse of any discipline or method, to see everything in its own terms, to make its own
"particular craft usurp and occupy the universe" (50; 1.3.6). A university,

Newman says here, is an assemblage of learned people, "zealous for their own sciences, and rivals of each other," but "brought, by familiar inter-course and for the sake of intellectual peace, to adjust together the claims and relations of their respective subjects of investigation. They learn to respect, to consult, to aid each other" (77; 1.5.1). Biology makes up for what chemistry is not equipped to consider. History compensates for what literature cannot see. Each discipline is partial and in need of the others, which is what makes a university a university, that it is universal, a coming together of everything in order for each thing to be corrected and put into right relation.

For Newman theology is the most important piece of all, not just the condition of all knowledge but the corrective of all disciplines, because when theology is missing from the curriculum, the other disciplines inevitably try to become theology, to claim absolutes that they have no business claiming. Science is just science, literature just literature. But without theology to remind them of this, they tend in their narrowness to develop the "absolute convictions of their own conclusion," the very "obstinacy of the bigot, whom they scorn," exceeding "their proper bounds" and "intruding where they have no right," teaching wrongly "where they had no mission to teach at all" (61, 59; 1.4.4, 1.4.2).

Whether or not theology should be formally taught on a secular campus, a Christian faculty member has the obligation to return from faith and to cross the line and to argue, on campus, from the center of it, that the line be identified and that the line be acknowledged and that the line be respected, whoever is crossing it. The question, Moberly says, is not whether Christianity should be allowed to speak somewhere on the periphery, tolerated among whatever else is seen as peripheral and unim-portant. The question is "what can Christian insight contribute to enable the university *to be the university*" (26). The question is whether Christianity has something central to offer to the very identity of the uni-versity. And it does: it offers an awareness of complexity, it professes the mystery, and it insists that the university profess this mystery rather than claiming to have mastered it once and for all. In its own honesty—when it is honest—faith calls the university to honesty, to recognize its limita-tions and so to respect what at heart it is always professing: that the world is a big place, that easy answers won't do, that what is and what seems to be are never the same.

And that commitments are never generic, never unembodied. Christianity is uniquely situated to call the university away from the hyprocrisy of the free-floating and the anti-institutional, to help the uni-versity recognize the material culture that embodies its own values as institution: the private offices, the parking lots, the PCs and the Xerox machines, the commencement exercises and the committee meetings, the seminar tables. Christianity can join with feminism and ethnic studies to challenge Melissa and Tina and all our students to see how they, too, are embodied, from their Gap jeans to their designer skateboards to their bleached hair. It can join feminism and ethnic studies in challenging the hypocrisy of the generic and so the uncommitted.

In this sense the image isn't of racing over to the Good Friday liturgy in the church, across campus and across Monroe Street, blocks away. In this sense the image is of the communion service on Wednesdays at noon, over in the Memorial Union, in the center of campus, above the Burger King and Woodstock's Pizza, just over from the bookstore. We gather our chairs around a seminar table. We lay an altar cloth over the laminated wood. Students are swirling all around outside, eating their lunches, talking, milling in the halls outside the door. And there inside we are praying for mercy, there inside we are praying out of our joy or our sadness that day, there students and faculty are joining hands and opening themselves up to the grace of the great thing that is in the center of that room as it is in the center of us all: the mystery of identity, which is the mystery of Christ. This is a model for what the classroom itself might be, a circle, not a lecture hall; a gathering in silence and humility, not a competition, not the production and consumption of knowledge, day after day, but a living together with the questions.

I open the pyx and remove the body of Christ: take and eat, I say. Consume who you are. And we go out into the world, nourished and transformed. "As those who are chosen, blessed, broken and given," Nouwen says of us as eucharistic people, "we are called to live our lives with a deep inner joy and peace. It is the life of the beloved, lived in a world constantly trying to convince us that the burden is on us to prove that we are worthy of being loved" (*The Life of the Beloved* 103). But the burden of proof is on the university finally. We know we are loved. We know we are worthy. We know we are free.

This is what the Christian has to offer the university as the world, a testimony to the mystery inside of us all, a proof that is finally not a burden but a gift.

## In the Wilderness

But even in the campus Mass we are separate from the university. Even at its heart we are in exile.[39] We still have to walk out the door and out into a world radically different than the one that with all our flaws and limitations and tackiness we have tried to foreshadow inside. This is the paradox of faith, that I can critique the university only from outside of it. I can make a difference only by maintaining difference, staying on the other side of the line, grounded in a source of strength that is other.

Wills call this an "American paradox": "that our churches have influence because they are independent of government" (*Under God* 380). Carter argues that this is the paradox that the founding fathers actually had in mind when they established the first amendment. In his view the first amendment's separation of church and state was really intended to protect religion from the state, not the state from religion. It was designed to keep religion free from government regulation, and this because such freedom of expression is finally essential for the government itself. The government knows that it needs to be resisted. It knows that to be truly democratic, it needs a critique, and that such a critique can only come from organizations not dependent on its own power, and that the only organizations not dependent in this way are the churches, organizations with allegiances beyond the power of any government. The founders, in other words, intended to give religion a special place within the state, and they did this because in the end they distrusted the state, unchecked. "To be consistent with the Founders' vision and coherent in modern religiously pluralistic America, the religion clauses should be read to help avoid tyranny—that is, to sustain and nurture the religions as independent centers of power" (124).

The civil rights movement is perhaps the best example. It could not have been effective in opposing the government if it had been sponsored by the government, on its payroll. The Christian community gave Martin Luther King and the others the strength to resist persecution at the hands of the state, to endure the beatings and the imprisonments and the murders. The closer the religions move to the sources of secular power, the less effective they are. Without distinction, there is no resistance. Christianity must be grounded in an alternate source of meaning, it must be grounded in God, not the state, if it is to speak the truth to power.

And this is a theological, not just a constitutional issue. It's a spiritual issue, one of the central themes of the *Divine Comedy*, that the church is always corrupted when it loses its own identity. In the Heavenly Pageant that concludes the *Purgatorio*, Dante sees the Triumphal Chariot of the Church drawn by the Griffon of Christ and accompanied by a procession of prophets and evangelists and allegorical figures. But then the chariot is tied to the Tree of Good and Evil and attacked by the Eagle of the Roman Empire and the Fox of heresy. The Eagle returns and covers the chariot with feathers that represent money and material wealth while Satan the dragon rips at its foundations. Slowly, before Dante's eyes, the church is transformed into a Monstrous Beast on which rides the Harlot, the Corrupted Papacy, attended by the Giant of the French Monarchy. This is what happens when the church crosses the line, back into the secular world. It becomes a beast, a whore, and that's always the threat. The Eagle is always attacking (Canto 32).

Earlier in the *Purgatorio*, on the level of the wrathful, Marco Lombardy explains why the politics of Italy and of the world have become so corrupted. "Rome used to shine in two suns," Marco says, one the church and the other the state. "Each showed her its way: / one to the ordered world, and one to God." But the state seduced the church, the church succumbed, and now confusion and corruption reign. "Since the Church has sought to be / two governments at once, she sinks in muck, / befouling both her power and ministry" (16.106–9, 127–29).

Even David, the beloved king, is corrupted when he becomes the king, seduced into wrongly using his power. A prophet must come to accuse him, the prophet Nathan, and prophecy always comes from outside, from the wilderness. Only in the wilderness can we be prophetic. Only in the wilderness can prophecy avoid what in a later time we call conflicts of interest, which is why John, too, comes out of the wilderness, speaking the truth to Herod. Jesus so speaks the truth to the Jews and the Romans in power that they kill him. Render unto Caesar what is Caesar's, Jesus says, don't confuse what is earthly and divine, and perhaps this is why they kill him, because they recognize the threat in this division, the prophetic threat—a threat not because it seeks power, but because it doesn't, because it questions power.

There are two cities, Augustine knows, the earthly and the celestial, and though we should do all we can as Christians to sanctify the world, we can never sanctify it fully, the kingdom will never fully come until the end of the world. It's the paradox of the incarnation itself. Jesus is both fully human and fully divine, both equally, one nature not swallowing up the other. As soon as we forget this, we lose the mystery. As soon as we forget this, we are back in the moral and philosophical morass of the Manicheans, who reduced the spiritual to the merely material and so reduced God to mere substance, not finally God at all. Only the incarnation can guarantee the real idea of God, and what the incarnation describes is paradox: an embodied truth that is yet not the body itself.

But we still don't get it, any more than the bumbling disciples. We can't grasp it. The historian James Bryce summarizes twenty-one centuries of church history from just this perspective, as a failure to understand the prophetic call of Christ: "The more the church identified with the world, the further did it depart from its best self. The Church expected or professed to Christianize the world, but in effect the world secularized the Church" (90).

It's a paradox I experience myself, directly, in the ebb and flow of my professional life since I've become a deacon. When I allow myself to get caught up in the departmental politics and professional ambitions—as I inevitably do—I lose not only my sense of God but my sense of my vocation as a teacher. My teaching blurs, loses power. It's when I am most centered in my prayer life—in those rare moments—it's when I am most

separate in my mind and my heart from the demands of the secular institution, that I come to love my teaching again. It makes sense again. It's
the paradox at the heart of my circuitous journey. I have to leave the university, to flee it, finding refuge in the seminary and the monastery. But
when I return, the university all at once makes sense again—but only
when I maintain my internal distance. My faith gives me strength to
remain a teacher within an institution that tends not to value teaching,
but only when I remember where this strength comes from. From
Christ. From the One.

Why do I cross the line? Because my heart is restless until it rests in
thee. Why do I stay on the other side of that line? Because only in God
is my soul at rest. As we pray in the *Salve Regina*, through Mary, the
mother of reading, through Mary, the figure of the intellectual: "Hail
Holy Queen, Mother of Mercy, our life, our sweetness and our hope. To
thee do we cry, poor banished children of Eve. To thee do we send up our
sighs, mourning and weeping in this valley of tears. Turn then, most gracious advocate, thine eyes of mercy upon us, and after this our exile, show
unto us the blessed fruit of thy womb, Jesus."

———

There is both pessimism here and optimism, realism and hope. "To
live divided no more," Palmer says, bluntly, "is to find a new center for
one's life, a center external to the institution and its demands. This does
not mean leaving the institution physically; one may stay at one's post.
But it does mean taking one's spiritual leave" (*Courage* 167). Palmer was
once a community organizer and still thinks like a community organizer.
He is far from recommending quietism. And yet what's both so practical
and profound in this statement is its recognition that institutions are limited, that institutions won't change in our lifetime, except so slowly, so
incrementally, that in the meantime we need to find for ourselves other
ways of staying alive and supporting each other. These are what he calls
"communities of congruence" and what Nouwen calls "communities of
resistance"—modeled on just such groups in both the civil rights and
women's movements. We do what we have to do to keep our jobs and get
by in the institution, we are smart and savvy, but privately we keep getting together and sharing our stories, deriving strength from this alternate source of power and meaning. The best way to influence institutions
is to stay healthy inside of them, but to stay healthy we have to stay separate. We have to cross the line.[40]

What defines Christianity is resistance, Tracy says. "Despite their
own sin and ignorance, the religions, at their best, always bear extraordinary powers of resistance. When not domesticated as sacred canopies for
the status quo nor wasted on their own self-contradictory grasps at
power, the religions live by resisting" (83–84). And the key to that resis-

tance is not to be domesticated, not to become a sacred canopy, grasping at power itself. "The chief resistance of religions is to more of the same" (84), which is to say, that religion then can't become more of the same. It must maintain its difference. As *Ex Corde* puts it, the whole point of evangelization is to "upset" the dominant culture's "criteria of judgment" (39).

A photograph. I am kneeling on the marble floor of the cathedral in Portland, head bowed, alb flowing out behind me over my shoes. My clasped hand are in the hands of the bishop, sitting on his throne, wearing his miter, and I am swearing my obedience to him. I am swearing my obedience to the will of the church and the mind of the church in a way that is entirely foreign to us in our democratic and American context—medieval, ancient. And it is. I am saying: I obey, I listen, I subordinate myself most of all not to the authority of this democracy but to another authority, the one that the bishop represents, the one that calls me, I believe, to become a deacon, to kneel there again in a few minutes while the bishop places his hands over my head and calls down upon me the power of the Holy Spirit to sanctify and ordain me.

In fact, in a brilliant and startling argument, Tracy challenges the common notion that individual religions are simply different expressions of the same basic insight. The great world religions do have much in common, he says, particularly a belief in the importance of decentering the ego, of dying to self. But to say that their individual differences are trivial is to deny them real authority. It's to assume that we already know what they're going to say, that they don't have anything new or challenging to offer us. Only if there is real difference is there real diversity, and only with real diversity is there real learning, anything more than repeating what we think we already know—complacently, beyond change, dismissing what might transform us. "If a pluralistic attitude is genuine, it must be willing to learn from anyone," and that means granting the possibility that behind the concrete details isn't simply more of the same (91). "A conversation that assumes, prior to the conversation itself, that all the religions are really the same can hardly help" (92). There is no conversation without genuine difference. We have to be willing to enter into "that unnerving place where one is willing to risk all one's present self-understanding" by seriously considering the possibility that the truth claim of the particular tradition is possibly true and possibly different than what we assumed to be true, not just a condition for understanding the tradition itself but for understanding our own lives (93). "The religious classic may be simply using another language to speak a truth I already know." Fine. But the "religious classic may be manifesting some reality different and other—even terrifyingly different and alienatingly other—from what I usually believe" (98). This is the possibility that we have to face. To refuse that possibility is to assert, arrogantly, that only we among all others have arrived at the truth once and for all, that only we among others have transcended all history and arrived at the ahistorical essences, unembodied. Particulars will never trouble us again. We have already crossed the line and we never have to cross again.

The state university celebrates diversity. It welcomes the multicultural. But for there to be true diversity the university must be open to the possibility that it doesn't finally possess the universalist truth behind all the individual manifestations, that somewhere in some particular manifestation of details may lie a truth it has never considered, a truth that is genuinely other, genuinely outside.

Religion is that other. Religion more than anything else is that other, because it has crossed the line. Because it is outside. Because it is particular.[41]

———

But by the same token, by exactly the same logic, religion must remain other. To guarantee diversity, religion must not pretend to be simply another way into what the secular university already knows and professes. It can't be more of the same. By its very nature Christianity must remain Moberly's "creative minority" within the more diverse world of the university, speaking the truth to power, speaking its own unique truth to a power that rests on another kind of truth entirely.

We can argue for general values only from a particular, committed position.

We are never not particular, we are never not committed. We might as well admit it.

I'm not really trying to make the university Christian. I'm trying to convince people to leave it. Not because it's bad: it isn't. We can have faith in the university, in its powers of analysis and description. It isn't evil and it isn't wrong, only partial, only limited. I'm not crossing the line in the classroom, I'm crossing the line by leaving the classroom. I'm saying: make your spiritual home elsewhere.

The role of faith is to bawl out the university as Beatrice bawls out Dante on the verge of Paradise. We have "turned our steps aside from the True Way," she tells us, "pursuing the false images of good / that promise what they never wholly pay" (*Purgatorio* 30.130–32). We have mistaken desire. We have taken the earthly as our end—our ambition, our institutional egos—when these things have value and worth only when subordinate to what is higher, in God.

## The War, the Stars, and the Cross

The line is blessed. The line is good. We cross it in the sense of making the sign of the cross above it, blessing it, because that tension and difference power a critique—and a critique that doesn't flow in only one direction, a critique that in the end may be even more vital for faith than for the university.

On the one hand the challenge is to the intellectual life, on two levels. Only God is the one, inviolate truth; and faith, as Newman explains in the *Apologia*, is always reminding the state and the university and secular world of this fact, holding itself up as an alternative to the relativism and formlessness and lack of center that defines what he calls "liberalism." Liberalism denies that there is a center, asserting that everything is equal to everything else, that there is no reference. But there is. There is a fixed point and it's God. It's Christ.

To put this another way, what faith is always doing, as we have seen, is offering a believing and committed liberalism over and against the tyrannizing influences of the university, resisting its claims that only reason can understand the world, only what is reasonable is real. It's always insisting that reality is multiple and shifting and elusive. Faith is always unmasking the university, calling it to recognize the situatedness and tentativeness and createdness of what it might otherwise profess to be universally and finally true.

But it works the other way around, too, the critique comes from the opposite direction, and as Christians this is finally even more crucial for us to understand. If the church unmasks the university, the university also unmasks the church. The university calls the church to intellectual humility, as it always needs to be called. The university calls the church to recognize and honor the line, even for its own sake.

"We aim at second naïveté through criticism," Ricouer says (351). Second naïveté is better than first, because it's mature and informed. We have sacrificed the naïve happiness of the child but exchanged it for the mature joy of the adult, and we've done this exactly through analysis, exactly by realizing that what we thought was fixed and easy is in fact shifting and mysterious. In our second naïveté, if we can reach it, through grace, we adopt our "myths" without "trying to disguise them as explanations" and so they don't harden, they don't become rigid, they don't become idols but remain icons, transparent to the truth rather than a false substitute, in the way (165). Critical assessment is always unthickening the image, unblocking the pathway between the image and the source of its power, showing us that the image is an image, that the truth is interpretation, and this is spiritually essential. It keeps us from pride. It teaches us that we are not God. It teaches us that without grace we are forever trapped inside ourselves and inside our own language. If our interpretations are not necessarily valid, perhaps others see something we have not. Perhaps their interpretations are no more partial than ours.

And critical assessment is the role of the university. It's the job of the university to unblock and unthicken the images so that we can see what's behind them. It's the job of the university to disenchant us—for the good, we realize as Christians, though we come to that realization across the line, in the freedom of our own faith and choice, within our own community and tradition.

In its inspired pastoral constitution on the Church in the Modern World, *Gaudium et Spes*, Vatican II proclaims that "those also have a claim on our respect and charity who think and act differently from us in social, political, and religious matters." In fact, the "more deeply, through courtesy and love, we come to understand their ways of thinking, the more easily will we be able to enter into dialogue with them" (193). The church "deeply appreciates what other Christian churches and ecclesial communities have contributed" to our understanding of God, as it deeply appreciates the contributions of non-Christian religions. As the bishops put it in their letter on campus ministry, "since no single community can monopolize the gift of wisdom, the Church joins with the university and others in the search for wisdom" (5). This is the church at its best, the church as it really is, in its heart, but it's so easy to forget that. It's so easy for all of us, in or out of churches, to forget the struggle and the complexity that we've experienced in our acts of interpretation.

The university reminds us.

Religions must be able to resist the illusory models of pure autonomy and easy coherence, Tracy says. They must be able to recognize when they have grasped for a power that by definition they can never claim to possess:

> The religions, in fact, are even more intensely pluralistic and ambiguous than art, morality, philosophy, and politics. Given the nature of the subject matter of religion, this is necessarily the case. For religions do claim, after all, that Ultimate Reality has revealed itself and that there is a way of liberation for any human being. (86)

Because the very nature of Christianity is to argue for a reality beyond all language, even its own, its own language must always be subjected to "retrieval, critique, and suspicion" (86). That's why the church needs the university: to be suspicious of it. Yes, we must accept the "thoughts" that we apply after the process of analysis and thickening, the thoughts we wager, but the very nature of these thoughts immediately requires us to begin the interpretive cycle again. The cycle becomes a spinning wheel, a turning globe, a planet, and it's always moving. What the dogma proclaims is a reality before which we must be joyously humble and subordinate, kneeling before it. What the dogma proclaim is a reality before which we must always take apart those very proclamations, take them apart and throw them away and start over again, but joyously, in prayer. What the dogma proclaim is always their own inadequacy and so we can never rest in them. What they proclaim is the need for constant interpretation and critique.[41]

The university is the place of critique. The university is where faith continues to discover and rediscover its own otherness, its own difference, its own need.

In the *Apologia* Newman describes this dynamic not as a dialogue but as a kind of "warfare" between the "infallibility" of the church and the creative and analytic power of human reason. "It is necessary for the very life of religion [. . .] that the warfare should be incessantly carried on." Every exercise of infallibility, he says, "is brought out into act by an intense and varied operation of the Reason, both as its ally and as its opponent, and provokes again, when it has done its work, a re-action of Reason against it." And so the will of the Holy Spirit works itself out in the flawed and varied realm of human bodies and beings, "ebbing and flowing" like "the tide" (225). The university is the ebb, the church the flow. Or: without an opponent, the opponent of the university, this necessary warfare cannot be carried on.

Moberly makes exactly the same point, even though he rejects the very idea of "infallibility," at least in one sense of that word:

> While we are ourselves assured that the whole truth is to be found in Christ, we have to recognize that it is not in the possession of Christians, either individually or collectively. [. . .] Any implied claim to infallibility is unchristian, since it clashes with Christian insight into human creatureliness and human corruption. (104)

Newman would agree, if by "infallibility" Moberly means the pretensions of merely human activity. It's Newman, after all, anticipating another great Vatican II document, *Lumen Gentium*, who makes it clear that this church that might otherwise, in another context, be described as "infallible," is finally "but the expression in human language of truths to which the human mind is unequal" (*Apologia* 44).

Newman would perhaps even agree with Moberly's startling conclusion:

> It follows that an all-Christian university, if we could have it, would be defective. We have indispensable lessons to learn from the heretic, however wrong he is on fundamental issues. He is needed both as a test and as a contributor. (105).

The sciences and the liberal arts even in Newman's Catholic university are allowed to function independently and without censor except at the extremes. Newman insists on the distinction between the Christian and the gentleperson, and this is in the nineteenth century. Much has changed by the time that Moberly is writing, in the twentieth, as much has changed now, in the twenty-first. "In the present state of the world," Moberly says, "Christians themselves ought not to want an all-Christian university" (105). Even now, especially now, we who are Christians teaching at the public university are teaching where we are called to be, as Christians, as believers. We are graced in our profession and our place. We are called.

------

Three images from the stars.

In *Teaching Christianity* Augustine describes himself as a "finger" pointing to a star. We can choose to look or not to look. All he can do is point (101).

Dante's *Purgatorio* ends with the same word as the other two canticles of the *Divine Comedy*. After descending into hell and climbing the seven story mountain, guided by Virgil and what he represents of human culture, Dante is now "ready for the stars." He is ready to ascend.

In a wonderful passage from a letter, centuries later, the poet Coleridge describes the relation between religion and reason:

> Religion passes out of the ken of Reason only where the eye of Reason has reached its own Horizon; and that Faith is then but its continuation: even as the Day softens away into the sweet Twilight, and Twilight, hushed and breathless, steals into the Darkness. It is Night, sacred Night! The upraised Eye views only the starry Heaven which manifests itself alone: and the outward Beholding is fixed on the sparks twinkling in the aweful depth, through suns of other Worlds, only to preserve the Soul steady and collected in its pure Act of inward Adoration to the great I AM, and to the filial WORD that re-affirmeth it from Eternity to Eternity, whose choral Echo is the Universe. (qtd. in Holmes 412)

The university is the daytime, faith the night.

The university is the *inferno* and the *purgatorio*, faith the *paradiso*.

The university is the finger that points, faith the stars that we can choose to see.

The university confronts us with the vastness of interpretive possibilities, with the mystery and complexity beneath the convenient and simplifying names that we assumed to be the reality itself. How we respond is up to us. We can turn away. We can deny and evade. We can despair. Or we can, with Coleridge and Dante and Augustine, open ourselves up to awe. Even as we are dwarfed, we are ennobled.

---

The choice is ours. The revelation is never so clear as to compel belief, which is why reason is never enough. The wager is required, and that wager is faith, and faith means surrender. It means dying.

We must die to live and the university wants us only to live. Or it's the reverse: the university is always killing us, always shattering our beliefs, tearing things apart. It's only across the line that we can live.

We must die and we must live and the two are always connected. There is no resurrection without crucifixion, and until the second coming, our resurrections are always tentative. Crucifixion always follows. There is no paradise without the *purgatorio*. The way up is the way down.

That's why we need the university: to crucify us.

We need the university so that we can run away from it, hurrying across campus to venerate the cross. We need the university to define what should be worshiped and what shouldn't. We need the good and sincere but sometimes lazy and jeering students to remind us what we also know in the sinfulness of our own hearts, that this world is not enough.

We need the cross to remind us that the self is to be died to. We need the cross to teach us how the self must rise.

---

And we are standing behind it, holding it up with our arms, resisting the pushes and the shoves, adjusting it here and there, keeping it upright even as our arms grow numb—it is shifting and slipping—it is the spar of a ship, a huge, wooden spar, shifting and creaking as the wind takes the sails.

It is a tree, a giant tree, and we are standing beneath it, looking up at the sky.

It is all the trees there ever were, it is a forest, an ancient forest, vast and deep, and we are walking and walking inside of it, further and further in.

# Conclusion

What I've done in this book is used my own experience to reflect on the experience of all Christian faculty who finally have to cross the line in their teaching and their faith. The line is hard to define but nonetheless real and good—good for us both as intellectuals and as Christians. Without it, the necessary and creative tension between faith and reason is no longer possible.

We can't finally live on both sides of the divide. We can't avoid the challenge and the choice. There's important and productive and inspiring overlap, moments in the classroom when the boundaries seem to collapse and there is no tension, there is no gulf. But in the end my argument has been that to live in faith requires an intellectual as well as a personal sacrifice, an intellectual as well as a personal honesty. The difficult and shifting border that I've been describing must be crossed and is always being crossed, and the most important contribution we can make as Christian faculty is to keep crossing that line and professing that we have.

But the line doesn't just exist for us, and we're not the only ones who cross it. Our students cross the line, too, all the time, and their experience deepens and clarifies our own call as believers.

One day in spring I was teaching my Advanced Composition class, using Tom Junod's fine essay about Mr. Rogers, one of my heroes, and in it there was a line I really liked. Mr. Rogers is getting out of a taxicab in New York City. A homeless man is sitting on the sidewalk, leaning against the wall of a building, and when he sees Mr. Rogers—Mr. Rogers himself, of Mr. Rogers's neighborhood—he blurts out: Holy Shucks, it's

Mister Flipping Rogers (or words to that effect). I have a weakness for profanity, I have to admit, and here, in this context, the string of those words struck me as so earthy and funny and sharp that I couldn't stop repeating them when we turned to the students' own work. Whenever I saw a line that I liked in their own essays, I'd burst out myself: Holy Shucks, it's Mister Flipping Rogers. Over and over again. I must have said it thirty or forty times that period, just riffing, unthinkingly.

The next day a student from the class came to my office, a very good student, a single mother returning to school for a masters in teaching. She started talking about how I'd been repeating that line from the essay, and I thought, oh no, here it is, I should have watched myself. Once again I should have thought before I opened my mouth.

But before I had a chance to apologize, she stopped and turned. She wanted to talk about becoming Catholic, she said. She wanted to talk about her spiritual journey and about coming into the church, and it was because I kept repeating that line in the essay. She knew I was Catholic and she thought, well, if he's got a sense of humor anyway, maybe it's alright after all. A year later, at the Easter Vigil, she was dunked in the water, fully immersed, coming up sputtering and smiling, then later confirmed.

Through the grace of God my thoughtlessness became a way in for that young woman, a young woman who felt crowded out of the church, who couldn't see how to get to Jesus through the front door. She knew Jesus was in there, and he is, he really is, in the church as in the house in the famous reading from Mark, the house in the second chapter where Jesus has come to teach. But all of us Christians were taking up the space, blocking the way, and like the friends of the paralytic in Mark's story, who took off the roof and lowered him in from above, my student had to take off the roof of the church and lower herself in. My office was the back door.

It was her assumptions about the church crowding her out in a way: that the church is full of disapproving moralists and terrifying rules and that you have to toe the line and sit up straight even to ask about it; that to be Catholic means to abandon everything about you that makes you human, like a sense of humor, or a sense of the real world. And it was my privilege to be the one who could show her, through my own obvious humanness, that no, that's not true.

Although in another way maybe those aren't just assumptions, or they are assumptions that sometimes Catholics and other Christians justify. Several days later this woman gave me a draft of an essay describing a childhood experience in a church where the preacher screamed about sin and damnation and scared her away for years, until now, and it's not just people in that church who do that. It's all of us. As G. K. Chesterton puts it, "The Christian ideal has not been tried and found wanting. It has been found difficult, and left untried" (48). We are all of us so often second- and third-rate Christians, we are so often Pharisees, sinful people who distort the grace we've been given, sticking to the rules and making everything technical and literal instead of falling back in humility before the mystery of God's love.

That's why Pope John XXIII convened the Second Vatican Council. His metaphor was of opening the windows and letting in the air, but the idea is just the same as in the gospel. Sometimes we have to raise the roof. Sometimes we have to open up a hole, come at things in a new way, backwards or at an angle, the sun has to come through, and not just at Vatican councils but maybe in universities, too.

It's the student who has crossed the line here, coming to my office within the university not to talk about things academic but things spiritual. That's legal, from both our perspectives. The university lawyer tells me that I can't "solicit" for my ministry using my university phone number, e-mail, or office, but that it's legal and proper for me to talk about spiritual things within the university if students have come to me on their own accord. The point is that sometimes they do. It happens a dozen times a term. A student comes to my office to talk about some academic issue but halfway through, the conversation changes, I can feel it, and it's time to shift gears, put on my other hat. It's not that I have any special wisdom but that ordination has identified me as someone who can be talked to about spiritual things, safely, without risk of ridicule. And they come, every term a handful come, and what that suggests to me is that students, too, feel the inadequacy of the university. They too long for something that the university not only doesn't provide but sometimes actively wars against.

The university is the house and sometimes we have to remove the roof. Sometimes the students do.

————

Sometimes we convert our students and sometimes our students convert us.

Of course we want to convert them—all teachers do: to openness, to precision, to fact, to intellectual humility. As a teacher who teaches Christian classics, my hope is for students to arrive at just the maturity and complexity that Mari shows here:

> I thought that I knew what Christianity was. Before this class, if I took an exam that asked, "What is Christianity?" I would have written a clear and concise answer: "Christianity is the belief that Jesus Christ is our savior. Christianity has been the predominant Western faith for the past 1500 years, and has many branches and sects. The two main

divisions are Catholics and Protestants. Martin Luther led the
Protestant revolution. Christians believe in both the Old and New
Testaments of the Bible." Now, I am not sure. I would give that same
question a different answer: "Christianity is a trust in the mystery of
God. All Christians believe, fundamentally, that Jesus is the spoken
word of God, and that he was the infinite embodied in the finite. God
is infinite and humans are finite, yet we were created in the image and
likeness of God. Somewhere within the depths of our soul we also contain a bit of God's timelessness." I could go on and on. Before reading
the *Confessions*, I thought that I could give a concise definition of
Christianity. The more I learn, the less I know. The more I learn, the
longer it takes to explain nuances that I do not understand. I was found
and now I am lost.

Yes, we want our students to find themselves, but in another sense we
want them to do just what Mari does: to lose herself, as Augustine loses
himself.

What's troubling and problematic—even after all I've said, even after
all the reflections and qualifications of the last six chapters—is when students go further than this, converting not just to the intellectual position
that I share with my colleagues but to my own spiritual point of view. No,
I don't proselytize in the classroom. I identify myself believing, I don't
urge others to believe. But simply by being who she is, a teacher influences students, simply by standing in front of them for ten weeks being
who she is, and since who I am is Catholic, it's certainly possible that students may be influenced by Catholicism.

It's not mostly me that influences, of course, it's the readings: the
Bible, Augustine, Dante. Immersed in these works, even at a state university, how can students not now and then come to religious insights that
apply to their own lives? It's not just the content of the works, their
themes, that might convert them. It's their complexity, it's the sense of
wonder they invoke, it's the sense even of confusion. If Augustine is converted by becoming confounded, whenever we succeed in getting our
students lost, there is at least a chance that they may end up believing.
We show them the night sky, we look up and point, and when students
see the stars, who knows but that they might be filled with awe?

Even the experience of interpretive frustration can lead, inadvertently, to faith. Reading literature teaches us the limits of our own knowledge, our inevitable subjectivity, our dependence on language itself.
What we learn through reading, as Gadamer says, is "the knowledge of
the limitations of humanity, of the absoluteness of the barrier which separates [us] from the divine," and this is ultimately, by its nature, "a religious insight." It is the experience of "human finitude" (37). Who knows

where this experience might lead? Perhaps to the next step: the realization of our need, for God and for each other.

I don't mean that there's a rush of conversions. As a preacher I know how difficult it is to move anyone to faith even when you're standing in the pulpit trying as hard as you can to do just that. Preaching has not been notably effective over the centuries, least of all mine. Even Jesus doesn't convince. By the end he is alone on the cross, all his followers gone.

There isn't any danger here for my secular colleagues to worry about, but there is an issue, and it's the students who raise it finally. They are in a sense more naïve about the separation of church and state and the boundaries between reason and faith. Many say they sign up for the Western Civilization survey because they want an opportunity to explore their faith and reflect on their own spirituality. My first reaction is embarrassment. My first impulse is to clarify: that's not what this class is for, it's an academic class, we're analyzing, not leaping into faith. But the students don't see those distinctions, and there's something to be said for that. There's an important issue embedded in the actual lives and practices of our students, in the academic version of what St. Basil calls the "truths unintentionally transmitted by custom."

Abby writes that she "struggled throughout the course to distinguish between an academic reading of these texts and a spiritual reading," but that in the end she found "that the value of reading them lies in the intermixing of the spiritual and academic." She explains: "At first I experienced a feeling of abandonment when I realized that the Bible is not intended to prove the objective truth of Christianity, but eventually I began to see the beauty that lies in the mystery of God revealed by the text." First she experienced disillusionment and disenchantment in just the way that Ricouer means it. She experienced the struggle of critical assessment. But eventually for her that very unthickening of the image led to a greater faith, a faith now in mystery, in the mystery itself, not in narrow human images of that mystery. "Learning to see the work of Mark, Augustine, and Dante as stories created to interpret a mystery experienced by the authors allows me to experience these mysteries through their eyes." Abby doesn't know and doesn't care about the critical theory that would expose such personal identification as naïve. She is reading to live.

Yet her reading is not all that naïve after all. What deepens her faith is exactly her awareness of her own "terministic screens"—that term again from Burke—her awareness of the interpretive frames of reference that she has brought to the text:

> The terministic screens of the authors, including the time and location
> in which they lived, affect their writing just as my own screen affects

my reading. My fear of reading the Bible as literature was really my fear of accepting the impact of these screens. I preferred to view God as above all of these screens and interpretations, but I have found that in fact it is through these screens that I can come to see more of God. It's not that God is changed or influenced by these screens, but that we as humans, in our weakness of mind, can only see God as through a screen. Rather than restricting my experience of God to the academic, as I feared would happen, my heart and mind have been opened to an endless supply of experiences of God provided by listening to the experiences of others, past and present. This is challenging to my own faith, but rather than fearing this challenge as a threat to my beliefs, I embrace the opportunity for growth and new understanding.

What every teacher wants is change in the students. We want them to be different going out than they were going in, even if more confused. What every teacher wants is the acceptance of complexity, the awareness that things are more complicated than they first appeared. Abby demonstrates both, beautifully, eloquently—change and the awareness of complexity— and that intellectual enlargement or growth has immediately and quite naturally led to an enlargement of her faith in God. It's his complexity that she sees, it's her own humility that she experiences, in the face of that greatness.

Mari earned an A in the course for her capacity to articulate her own change and deepening, a change and deepening that didn't lead to faith. But in Abby's case, faith has deepened intellectual understanding and intellectual understanding has deepened faith. She has believed and so understood, she has understood and so believed, and frankly it's hard for me to separate the faith from the understanding in explaining why I gave her an A+ except to say that it's an A+ partly because she herself refuses to distinguish in any simple way between faith and under-standing.

One day I receive an e-mail from a student I don't remember at first, an undergraduate who took the Literature of Western Civilization a year before and has now transferred to another school. It's an e-mail that com-plicates the question still further. Jason writes that he was "raised in a Baptist church and had Baptist ways," reading the Bible literally from the time he was a child. "Your class was extremely hard for me to take." He couldn't believe some of the things that I was saying: "According to how I was raised, blasphemy was flowing from your mouth and you were a terrible heretic bound for hell."

But gradually something started to shift:

> I did have one internal conflict I faced, however, walking into your
> class every day telling myself how awful your teachings were. I found

myself fighting the same feelings over and over again: what you were teaching made sense. This was awful because it couldn't make sense—you were going to hell! I couldn't listen to you! But the problem was all of the gaps in the Bible that you were talking about had never made sense to me growing up Baptist. You were right that they were there and I had to look at them. And then you began to answer some of my questions and explain how to read past these gaps. You made things make sense. I realized I had been looking at everything through glasses that were made for me and placed on me. You helped to remove them and I began to listen as well as see.

The e-mail concludes with an update on this life since leaving OSU: that he's not going to the religious college that he planned to attend, that he's reading lots of books in his free time, that he's even registered for the Pacific Green Party!

I've been teaching long enough to know that most of what happens in a class has nothing to do with me, the good and the bad; that students are ready to learn or not ready to learn; that sometimes I have the privilege of being the one who can be the door or the opening in the roof; that the classroom is defined by the fall, just like everything else; that the classroom is available to grace. I share this story partly as a way of celebrating the many students I have had who respond with intelligence and generosity to what I try to teach, who want it and get it, who make teaching worthwhile. But more, I share this to make even fuzzier the fuzzy line that I have drawn between reason and faith, the university and the church. This fine young man has been converted, partly through what he experienced in my class—his faith has been changed, it has been lost, and a new faith found—and this has come about exactly because of the work of reason, exactly because of critical thinking, exactly because he has done what a university wants him to do and thought long and hard about what no longer seems obvious. The reason that it's hard to separate reason from faith is that sometimes reason naturally leads to faith. It opens things up. It reveals the icon as image, it lets in the mystery again. And when that happens, it's very hard not to respond. It's very hard not to hunger and thirst for more of the beauty and the sweetness that's been glimpsed.

This young man's parents were justified in worrying about sending him to the university. He did lose his faith, and discovered a new one.

———

Sometimes students believe before the class begins, their faith is already there, and it continues to express itself throughout the term, unfazed. Randall comes to my office, enthused about literature and writing and the love of God, an evangelical student, active in Campus

Crusade for Christ. God is so "awesome" he says, grinning, talking about how the journal he's been writing has deepened his faith, and I can't help but be heartened and warmed. Lindsay, another evangelical student, writes after the course is over to thank me for "strengthening my faith and allowing me to share with you how the Lord has changed my life," even though I've quietly cut her off every time she's tried. Yet when she blesses me in this final e-mail, I feel blessed, for days: "I pray that the Lord blesses you each and every day of your life," she says, and I say amen. Amen, I say.

Who am I to challenge what is so deep and sincere? What these students praise has flowed out of them and into the class, what they thank me for is a love and a faith that comes from God, a love and a faith that no professor should try to undermine. Who am I to say that such faith can't coexist with the critical thinking that I have tried to demonstrate or that it might even have in some way been aided by it? Who am I to say what is first and what is second naïveté?

Isn't their conviction what I long for myself?

Sometimes students are already engaged and engaging thinkers, long before they encounter me. Often. One Friday a student came to my office during office hours. I was irritated at first. I had work to do and memos to write. But he wanted to talk about his spiritual life and the reading he's been doing—he's not accepting anything, he's not believing anything—and he's a smart and sincere and personable guy. After a few minutes I relaxed and settled back in my chair. Here was a man genuinely alive, genuinely seeking the spirit, and the spirit was already in him. I could feel it welling out of him and into the room, and something started to well up in me, too, as he talked. He's got thousands of questions right now, thousands of doubts, the good, healthy kind. He's not a believer and probably never will be, but he's got enthusiasm, and joy, and hope, and talking to him I felt better than I had in days. I felt like myself again.

How does God call us? Moment by moment, person by person, even at Oregon State University.

———

Johanna's wedding, a spring day at Silver Falls, by a river and among the trees. Johanna is a graduate student and teaching assistant, a fine, disciplined student, but here she is in a flowing white gown smiling at the man who is now her husband, a Ph.D. candidate in microbiology. I am standing in front of them, in my alb and my stole, and the wind is moving in the fir trees, and Johanna is smiling and I am saying the words, the congregation is laughing and clapping.

Rhonda and John, Amy and Scott, so many others, couples who come to my office and ask me to come into their lives in this other way, for just a moment. May the Lord bless you, I say to the bride, my student. May the Lord bless you, I say to the groom, my student. But it is they who are blessing me.

A few years ago another of my students came and asked about being Catholic, and it was my honor to sponsor her for confirmation and introduce her to the church. Later, as she finished her Masters degree, she started feeling another call. School seemed to be paralyzing her. School was the house with the low and constricting roof, it wasn't answering to a deeper need, and it was given to me to ask if she had ever considered the religious life. She looked at me like I was crazy. A nun?

But several years later I stood in the chapel at Queen of Angels Monastery at Mount Angel as this faith-filled young woman became a novice, the first formal step towards becoming a Benedictine. What a moment that was, seeing her there, so happy, all the other nuns welcoming her.

It was God calling her. I was just one of a number of others helping her hear that. And it was a gift to be able to do that, a gift to me, a grace—a grace that we all are given, I think. Now and then we are all given a moment when we can make a difference for someone else. We are the ones looking at a friend over a cup of coffee—we are the ones who can say: you need help. Here, here's a number you can call. Here, let me drive you. Or maybe it's given to us just to smile and say yes, this is good, this is wonderful. Or maybe it's given to us just to listen, just to be there.

Even at Oregon State. This young woman wasn't Catholic before she started graduate school. When she left she was on her way to the monastery.

Students cross the line. They move back and forth from church to university all the time. Students I minister to at the Newman Center take my classes, students who have taken classes with me sometimes attend Mass or go on retreat. And they make whatever connections they make then. They are pulled in whatever way they are pulled. And I am pulled then, too. Their faith moves me, it deepens and complicates me, it crosses my lines in so many ways that some days I am back in the sea of stories, bobbing and confused, but joyous, alive, humbled, grateful to be in the presence not just of God but of the generosity and humaneness of these young men and women.

---

A woman comes to my office, a senior English major, and in a few minutes the conversation has shifted as it sometimes does. She is crying. Do you want me to listen now as a deacon, I ask her, not as a professor, and she nods through her tears. She has lost her baby, she tells me, she has miscarried, just a few days before, and she is very shaken by the experience. She is grieving over the loss of that hope and that possibility. "Where is my baby?" she asks me. "Is my baby in heaven?"

This woman isn't Catholic, and it occurs to me for a moment that maybe I could explain Catholic teaching on the origin of life and the grace of God. This woman is an insightful reader and writer, and it occurs to me for a moment that maybe I could talk a little about Augustine's theology of grace and the mercy of God. But through that very grace I am able to wait and to resist the temptation to talk. Through that grace I am able to realize what is obvious, that this person is in tears and that she needs not language, not ideas, not theology, but consolation.

May I pray with you?

May I take your hand?

It's so warm when I take it, her hand is so warm. And we sit there together, our chairs facing, and we pray together, our heads down, right there in my office in Moreland Hall, behind the closed door. Then I look up and lift my hand and make the sign of the cross above her: "May the Lord bless you and keep you, may the Lord make his face to shine upon you and be gracious onto you, may the Lord lift up his countenance upon you and give you his peace."

---

Holy Thursday, St. Mary's. Several of us have taken our positions at the top of each aisle, sitting on chairs, a basin of water in front of us, and we are washing feet. The people come up one by one, take off a shoe and a sock, and sitting in the chair across from me, extend their foot for me to wash in the water. I put my right hand on their heel and pour the water with my left, three times, then dry them off with a towel, enacting two thousand years later the gesture of Jesus the night before he died, at the last supper, when he got down on his knees and bathed the dusty feet of his disciples.

It's an intimate thing, to touch a stranger's foot. Some are delicate and veined. Some are hard as horn, gnarled. Small. Large. White. Brown.

I look up and there is Abby. I look up and there is Anna. I look up and there is Alicia. My students are standing there, waiting, they are coming forward and sitting in the facing chair. And I'm reaching out to cup their heel in my hand. I am touching the skin of their feet, pouring out the water.

This is what Jesus the greatest of teachers instructed all of us to do: to kneel before our students and wash their very feet. To die to ourselves. To humble ourselves. To empty ourselves out. And what moves me is not that I have achieved this in any way more than liturgically but that the students have come for this, too. They have come to feel the water, they have come to be cleansed, and in coming they cleanse me, too.

They are crossing the line, and I am crossing the line, and for now we are all together. For now we are all in the presence of the Lord. We are in the kingdom.

# Notes

1. Though a number of scholars have explored the history of faith and the university, particularly from the point of view of the religious college—see note 3—I believe that I am the first to focus on these questions from the perspective of the secular university. But as Burtchaell argues in *The Dying of the Light: The Disengagement of Colleges and Universities from their Christian Churches*, in this respect there really isn't much difference between religious and secular institutions. Even in most church-sponsored colleges and universities, faith is no longer an integral part of the intellectual life on campus and hasn't been for a long time. In fact, faith may never have been central in these institutions, Burtchaell suggests, not in any real sense, since in the eighteenth and nineteenth centuries their curriculum was merely classical, not theological, a matter of learning Greek and Latin. Certainly now, given the need to compete for students, religious colleges and universities tend to downplay their religious heritage, though Robert Benne discusses several notable exceptions in *Quality with Soul*. As a result, on many of these campuses the majority of faculty and students are not believers, a factor that in itself changes the character of the institution. Though faith and reason may be more in harmony at such places than at public institutions, day to day—in the classroom, on hiring and tenure committees—my Christian colleagues at Christian colleges and universities say that their situation is much the same as mine at Oregon State.

And the problem isn't limited to Christian colleges. In "Jewishness and Judaism at Brandeis University," Marvin Fox observes that at this ostensibly Jewish institution, "the most urgent questions that face a religiously committed Jew in any American university receive no answers or even any consideration." As at Christian colleges, too, as at any secular university, faith is something to the side, on the periphery. "We do nothing institutionally to help our students deal with the issues generated for religion by our whole range of academic subject matter. [. . .] Such concerns stand outside the orbit of a nonsectarian university. [. . .] We do not, because we may not, address the deepest religious questions, even those that are specifically generated by the academic setting in which we spend our lives" (469).

Richard Hughes notes these same tensions and problems in religious and former religious colleges, like Pepperdine, where he teaches, a college founded by the Churches of Christ. He then goes on, in *How Christian Faith Can Sustain the Life of the Mind*, to make an argument very similar to the one that I make in the next few paragraphs in the context of the secular university. There's much of intellectual value in the Christian tradition that first formed these colleges, he says, much that should be reclaimed, however poorly realized in the past. In fact, for Hughes personally faith is the foundation of the intellectual life. "Precisely because I am a Christian scholar, I seek to maintain an open classroom in which my students can raise any questions they wish. Precisely because I am a Christian scholar, I seek to nurture in my students a hunger and thirst for truth. Precisely because I am a Christian scholar, I encourage my students to critically assess not only the perspectives of others, but their own" (9).

2. This theology is often described not just as "postmodern" but also as "post-liberal" and "post-conservative." The last chapter of Douglas Sloan's *Faith and Reason: Mainstream Protestantism and American Higher Education*—"Postmodernism and its Postmodern Prospects"—is a fine survey of both the Protestant and the evangelical versions of this movement (212–37). Stanley Grenz and John Franke's *Beyond Foundationalism: Shaping Theology in a Postmodern Context* is a book-length study of the evangelical approach. Conservative and evangelical Christianity has depended on an "epistemological foundationalism," Grenz and Franke explain, a belief in the "absolute, incontestable certainty" of ideas that can be expressed in the form of propositions. The Bible is understood as the source of these propositions, ready for systematizing and logical arrangement. But a number of conservatives and evangelicals are now attempting

to develop a method for doing theology in a postmodern framework, a method that is neither liberal nor "propositional" or "foundational." The move is from "a realist to a constructivist view of truth and the world," a move based on a "chastened rationality" that accepts the complexity and situatedness of knowledge while not giving up on the idea that reality can nonetheless be known, that knowledge is nonetheless possible, in some way (23). Sloan calls this a "true postmodernism": "postpositivist, postreductionist, postrelativist" (xiii). The introduction to Dan Stiver's fine *Theology After Ricouer* is also a useful overview of the development of this "more embodied and holistic view of the world," this "epistemological holism" (11). See also Nancey Murphy's *Beyond Liberalism and Fundamentalism: How Modern and Postmodern Philosophy Set the Theological Agenda*.

My argument in this book is grounded in the work of Ricouer, as well as of the Catholic theologian David Tracy, and it's exactly here that my thinking intersects this new evangelical theology. As Stiver demonstrates, we share an interest in the same figures—Stiver's whole project is to show the usefulness of Ricouer for the postmodern Protestant agenda (87). Postmodern theologians are also very interested in Tracy, as well as in the earlier philosophy of Gadamer. It's in our mutual concern with tradition, with culture, and with the constitutive power of symbol that Protestant, evangelical, and Catholic theology seem to be coming together.

3. I have found several books particularly helpful in piecing together the complex history of the university. Jean LeClercq's *The Love of Learning and the Desire for God* explains the idea of education in Benedictine monasticism, the origin of the university in medieval Europe. George Marsden's *The Soul of the American University*, after summarizing the history of the university in Europe during and after the Reformation, tells in great detail the story of American higher education, emphasizing the complicated relationship between church and state. Though it focuses on the rise of the English Department, Gerald Graff's *Professing Literature* also gives a good sense of the development of specialization and disciplinarity in the university as a whole, emphasizing the role of practical politics and economics in the establishment of academic culture as we know it today. Marsden and Graff inform my discussion throughout this book. Kurt Spellmeyer's recent *Arts of Living* is a principled attack on the professionalism that Graff describes and an argument for a new vision of the humanities, one closer to the needs of students and the world. Stephen Carter's *The Culture of Disbelief* looks at these questions from the perspective of constitutional law, arguing that we have misunderstood the intentions of the founders and created a false wall

between church and state. My argument in the final two chapters very much depends on Carter's fine and insightful analysis.

A number of other books have deepened and complicated my sense of this topic. Burtchaell's *The Dying of the Light*, as I've mentioned, follows Marsden with an exhaustive history of the gradual disengagement of religious colleges from their Christian heritage. Philip Gleason's *Contending with Modernity: Catholic Higher Education in the Twentieth Century*, tells the story for Catholic institutions. Benne's *Quality with Soul* describes the efforts of a few religious colleges to "keep faith with their religious traditions," as he puts it, re-establishing the connections that have pulled apart for the majority. *Models for Christian Higher Education*, edited by Richard Hughes and William Adrian, collects a number of essays exploring the place of religious colleges in contemporary higher education, as does *The Future of Religious Colleges*, the proceedings of a 2000 Harvard conference on this subject, edited by Paul Dovre. Several studies since Marsden have also stepped back to look again at the role of religion in the larger history of American higher education, emphasizing its role in the public university. Warren Nord's *Religion and American Education: Rethinking a National Dilemma* argues for "restoring the tensions" between faith and reason by allowing religious texts and ideas to be taught in state sponsored schools, an idea that I will draw on in my final chapter. Jon Roberts and James Turner's *The Sacred and the Secular University* suggests that the split between religion and higher education isn't the result of an inherent theoretical conflict but of the institutional forces of academic specialization. Julie Reuben's *The Making of the Modern University: Intellectual Transformation and the Marginalization of Morality* focuses on the transition from the nineteenth to the twentieth centuries, when the university gradually relinquished its role as a teacher of moral values.

Several further books about the history of higher education have also challenged and intrigued me. While providing a very useful overview of postmodern Protestant and evangelical theology, Sloan's main purpose in *Faith and Reason* is to show how mainstream Protestantism eventually surrendered the public university to the false rationalism of the sciences. I come back to his argument again and again in the chapters and notes that follow. Mark Schwehn's *Exiles from Eden: Religion and Academic Vocation* reflects on the implications of the author's own move from a larger comprehensive university to a small church-sponsored institution, arguing in the process for a more spiritually committed curriculum and a greater emphasis on the spiritual vocation of teachers. I draw on Schwehn's insights several times in chapters five and six, along with Hughes's analysis in *How Christian Faith Can Sustain the Life of the Mind*. George Dennis O'Brien's recent *The Idea of a Catholic University* has been a touchstone throughout my analysis. (See also Jaroslav Pelikan's reflection on Newman's classic, *The Idea of the University: A Re-examination*.)

4. Except where noted otherwise, all my citations from Tracy are from *Plurality and Ambiguity*.

5. I am thinking, for example, of Allan Bloom's best-selling *The Closing of the American Mind* and its attack on the instinctive relativism of students in the 1980s. My own critique of relativism in chapters five and six owes something to Bloom's. I certainly share his commitment to the "rational quest for the good," as well as his sense that truth exists, finally, outside of history and culture. What I resist is the tone of Bloom's form of Platonism, as well as its confidence. "The United States is one of the highest and most extreme achievements of the rational quest for the good life according to nature," he says, a statement that strikes me as both inaccurate and chauvinistic (39). What I resist, too, is Bloom's impatience with students. For me the problem with their relativism is not its relativism but its immaturity. It's generous but unformed. The key is not to abandon such generosity but to develop and discipline it. There's wisdom here, an instinctive understanding of the values of pluralism as well as of the central insight of Platonism itself: that the truth is beyond any one of us, that for all its virtues, reason can only take us so far.

6. This is Garry Wills's own translation, in his short biography, *Saint Augustine*, of a line from one of Augustine's less accessible sermons. Later in my introduction, I also use Wills's translation of a line from another less accessible work, *Enarrationes in Psalmos*, Augustine's voluminous commentary on the Psalms: "Pride asserts, humility testifies" (Wills xvi).

7. Because it asks local bishops to "watch over" the Catholic character of faculty and students at Catholic universities (43), *Ex Corde Ecclesiae* has been a controversial document for Catholic intellectuals. But while there's good reason to be concerned about the practical effects of this particular recommendation, in general *Ex Corde* makes the same point that I am making in this book, that though reason is the "minister" of faith (6), in the end faith and reason are not the same.

On this theoretical level, too, everything I say in the following chapters applies not just to Christian faculty at state universities but to faculty in religious universities as well. After all, I ground my argument in Newman's *The Idea of the University*, a book that describes the formation of a Catholic university and that insists, as I will explain in chapters five and six, on the boundary between the "gentleman" and the "Christian." John Paul II is likewise careful to talk about the "institutional autonomy" of Catholic colleges and universities and to support the idea of academic freedom (12). Certainly all but the most sectarian institutions, Catholic, Protestant, or evangelical, are careful to distinguish between the academic and evangelizing mission of their schools. Students and faculty are evaluated by performance, not piety. Conversion is not required for graduation or promotion. In other words, though it's possible to lament the separation of faith and reason at religious schools, it's also possible to see faith and reason as existing in a necessary tension, by their nature. Again, see Burtchaell for the history of religious colleges in America. See Gleason and O'Brien for a discussion of the situation in Catholic universities, a discussion that applies directly to Protestant and evangelical institutions as well. O'Brien's analysis of *Ex Corde* in chapter nine of *The Idea of a Catholic University* is particularly nuanced.

For an analysis of the practical realities of academic freedom in religious colleges and universities, see Charles Curran's *Catholic Higher Education, Theology, and Academic Freedom*. What makes this book of special interest is that Curran, a moral theologian, was censored by the Vatican and excluded from teaching Catholic theology because of his outspoken views on abortion, contraception, and other issues. It was a celebrated case and represents just the dangers that many Catholic academics see in the paragraph in *Ex Corde* about the overseeing role of the bishops.

8. See Stiver's *Theology After Ricouer* for an in-depth and theologically sophisticated reading of Ricouer's entire career, a reading that puts Ricouer in the context both of postmodernism and of contemporary theology, Catholic, Protestant, and evangelical.

## CHAPTER I

9. See O'Brien's discussion of "truth" and the Catholic university in chapter 2 of *The Idea of the Catholic University*, a discussion that depends on an analysis of Pope John Paul II's encyclical, *Fides et Ratio*, an effort to reassert the traditional methods and values of theological reasoning. It's not just science that's rational. Faith is, too, in different ways. Theological reasoning involves reasoning *towards* a faith position but even more, finally, reasoning *from* such a position, that is, reflecting in a sustained and rational way on what is first accepted as revelation. The acceptance of revealed truth becomes the premise for syllogistic reasoning—reasoning that takes place, furthermore, inside the terms and methods and judgments of tradition.

As O'Brien puts it, "by allying faith with reason," theology seeks to establish that Christian religion, "no less than rational science, lays claims upon the individual that go beyond subjective interests and position" (24). See also the first chapter of Bernard Lonergan's *Method in Theology* for an explanation of how theology performs its acts of reasoning, as well as Ben Meyer's appropriation of Lonergan's "critical realism" in *Critical Realism and the New Testament.* Lonergan, Meyer says, "retrieved the conditions of the possibility of real meaning and real value" (7). Nancey Murphy's *Reasoning and Rhetoric and Religion* lays out the methods of theological reasoning in the form of a textbook, extending the standard chapters on logic and logical fallacies to the realm of religion. There is a "rationality of religion," she says, and a corresponding way of making and supporting claims about revealed truth and matters of faith. Sloan makes an interesting case for the validity of "ecstatic reason" in the theological method of Tillich (116) and in general argues for the rationality of religion as a subject of discussion in the university.

As we will see in *The Idea of the University*, Newman certainly thinks of theology as in part a rational method. Theology should be taught at the university because it's *true*. "A university, I should lay down, by its very name professes to teach universal knowledge: Theology is surely a branch of knowledge: how then is it possible for it to profess branches of knowledge, and yet to exclude from the subjects of its teaching one which, to say the least, is as important and as large as any of them?" (25). Newman's *An Essay in Aid of a Grammar of Assent* is an in-depth analysis of the process of conversion, a process that involves the cumulative weight of experience, emotion, and reason.

10. All my Biblical quotations are taken from *The New Oxford Annotated Bible* (New Revised Standard Version).

11. See Stiver's *Theology After Ricouer*, especially pages 56–78, on Ricouer's notion of "the hermeneutical arc"; and pages 100–117, on Ricouer's *The Symbolism of Evil* and his understanding of symbolism, metaphor, and narrative.

## Chapter 2

12. N. T. Wright explains in *Jesus and the Victory of God* that the term "Son of God" is in fact quite ambiguous and doesn't necessarily indicate the divinity of Jesus. The phrase is "not completely unique" in Jewish scripture and imagination—it is used in other contexts in the Old Testament—though its use by Jesus is nonetheless "very remarkable" (648–51).

13. A new Bible as Literature movement, led by Frye in *The Great Code* and continued by Alter in *The Art of Biblical Narrative*, *The Art of Biblical Poetry*, and *The World of Biblical Literature*, has tried to shift the study of the Bible in just this direction, away from the atomizing and deconstructing that characterizes the historical/critical methods of the nineteenth and twentieth centuries and towards a greater appreciation of the artistry of the redactors. The result of historical criticism was to "eclipse" the Biblical narrative itself, to borrow the title of Hans Frei's *The Eclipse of Biblical Narrative: A Study in Eighteenth and Nineteenth Century Hermeneutics*. The power of the stories, as stories, had been forgotten. In response, Alter and others focus on the coherence that the redactors have created, on the Bible as a whole book, intentionally assembled, and on the patterns and intricacies to be found in the text itself. There is a "surprising degree of artful coherence in the final version of the text" of Genesis and all the books of the Bible, Alter says in *The World of Biblical Literature*. To argue for this is to argue "for the art of the redactor or for that of a powerfully integrative writer using earlier sources whose work the redactor merely polished" (4). My own reading of Genesis and the way that I teach it is everywhere influenced by Alter's assumptions and methods. In Ricouer's terms, the effort is to stand "in front" of the text rather than "behind" it, an effort that tends in the opposite direction of secular literary criticism in the last fifty years, which has gone from an early New Criticism that focused on the text itself to the current concern with historical and cultural contexts. A course in the Literature of Western Civilization, in which the Bible is read "as literature," may be the last place in an English Department where a text can be studied again, in keeping with current theory, as a work in itself, the challenges on and not off the page.

14. Certainly Mark is writing under the influence of a strong belief in Jesus. In a classic piece of Biblical scholarship, C. H. Dodd argues that the narrative structure of the gospel actually reflects a set of very definite beliefs, beliefs passed on to Mark by the believing community. "The outline which we have recognized as existing in fragmentary form in the framework of Mark may well have belonged to a form of the primitive kerygma" (399)—that is, a form of the early church's proclamation of faith.

15. What I am arguing in this section presupposes a Christian environmentalism. For a discussion of the complexities of this subject, see H. Paul Santmire's *The Travail of Nature: The Ambiguous Ecological Promise of Christian Theology*. As Santmire demonstrates, there are really two conflicting impulses towards nature in Biblical theology and Christian tradition, what he calls the "spiritual" and the "ecolog-

ical." The spiritual impulse emphasizes the need of the human person to rise above the body and so tends to lead to estrangement from the natural world. But the ecological impulse emphasizes "the human spirit's rootedness in the world of nature" (9). In my discussion here I am obviously emphasizing the latter. See also John Carmody's *Ecology and Religion*.

16. My understanding of Gadamer's very complex argument comes through Louth's wonderfully lucid summary and analysis in *Discerning the Truth*, 29–44. See also Stiver's discussion of Gadamer. "In a sense," Stiver says, "Gadamer is saying that we cannot bracket ourselves from interpretation, only bringing in ourselves and our assumptions at a later stage. We come with all of our presuppositions at the beginning" (46). Or as Stiver later puts it, summarizing the essence of Gadamer's thought, "our presuppositions *enable* our understanding, as well as sometimes *disable* it" (49).

17. I don't mean to imply that our naming or our interpretations are random, choices we make without reason. As I noted earlier, in note 8, theology has its own reasons and its own form of reasoning. In comments on an earlier draft of this manuscript, David Leigh, S.J., clarifies this point further, drawing on Lonergan's method: "In some places you imply that all human knowing is merely searching and hypotheses, with no way of reaching even a tentative or probable truth. It seems more accurate to say that some searching gets farther towards the truth, that some hypotheses have more evidence to back them than others, and that faith does reach a sort of certitude, even though the truth one believes in may include much mystery, and the grounds for the belief may be through testimony and experience rather than intrinsic evidence." In other words, though the wager or leap of faith is finally a leap, there's also at least some evidence, some reason, for our making it.

CHAPTER 3

18. Spellmeyer says that the reasons for the hyperspecialization and remote professionalism of the contemporary humanities are economic, not theoretical. He is both blunt and eloquent: "The truth is that the modern humanities have largely taken up residence in the university, and there they have remade themselves into specialized professions on the model of physics or medicine. As a consequence, they have a powerful vested interest in persuading us that the arts and ideas come from far away and are created by humans quite unlike ourselves. The arts as scholars often represent them seem remote and difficult, demanding almost superhuman levels of

erudition, but such qualities have less to do with the arts themselves than they do with the need to make distinctions between the experts and the amateurs" (6). Interestingly, Spellmeyer later suggests that religious communities, whether traditional or nontraditional, can become alternate—and valid—sites for engaging in the process of genuine education that the universities have abandoned.

19. In the next few pages I am following LeClercq's *The Love for Learning and the Desire for God*. It's a splendid book, both scholarly and contemplative, and its thesis is exactly the paradox that I am trying to describe. "In the life of St. Benedict," LeClercq says, "we find in germ the two components of monastic culture: studies undertaken, and then, not precisely scorned, but renounced and transcended, for the sake of the kingdom of God." This is very much the pattern that I found myself following in leaving the university for the seminary, then returning (see the introduction). "All Benedictine tradition was to be made in the image of St. Benedict's life [. . .] It was to embrace the teaching of learned ignorance, to be nurtured by it and to transmit, recall, and keep it alive face to face with the cultural activity of the Church, as an inevitable paradox" (12).

20. See Graff, ch. 6, "The Generalist Opposition." "The generalists were spokesmen for the missionary view of literature they inherited from Arnold, Ruskin, and other Victorian apostles of culture. [. . .] It was because they believed that Arnoldian culture should exert national leadership that the generalists eagerly supported the professional ambitions of departments of English and urged the legitimation of American literature as a college subject. Yet this larger vision of cultural leadership was precisely what led the generalists to find fault with those departments for betraying this leadership responsibility to professional interests" (81–82).

21. By "true" Lewis seems to mean literally and historically true, that what is fictional in the great myths of other cultures gets acted out in Judaism and Christianity through historical events and the life of the person of Jesus. As he says later in "Modern Theology and Biblical Criticism," the Gospels read to him like "realistic narrative," like "reportage" that is "pretty close to the facts" (*Christian Reflections* 155). Humphrey Carpenter calls Lewis "very nearly a fundamentalist" in this sense (155), though this may be stretching the point. See, for example, Lewis's letter to Clyde Kirby of May 7, 1959 (*Letters* 479–80) where he is more nuanced in his views. In fact, what Lewis goes on to argue in "Modern Theology and Biblical Criticism" isn't that every miraculous occurrence described in the Bible necessarily happened literally and historically, but that it's illogical to begin reading the Bible by making the opposite assumption, that such

events *never* could have happened. Lewis doesn't insist on the miraculous, he just doesn't rule it out (158–59). For my own part, I don't necessarily mean literal or historical truth when I borrow this idea of truth from Lewis and Tolkien but truth in a more general and undetermined sense—including psychological and philosophical truth, truth that is finally mysterious—beyond the categories of literal and symbolic altogether.

22. Carpenter quotes from an unpublished manuscript by a former student of Lewis's, Derek Brewer, describing Lewis's reaction to his debate with Anscomb. "He was obviously deeply disturbed by his encounter with Miss Anscomb, who disproved some of the central theory of his philosophy about Christianity. I felt quite painfully for him. Dyson said—very well—now he had lost everything and was come to the foot of the cross" (217).

## Chapter 4

23. Here again I want to correct the impression that leaps of faith are entirely arbitrary, without any justification. As Leigh explains in his letter on the earlier draft of the manuscript, "you sometimes imply that presuppositions are mere blind assumptions, whereas many philosophers try to argue and ground their presuppositions either philosophically through reasoning, or through faith based on some evidence and experience." In the scene in the garden in the *Confessions*, for example, Leigh says, Augustine finds himself "not through a blind leap but through an act of trust based on experience, some understanding of God, and the communal support of other believers and of Scripture and its truths." The leap of faith, for Augustine and for all of us, is based partly on evidence: of our joy, of our sense of the world, of our experience of tradition.

24. In *Faith and Reason* Sloan describes the roots of this postmodern assumption in the neo-orthodox theology of H. Richard Niebuhr, Reinhold Niebuhr, and Paul Tillich:

> For all three theologians the nature of personal knowledge and of the meaning of the encounter with the Divine are disclosed only through symbols, not through the propositions of discursive, analytical reason. Here again was an attempt by necessity to broaden the dominant modern conception of knowledge by arguing that the denotative signs and labels of ordinary reason can not express the nuances and connotations of the fullness of reality. Religious language and religious knowing, they maintained, are essentially symbolic. (118)

Sloan worries that this notion of symbol inadvertently creates a distinction between subjective and objective knowledge, conceding hard knowledge to science. But what postmodernism does is deny the subject/object distinction in the first place. Symbolic knowledge is real knowledge of the real world, however sometimes indeterminate, and is, in any event, the only kind of knowledge we have. There is no "objective" truth in either the Enlightenment and Modernist all-or-nothing sense.

25. See Robert Grant and David Tracy, *A Short History of the Interpretation of the Bible*, a clear and accessible introduction to this complex history; and James Kugel and Rowan Greer, *Early Biblical Interpretation*, a more detailed study. For an understanding of Catholic teaching on the Bible, see Pope John Paul II's own biblical commission in *The Interpretation of the Bible in the Church*. This document, representing official church teaching, calls fundamentalism "intellectual suicide," injecting into life "a false certitude" and confusing "the divine substance of the biblical message with what are in fact its human limitations" (73). Nineteenth century Catholicism does share in the fundamentalist reaction to modernism and the new Biblical criticism, but now, for Catholics as for mainstream Protestants, the Bible is understood again as it was for most of its history, not as a mere repository of "ready answers to the problems of life," containing "an immediate answer to each and every problem," as the Pontifical Biblical Commission puts it, but as a guide in a deeper and truer sense, a source for encountering the mystery (75). Representing the Protestant consensus, Peter Gomes in *The Good Book* warns us away from "bibliolatry," or "the worship of the Bible and the making of it an object of veneration, of ascribing to it the glory due to God" (36).

26. The acceptance of imprecision is another way in which my description of orthodoxy isn't only Catholic but very much in keeping with postmodern Protestant and evangelical theology. In the model that Grenz and Franke advance in *Beyond Foundationalism*, theology isn't simply a matter of retrieving Biblical truths but a process involving the "interplay" of the spirit, which speaks with authority through the Bible; of tradition, which provides the framework for interpretation; and of culture, which gives context for our own reflection. For truth this complicated and contextualized, as Stiver puts it, "understanding is primarily conveyed through analogical language and need not be reduced to univocal language," a view shared, too, by McClendon, for example (12). Stiver concedes that "such knowledge may seem too uncertain and too imprecise," but insists that "it is an illusion to think we can do better" (13). What Christians need to

accept is the "rough and ready" ways of proving and disproving that an embodied faith requires, the fact that reason is always "situated" (14)—though such a view of faith is finally sufficient, is finally satisfying, finally works. It's time to move beyond modernism's insistence on an all-or-nothing certainty, Stiver says. We can never have certainty. What we can have is the fullness and reality of lived experience (12–13).

27. My understanding of the Greek comes from professor Elaine Park of Mount Angel Seminary. My specific definitions are from Strong's *Exhaustive Concordance of the Bible*.

28. In *Exiles from Eden* Schwehn calls this kind of inquiry "spirited inquiry." "All higher learning depends," he points out, "not simply upon the possession of certain cognitive skills but also upon the possession of moral dispositions or virtues that enable inquiry to proceed" (42). As epistemologies differ, so do virtues. In the purely instrumental view of reason that still dominates too much of the academy, the virtues are those of clarity, honesty, mastery, and so on—all necessary and good, but limited. What Schwehn argues for is an epistemology of learning that also includes what he calls more "communitarian" virtues like charity and friendship. These moral dispositions are necessary for genuine knowledge, he says. "The pursuit of truth is linked inextricably to care taken with the lives and thoughts of others" (42)—and this effort to care for others, this instinct to consider the community, Schwehn insists, is broadly spiritual and even specifically Christian. As he later puts it, "certain spiritual virtues are indispensable to learning" (94).

In *How Christian Faith Can Sustain the Life of the Mind*, Hughes identifies these spiritual virtues as openness, compassion, and skepticism (40–41). Later he suggests that Christian faith necessarily results in what he calls "teaching with passion" (124).

## CHAPTER 5

29. Burtchaell concludes *The Dying of the Light* with this compelling statement. Notice how in the course of celebrating the power of Biblical theology, he also condemns the inadequacy of much Christian education and many Christian educators, now and in the past. This is his assessment of the history of religious colleges in America: that even when they dominated higher education, they by and large failed to provide a credible approach to faith. But this isn't my emphasis for now. What's relevant for my purposes here is Burtchaell's strong affirmation of the intellectual complexity and value of Christianity, exactly the affirmation that I felt myself

wanting to make in class that day: "What the academicians ignore, partly because they do not wish to know it and partly because their Christian colleagues have so feebly manifested it, is that the gospel within the church has continually been the center of intense and critical dialectic: textual, hermeneutical, historical, intercultural, philosophical, theological" (850). The irony of the history of religious colleges, Burtchaell says, is that religion lost its footing in the university at exactly the moment it was discovering the tools to make it academically respectable—that is, in the nineteenth and twentieth centuries, with the development of Biblical studies, and now, in the twenty-first, with the development of a postmodern, post-liberal, and post-conservative theology (822).

30. Marsden makes a similar argument in the conclusion of *The Soul of the American University*. "Tolerance, one would think, ought to include tolerance of religious viewpoints, including religious viewpoints in the academic life. Pluralism, one might otherwise suppose, would encourage first-class citizenship within universities for the widest feasible variety of cultural expressions. Since religion is integral to some cultures, one might expect that a commitment to diversity would entail the encouragement of intellectual expressions of a variety of religious perspectives." But no. In fact, "pluralism as it is often conceived of today seems to be almost a code word for its opposite, a new expression of the melting pot ideal. Persons from a wide variety of races and cultures are welcomed into the university, but only on the condition that they think more or less alike. Though the leadership may no longer be all northern European male, the establishmentarian impulse toward homogenization still prevails. Religious viewpoints that do not blend into the multicultural melting pot are excluded" (432–33). Marsden also comments on the issue of the first amendment in this last chapter, sounding much like Carter: "The government should not interfere with the free exercise of religion. If this constitutional principle is taken seriously, nonestablishment might seem better accomplished by encouraging varieties of religious expression, rather than discouraging them" (435).

31. Tracy's *Plurality and Ambiguity* is a remarkable book, both challenging and deeply rewarding, carrying forward the ideas of his earlier and seminal work, *The Analogical Imagination*, to make an argument about the relation of faith and reason in contemporary, pluralistic society. We understand God and we understand each other, Tracy says in this earlier work, only through analogies, comparisons which capture part of the reality of the other but always fail to capture its fullness and wholeness. In an analogy, the image is both like and unlike what it represents, and it's the difference that should lead us

to epistemological humility and charity towards others. Tracy is also heavily indebted in *Plurality and Ambiguity* to the ideas of Ricouer, extending the notion that "mystery gives rise to story gives rise to thought" and considering its broader implications. The rest of my discussion in these two chapters interweaves Ricouer and Tracy, though in the end, in the last chapter, I am most dependent on the intricacies of Tracy's dense and powerful analysis of the nature of theology in *Plurality and Ambiguity*.

Note, too, in the next two chapters the close similarities between Tracy and the postmodern evangelicals. Sloan's summary and assessment of the postmodern evangelical project nearly works as a summary of Tracy's aims and assumptions in *Plurality and Ambiguity*:

> The emphasis on the community does underscore the social nature of human life. [. . .] The emphasis also on life practices can express a basic appreciation of the importance of a deep, tacit participatory knowing that must be nourished by tradition, communal experience, and social responsibility. Above all, the central importance given in this perspective to narrative and story as providing identity and meaning to the community to its members could be truly radical. Language and narrative are potentially among our primary ways of apprehending and nurturing the qualities of existence and the immaterial relationships that are the source of its meaning. (223)

It's no wonder that the evangelicals have been turning more and more both to Ricouer and to Tracy as they try to engage the challenges of postmodernism.

32. In this sense I disagree with Cantell Smith's thesis in *Faith and Belief: The Difference Between Them*. Faith for him is an attitude of trust towards the infinite, while belief involves the statement of particular creeds. The scandal always comes with belief and its specific commitments, not with faith and its general attitudes—faith is too general for risk, too open-ended. But that's just the point. A faith without belief is mere intention, mere idea, formless and so unreal.

33. I realize that in quoting Tillich I'm risking the charge of "universalism." It's a tricky issue. Barth and Tillich are the fathers of the theological renaissance of the twentieth century and so of postmodernism, but Barth is the conservative father of the post-conservatives, Tillich the liberal father of the post-liberals. Earlier in this quotation Tillich says it bluntly, that "no particular religion matters, neither ours nor yours," a claim that in many ways Barth and others would contest, committed as they are to the absolute truth revealed in the Bible. In fact, I would contest this claim. My argu-

ment here is that the particulars do matter and that only particulars
matter, the concrete here and now. But what I'm also suggesting is
that God exceeds all language, including our own. What I doubt isn't
God but human understanding of God, a doubt that Barth certainly
shares. The righteousness of God is a fact, he says in *The Word of God
and the Word of Man*. But "we shall hardly approach [this] fact with
our critical reason. [. . .] It sees what is human but not what is divine"
(9). Ultimately what I'm arguing for here is the infinite mercy of
God, a mercy beyond our capacity to comprehend. This is Clark
Pinnock's point in *A Wideness in God's Mercy*, a point he supports with
an exhaustive survey of the Bible: that though salvation can be found
only in Jesus Christ, there is in God a "boundless generosity" that
works in ways we must not presume to limit or judge but can only
accept on faith (153).

In *Tracing the Way*, his survey of world religions, Hans Küng
solves this problem by simply admitting it. There are many similarities between the major world religions, he demonstrates. But this
doesn't mean that "the dogmatic differences" which exist between
religions can be simply "done away with." Those differences are real
and important, Küng concedes. For him the issue isn't the "unity" of
religions but "peace between the religions," "an essential presupposition of peace among the nations" (76). What exactly these dogmatic differences might be, Küng chooses not to say. This isn't his
focus, as it isn't mine.

See also Hughes's discussion of the paradoxes of the universal
and the particular in *How Christian Faith Can Sustain the Life of the
Mind*. Christians must "break through the particularities" of their
own tradition while at the same time honoring those very particularities. "The paradox lies in the fact that when we affirm a particularity, we break through it at the very same time, only to affirm it again
and break through it again, and on and on we go, simultaneously
affirming and breaking through, affirming and breaking through,
affirming and breaking through" (31).

34. In my discussion of this story I am quoting the New American Bible's
translation, since it uses the word "scholar." The New Revised
Standard Version, which I quote in the rest of the book, translates
this as "lawyer," a less helpful word for the point I want to make.

## Chapter 6

35. However defined, the presence of "great things" necessarily changes
the process and purpose of learning. As Mark Schwehn puts it, echoing Palmer, in this view of education "academic life [. . .] depends

upon such spiritual virtues as humility, faith, self-sacrifice, and charity" (45).

36. See again Graff's discussion of the "Generalist Opposition" to the
rise of professionalism in English studies in the late nineteenth and
early twentieth century. Many of these generalists were ministers, in
fact. They all, as Graff puts it, "channeled into literature emotions
that, a half-century earlier, would have likely been expressed in evangelical Christianity, Unitarianism, or Transcend-entalism, investing
the experience of literature with the redemptive influence their min-
isterial ancestors had attributed to the conversion experience" (85).
Graff sees this as naïve, but I don't. In a sense what I experience as a
contemporary minister who is also a teacher is exactly this conjunction of the literary and the religious—this is the experience I
describe in Chapter 3, in my teaching of Odysseus. In a sense this is
also what Palmer is urging for faculty in all disciplines, a return to an
understanding of the "redemptive" power of education, but seen
now exactly from the point of view of postmodernism, both accepting its premises and moving beyond its limitations. As Tracy would
say, what now? Yes, this is all true, the indeterminacy of knowledge,
but what do we do now? Is this enough? And the answer, of course,
is no. The answer is that it's time for a leap, a wager, a second
naïveté, and this second naïveté, I'm suggesting, might be enacted
pedagogically through a return to something like the "Generalist
Opposition."

37. Stiver puts it this way: "what has happened, ironically, is that reason
has moved closer to faith. The hermeneutical texture that has long
been recognized in theology—involving multiple interpretations,
personal judgment, conviction, passion, argument but not proof—is
now seen from a postmodern perspective as characterizing knowledge in general. Instead of theology being marginalized and suspect
as an intellectual discipline, it belongs in the game" (14).

38. Here again my argument intersects that of evangelicals who "appeal
to postmodernism," as Sloan explains, "to bolster the contention that
all knowing is based on certain unspoken, unconscious pretheoreti-
cal assumptions, and that the Christian ones are entitled to a fair
hearing along with the others" (230).

39. What Schwehn means by "exile" in *Exiles from Eden* is the idea that
faculty at small colleges are in a kind of forced exile from the larger,
comprehensive universities where the real action is. This is an idea
he rejects. The research that defines the work of such large institutions isn't the only kind of valuable work that an intellectual might
do, Schwehn says. Teaching, too, is a vocation, equal if not greater in
status, and so in the end there is no exile for faculty at smaller

schools, not if they are called to teach. I very much agree. But what I mean by "exile" here is the more traditional Christian notion that in a sense we are always in exile in our lives on earth, whatever our work or vocation, that until we are wholly joined in God we are never complete.

40. In this sense I finally disagree with Sloan in *Faith and Reason*. His argument in the end is that there's something wrong in how campus ministries have been banished from the intellectual life of the campus, slowly moving further and further out until now they exist only on the periphery. Faith is reasonable, he says, echoing Newman in one sense. To place it on the periphery is to suggest that it isn't, that it's not important, that it's a matter simply of lifestyle and feeling. And Sloan is partly right. Christianity should certainly be located in the center of the university—in the communion service, in the Memorial Union—speaking the truth to power. But what Newman himself realizes is what Augustine realizes, what's central to Christianity itself, that to speak the truth to power the communion service has to be in the university but not of it, drawing on a source of strength that isn't less than reason or at odds with it but simply far beyond it, not reducible to it.

41. O'Brien asserts that the Catholic university—and by extension, any Christian university—should be a "contrarian university," publicly opposing the values of secular institutions. See chapter 11 of *The Idea of a Catholic University*. My argument is that Christians within the secular university should model such a contrarian community—but also, that to be truly contrarian, these Christians require the secular university. Without opposition there are no contraries.

    Warren Nord makes a related claim in the conclusion of *Religion and American Education*. Religious issues should be taught in the public university, he says—as issues, as subjects of analysis and discussion—exactly because they are contentious: "I am arguing for *restoring the tension* between the secular and the spiritual in education, for having public education mirror the many ways in which religion and modernity relate to each other. Students should be taught the conflicts; they should feel the pull of the contending alternatives if they are to be liberally (and constitutionally) educated" (380). In this sense, too, Nord is interpreting the constitution in much the way that Carter does. To be truly democratic, higher education must reflect our democracy's deep concern with religious questions.

42. In his plenary address to the Call to Action conference in November of 2002, "Enhancing Democracy: The Key to Religious Reform," James Carroll makes many of the points that I have been making in

this chapter. "Religious pluralism," he says, "begins with the acknowledgement of the universal impossibility of direct knowledge of God. Because of this universal ignorance, we should regard each other respectfully" (5). As Carroll insists, democracy and pluralism are key to the very nature of orthodoxy, an argument he develops more fully in *Toward a New Catholic Church: The Promise of Reform*.

# Works Cited

Allen, Woody. "The Kugelmass Episode." Pages 61–78 in *Side Effects*. New York: Ballantine, 1981.

Alter, Robert. *The Art of Biblical Narrative*. New York: Basic, 1981.

———, trans. *Genesis*. New York: Norton, 1996.

———. *The World of Biblical Literature*. New York: Basic, 1992.

Anderson, Gary. *The Genesis of Perfection: Adam and Eve in Jewish and Christian Imagination*. Louisville: Westminster John Knox, 2001.

Armstrong, Karen. *The Battle for God*. New York: Knopf, 2000.

———. *In the Beginning: A New Interpretation of Genesis*. New York: Ballantine, 1996.

Auden, W. H. "Effective Democracy." Pages 15–18 in *The Complete Works of W. H. Auden: Prose*. Vol. 2, *1939–1948*. Edited by Edward Mendelson. Princeton: Princeton University Press, 2002.

Augustine. *City of God*. Trans. Marcus Dods. New York: Modern Library, 1993.

———. *The Confessions of St. Augustine*. Translated by Rex Warner. New York: New American Library, 1963.

———. *Teaching Christianity (De Doctrina Christiana)*. Translated by Edmund Hill. Hyde Park, N.Y.: New City Press, 1996.

———. *The Works of St. Augustine: A Translation for the 21st Century*. Edited by John Rotelle. Hyde Park, N.Y., New City Press, 1996.

Barth, Karl. *The Word of God and the Word of Man*. Translated by Douglas Horton. New York: Harper and Row, 1957.

Basil. *On the Holy Spirit*. Translted by David Anderson. Crestwood, N.Y.: Vladmir, 1980.

Benne, Robert. *Quality with Soul: How Six Premier Colleges and Universities Keep Faith with Their Religious Traditions*. Grand Rapids: Wm. B. Eerdmans, 2001.

Bloom, Allan. *The Closing of the American Mind*. New York: Simon and Schuster, 1987.

Booth, Wayne C. *The Rhetoric of Fiction.* Chicago: University of Chicago Press, 1961.

Brock, Sebastian. *The Luminous Eye: The Spiritual World of Saint Ephrem.* Cistercian Studies Series 124. Kalamazoo: Cistercian Publications, 1992.

Bryce, James. *Modern Democracies.* Vol. 1. New York: Macmillan, 1921.

Buechner, Frederick. *The Alphabet of Grace.* San Francisco: Harper and Row, 1970.

———. *The Sacred Journey.* San Francisco: Harper and Row, 1982.

———. *Now and Then.* San Francisco: Harper and Row, 1983.

Burke, Kenneth. *Language as Symbolic Action: Essays on Life, Literature, and Method.* Berkeley: University of California Press, 1966.

Burtchaell, James Tunstead. *The Dying of the Light: The Disengagement of Colleges and Universities from their Christian Churches.* Grand Rapids: Wm. B. Eerdmans, 1998.

Campbell, Joseph P., with Bill Moyers. *The Power of Myth.* Edited by Betty Sue Flowers. New York: Doubleday, 1988.

Carmody, John. *Ecology and Religion: Toward a New Christian Theology of Nature.* New York: Paulist, 1983.

Carpenter, Humphrey. *The Inklings: C. S. Lewis, J. R. R. Tolkien, Charles Williams and their Friends.* Boston: Houghton Mifflin, 1979.

Carroll, James. *Toward a New Catholic Church: The Promise of Reform.* Boston: Houghton Mifflin, 2002.

Carter, Stephen. *The Culture of Disbelief: How American Law and Politics Trivialize Religious Devotion.* New York: Doubleday, 1999.

Carver, Raymond. "What We Talk About When We Talk About Love." Pages 117–26 in *The Story and its Writer: An Introduction to Short Fiction.* Edited by Ann Charters. Boston: Bedford/St. Martins, 1999.

Chesterton, G. K. *What's Wrong with the World.* New York: Dodd, Mead, 1910.

Ciardi, John, trans. *Dante's Purgatorio.* New York: New American Library, 1957.

Crossan, John Dominic. *The Dark Interval: Towards a Theology of Story.* Niles, Ill.: Argus, 1975.

Curran, Charles E. *Catholic Higher Education, Theology, and Academic Freedom.* Notre Dame: University of Notre Dame Press, 1990.

"Dei Verbum." Pages 97–116 in Flannery.

Denby, David. *Great Books: My Adventures with Homer, Rousseau, Woolf, and Other Indestructible Writers of the Western World.* New York: Simon and Schuster, 1996.

Dillard, Annie. "Living Like Weasels." Pages 29–34 in *Teaching a Stone to Talk: Expeditions and Encounters.* New York: Harper Collins, 1982.

Dodd, C. H. "The Framework of the Gospel Narrative." *Expository Times* 43 (1931): 396–400.

Dovre, Paul. *The Future of Religious Colleges: Proceedings of the Harvard Conference on the Future of Religious Colleges.* Grand Rapids: Wm. B. Eerdmans, 2002.

Elbow, Peter. *Writing with Power: Techniques for Mastering the Writing Process.* New York: Oxford, 1981.

Fagles, Robert, trans. *The Odyssey of Homer.* New York: Penguin, 1996.

Flannery, Austin, ed. *Vatican Council II: The Basic Sixteen Documents.* Northport, N.Y.: Costello, 1975.

Fowler, James W. *Stages of Faith: The Psychology of Human Development and the Quest for Meaning*. San Francisco: Harper and Row, 1981.

Fox, Marvin. "Jewishness and Judaism at Brandeis University." *Crosscurrents* 43.4 (1993–1994): 464–69.

Fox, Matthew. *Original Blessing: A Primer on Creation Spirituality*. New York: Putnam, 1983.

Frye, Northrop. *Anatomy of Criticism*. Princeton: Princeton University Press, 1957.

———.*The Great Code: The Bible and Literature*. New York: Harcourt Brace, 1982.

Gadamer, Hans-George. *Truth and Method*. Second revised edition. Translated by Joel Weinsheimer and Donald G. Marshall. New York: Continuum, 1999.

"Gaudium et Spes." Pages 163–282 in Flannery.

Gleason, Philip. *Contending with Modernity: Catholic Higher Education in the Twentieth Century*. New York: Oxford, 1995.

Gomes, Peter J. *The Good Book: Reading the Bible with Mind and Heart*. New York: Avon, 1996.

Graff, Gerald. *Professing Literature: An Institutional History*. Chicago: University of Chicago Press, 1987.

Grant, Robert, and David Tracy. *A Short History of the Interpretation of the Bible*. 2d. ed. New York: Fortress, 1984.

Grenz, Stanley J. and John R. Franke. *Beyond Fundamentalism: Shaping Theology in a Postmodern Context*. Louisville: Westminster John Knox, 2001.

Holmes, Richard. *Coleridge: Darker Reflections, 1804–1834*. New York: Pantheon, 1998.

Hughes, Richard T. *How Christian Faith Can Sustain the Life of the Mind*. Grand Rapids: Wm. B. Eerdmans, 2001.

Hughes, Richard T. and William B. Adrian, eds. *Models for Christian Higher Education: Strategies for Survival and Success in the Twenty-First Century*. Grand Rapids: Wm. B. Eerdmans, 1997.

Irenaeus. *Against the Heresies*. Pages 309–567 in *The Ante-Nicene Fathers*. Vol. 1. Edited by Alexander Roberts and James Donaldson. Grand Rapids: Wm. B. Eerdmans, 1956.

John Paul II. *On Catholic Universities: Ex Corde Ecclesiae*. Washington, D.C.: United States Catholic Conference, 1999.

Junod, Tom. "Can You Say . . . 'Hero'?" Pages 148–70 in *The Best American Spiritual Writing 1999*. Edited by Philip Zaleski. San Francisco: Harper San Francisco, 1999.

Kafka, Franz. *Metamorphosis*. Pages 117–26 in *The Story and its Writer: An Introduction to Short Fiction*. Edited by Ann Charters. Boston: Bedford/St. Martins, 1999.

Kaspar, Walter. *The God of Jesus Christ*. New York: Crossroad, 1984.

Keats, John. *Selected Poems and Letters*. Edited by Douglas Bush. Boston: Houghton Mifflin, 1959.

Ker, Ian. *John Henry Newman: A Biography*. New York: Oxford, 1990.

Korzybski, Alford. *Science and Sanity: An Introduction to Non-Aristotelian Systems and General Semantics*. 5th ed. Concord, Calif.: Institute of General

Semantics, 1995.

Kugel, James and Rowan Greer. *Early Biblical Interpretation.* Philadelphia: Westminster, 1986.

Küng, Hans. *Tracing the Way: Spiritual Dimensions of the World Religions.* Translated by John Bowden. New York: Continuum, 2002.

LeClercq, Jean. *The Love of Learning and the Desire for God: A Study of Monastic Culture.* Translated by Catharine Misrahi. New York: Fordham, 1974.

Leigh, David. *Circuitous Journeys: Modern Spiritual Autobiography.* New York: Fordham, 2000.

Leopold, Aldo. *A Sand County Almanac.* New York: Ballantine, 1970.

Lewis, C. S. *The Letters of C.S. Lewis to Arthur Greeves.* Ed. Walter Hooper. New York: Macmillan, 1979.

———. *Letters of C. S. Lewis.* Revised and enlarged edition. Edited by Walter Hooper. New York: Harcourt Brace, 1993.

———. "Modern Theology and Biblical Criticism." Pages 152–66 in *Christian Reflections.* Ed. Walter Hooper. Grand Rapids: Wm. B. Eerdmans, 1994.

———. *On Stories.* Ed. Walter Hooper. New York: Harcourt Brace, 1982.

———. *The Screwtape Letters.* New York: Macmillan, 1982.

———. *Surprised by Joy: The Shape of My Early Life.* New York: Harcourt Brace, 1955.

Lonergan, Bernard. *Method in Theology.* Toronto: University of Toronto Press, 1971.

Louth, Andrew. *Discerning the Mystery: An Essay on the Nature of Theology.* Oxford: Clarendon, 1989.

Marsden, George M. *The Soul of the American University: From Protestant Establishment to Established Nonbelief.* New York: Oxford, 1994.

McClendon, James Wm. Jr. *Biography as Theology: How Life Stories Can Remake Today's Theology.* 2d. ed. Eugene, Oreg.: Wipf and Stock, 2002.

Meyer, Ben F. *Critical Realism and the New Testament.* Princeton Theological Monograph Series 17. Edited by Dikran Y. Hadidian. San Jose: Pickwick, 1989.

Moberly, Walter. *The Crisis of the University.* London: SCM, 1949.

Murphy, Nancey C. *Beyond Liberalism and Fundamentalism: How Modern and Postmodern Philosophy Set the Theological Agenda.* Harrisburg: Trinity Press International, 1996.

———. *Reasoning and Rhetoric in Religion.* Valley Forge: Trinity Press International, 1994.

National Conference of Catholic Bishops. *Empowered by the Spirit: Campus Ministry Faces the Future.* Washington, D.C.: United States Catholic Conference, 1986.

*New American Bible.* New York: Oxford, 1990.

*The New Oxford Annotated Bible.* New York: Oxford, 1991.

Newman, John Henry. *Apologia Pro Vita Sua.* Edited by Ian Ker. New York: Penguin, 1994.

———. *Arians of the Fourth Century.* London: Longmans, 1868–1881.

———. *An Essay on the Development of Christian Doctrine.* Notre Dame: University of Notre Dame Press, 1989.

————. An Essay in Aid of a Grammar of Assent. Notre Dame: University of Notre Dame Press, 1979.

————. Newman's University Sermons: Fifteen Sermons Preached Before the University of Oxford 1826–43. London: SPCK, 1970.

————. The Idea of the University. Edited by Frank M. Turner. New Haven: Yale, 1996.

Nord, William. Religion and American Education: Rethinking a National Dilemma. Chapel Hill: University of North Carolina Press, 1995.

Nouwen, Henri. The Life of the Beloved: Spiritual Living in a Secular World. New York: Crossroad, 1992.

————. Seeds of Hope: A Henri Nouwen Reader. Edited by Robert Durback. New York: Bantam, 1989.

O'Brien, George Dennis. The Idea of a Catholic University. Chicago: University of Chicago Press, 2002.

O'Connor, Flannery. Mystery and Manners. Edited by Sally and Robert Fitzgerald. New York: Farrar, Straus, and Giroux, 1969.

Oliver, Mary. House of Light. Boston: Beacon, 1990.

Palmer, Parker. The Courage to Teach: Exploring the Inner Landscape of a Teacher's Life. San Francisco: Jossey-Bass, 1998.

————. To Know as We Are Known: A Spirituality of Education. San Francisco: Harper Collins, 1983.

Pelikan, Jaroslav. The Idea of the University: A Reexamination. New Haven: Yale, 1992.

Pinnock, Clark H. A Wideness in God's Mercy: The Finality of Jesus Christ in a World of Religions. Grand Rapids: Zondervan, 1992.

Pontifical Biblical Commission. The Interpretation of the Bible in the Church. St. Paul: St. Paul, 1993.

Price, Reynolds. Three Gospels. New York: Simon and Schuster, 1992.

Reuben, Julie A. The Making of the Modern University: Intellectual Transformation and the Marginalization of Morality. Chicago: University of Chicago Press, 1996.

Rhoads, David and Donald Michie. Mark as Story: An Introduction to the Narrative of a Gospel. Philadelphia: Fortress, 1982.

Ricouer, Paul. The Symbolism of Evil. Translated by Emerson Buchanan. Boston: Beacon, 1967.

Roberts, Jon J. and James Turner. The Sacred and the Secular University. Princeton: Princeton University Press, 2000.

The Rule of St. Benedict in English. Edited by Timothy Fry. Collegeville: Liturgical Press, 1981.

"Sacrosanctum Concilium." Pages 117–62 in Flannery.

Santmire, Paul H. The Travail of Nature: The Ambiguous Ecological Promise of Christian Theology. Philadelphia: Fortress, 1985.

Schwehn, Mark. Exiles from Eden: Religion and the Academic Vocation in America. New York: Oxford, 1993.

Shea, John. Stories of God. Allen, Tex.: Thomas More, 1996.

Sloan, Douglas. Faith and Knowledge: Mainline Protestantism and American Higher Education. Louisville: Westminster John Knox, 1994.

Smith, Wilfred Cantwell. *Faith and Belief: The Difference Between Them*. Oxford: Oneworld, 1998.

Spellmeyer, Kurt. *Arts of Living: Reinventing the Humanities for the Twenty-First Century*. Albany: State University of New York, 2003.

Stafford, William. *An Oregon Message*. New York: Harper and Row, 1987.

———. *The Way It Is: New and Selected Poems*. St. Paul: Graywolf, 1998.

———. *Writing the Australian Crawl: Views on the Writer's Vocation*. Ann Arbor: University of Michigan Press, 1978.

Sterk, Andrea, ed. *Religion, Scholarship, and Higher Education: Perspectives, Models, and Future Prospects*. Notre Dame: University of Notre Dame Press, 2002.

Stiver, Dan. *Theology After Ricouer: New Directions in Hermeneutical Theology*. Louisville: Westminster John Knox, 2001.

Strong, James. *Exhaustive Concordance of the Bible*. New York: Abingdon, 1890.

Thomas, Lewis. *The Medusa and the Snail: More Notes of a Biology Watcher*. New York: Bantam, 1980.

Tillich, Paul. *The New Being*. New York: Harper and Row, 1977.

Tolkien, J. R. R. "On Fairy-Stories." Pages 38–89 in *Essays Presented to Charles Williams*. Edited by C. S. Lewis. Grand Rapids: Wm. B. Eerdmans, 1966.

Tracy, David. *The Analogical Imagination: Christian Theology and the Culture of Pluralism*. New York: Crossroads, 1981.

———. *Plurality and Ambiguity: Hermeneutics, Religion, Hope*. Chicago: University of Chicago Press, 1987.

von Balthasar, Hans Urs. *The Word Made Flesh*. Translated A. V. Littledale with Alexander Dru. San Francisco: Ignatius, 1989.

von Hügel, Friedrich. *Letters to a Niece*. London: Harper Collins, 1995.

Wills, Garry. *Augustine*. New York: Penguin, 1999.

———. *Under God: Religion and American Politics*. New York: Simon and Schuster, 1990.

Wilson, A. N. *C. S. Lewis: A Biography*. New York: Norton, 1990.

Wright, N. T. *Jesus and the Victory of God*. Minneapolis: Fortress, 1996.

# Index